THE
PACKAGE DESIGN
BOOK
6

pentawards

THE PACKAGE DESIGN BOOK 6

6

TASCHEN

diamond

18

beverages

26

food

140

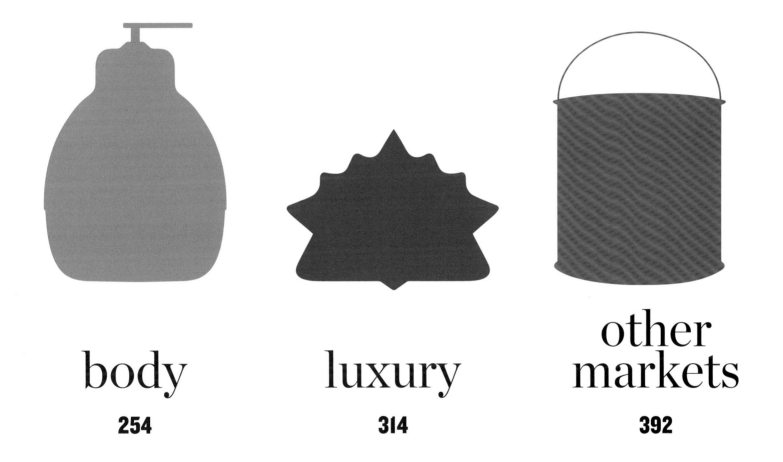

body

luxury

other
markets

FOREWORD

Jennifer Clements
Marketing Manager, Pentawards

Welcome to the sixth edition of *The Package Design Book* from the Pentawards, the world's leading and most prestigious competition for packaging design.

Across these pages you'll discover the very best packaging designs from the last two years, showcasing the winners from the 2019 and 2020 Pentawards competition. Each featured design has won a Bronze, Silver, Gold, Platinum or an exclusive Diamond Pentaward trophy, beating thousands of submissions from over 60 countries.

The winning entries were selected by an international jury, made up of an eclectic mix of individuals from the four corners of the globe. Since our last book we have extended our jury from 15 to 30 members, ensuring we have representatives of different nationalities, genders, skill sets, experiences and knowledge bases. From design directors and CEOs to design experts from the most renowned agencies that exist, these together create an unparalleled hive of knowledge, experience and creativity to judge the awards.

The design agencies, packaging companies, brands and individuals whose works are featured represent the very best creative minds in the business. They have pushed the boundaries of visuals and form to create designs that are both a pure expression of their brands' values and a delight for the consumers who buy them - and we're delighted to showcase their work within this book.

As well as growing our jury, last year we released the Pentawards Portal, an online hub for designers, brands and individuals featuring a global design directory, a winners' archive and our packaging design league tables. And we also had some firsts: we hosted our first ever online event, the Pentawards Festival which included a live Gala Ceremony, and we publicly announced the competition shortlist for the first time.

I hope you enjoy looking through these pages and feel inspired by these works that highlight the fantastic quality and variety of packaging design from across the globe.

VORWORT

Jennifer Clements
Marketing Manager, Pentawards

Willkommen zur sechsten Ausgabe von *The Package Design Book* von Pentawards, dem weltweit führenden und renommiertesten Wettbewerb für Verpackungsdesign. Auf diesen Seiten entdecken Sie die besten Verpackungsdesigns der letzten zwei Jahre und wir präsentieren Ihnen die Gewinner des Pentawards-Wettbewerbs aus den Jahren 2019 und 2020. Jedes der vorgestellten Designs hat eine Bronze-, Silber-, Gold-, Platin- oder eine exklusive „Diamond Pentaward"-Trophäe gewonnen und sich damit gegen Tausende von Beiträgen aus über 60 Ländern durchgesetzt.

Die Gewinner wurden von einer internationalen Jury ausgewählt, die sich aus einer vielseitigen Mischung von Mitgliedern aus allen Teilen der Welt zusammensetzt. Seit unserem letzten Buch haben wir unsere Jury von 15 auf 30 Mitglieder erweitert, um sicherzustellen, dass wir die verschiedenen Nationalitäten, Geschlechter, Fähigkeiten, Erfahrungen und Kenntnisse repräsentieren. Von Designdirektoren und CEOs bis hin zu Designexperten der renommiertesten Agenturen, die es gibt, bilden sie zusammen ein nie zuvor gesehenes Konglomerat an Wissen, Erfahrung und Kreativität, um die Auszeichnungen zu beurteilen.

Die Designagenturen, Verpackungsunternehmen, Marken und Einzelpersonen, deren Arbeit vorgestellt wird, repräsentieren die besten kreativen Köpfe der Branche. Sie haben die Grenzen von Optik und Form überschritten, um Designs zu kreieren, die sowohl ein reiner Ausdruck ihrer Markenwerte als auch eine Freude für die Konsumenten sind, die die Produkte kaufen – und wir freuen uns, ihre Arbeit in diesem Buch zu präsentieren.

Im vergangenen Jahr haben wir nicht nur unsere Jury erweitert, sondern auch das Pentawards-Portal eingerichtet, ein Online-Netzwerk für Designer, Marken und Individuen, das eine globales Designverzeichnis, ein Archiv mit den Gewinnern und unsere Ranglisten für Verpackungsdesign enthält. Und es gab auch ein paar Neuerungen: Wir haben unser erstes Online-Event veranstaltet, das Pentawards-Festival, inklusive einer Live-Gala-Zeremonie, und zum ersten Mal haben wir die Liste der engeren Auswahl für unseren Wettbewerb öffentlich bekannt gegeben.

Ich wünsche Ihnen viel Freude beim Durchblättern dieser Seiten und hoffe, dass Sie von diesen Arbeiten inspiriert fühlen, die die fantastische Qualität und Vielfalt von Verpackungsdesigns aus der ganzen Welt hervorheben.

AVANT-PROPOS

Jennifer Clements
Directrice marketing, Pentawards

Bienvenue dans la sixième édition de *The Package Design Book* des Pentawards, la plus grande et prestigieuse compétition au monde de design de packagings.

Vous découvrirez dans ces pages la crème des designs de packagings des deux dernières années, avec les lauréats des compétitions Pentawards 2019 et 2020. Chaque design présenté ici a remporté un Pentaward Bronze, Silver, Gold, Platinum ou le prestigieux Diamond, après avoir été retenu parmi les milliers de candidats originaires de 60 pays.

Les contributions gagnantes ont été triées sur le volet par un jury international éclectique, composé d'experts venant des quatre coins du globe. Depuis notre dernier ouvrage, ce jury est passé de 15 à 30 membres pour inclure des représentants de nationalités, genres, compétences, expériences et connaissances d'une grande diversité. Ensemble, les directeurs du design, les PDG et les experts en design des plus grandes agences forment une concentration sans pareille de savoir, d'expériences et de créativité pour décerner les prix.

Les agences de design, les entreprises d'emballages, les marques et les individus dont les créations figurent dans ces pages représentent les meilleurs esprits créatifs du secteur. Ils ont repoussé les limites du visuel et des formes pour concevoir des designs qui sont la pure expression des valeurs de leur marque et un véritable plaisir pour les consommateurs qui les achètent. Nous sommes ravis de présenter leur travail dans cet ouvrage.

Outre l'extension de notre jury, nous avons l'an passé lancé le portail en ligne Pentawards Portal, destiné aux designers, aux marques et aux individus : il présente un annuaire mondial du secteur du design, les archives des lauréats passés et notre classement des meilleurs acteurs en matière de design de packaging. Sans oublier deux premières : nous avons organisé notre premier événement en ligne, le Pentawards Festival, avec une cérémonie de gala en direct, et nous avons pour la première fois rendue publique la liste des candidats sélectionnés pour la compétition.

J'espère que vous aimerez parcourir ces pages et vous sentirez inspiré par ces créations qui transmettent la remarquable qualité et la variété du design de packagings à travers la planète.

PACKAGING IN 2020

Adam Ryan
Head of Pentawards

It's December 2020 and one thing is for sure, no one could have ever predicted that the world would be faced with so much uncertainty. Over the last nine months everything has changed, bringing two crises at once; COVID-19 and its economic fallout. It feels like a dream, but this is real life and we all are adapting to a new way of living.

However, these times have had a positive effect on humanity. We have seen beautiful acts of love and solidarity, nature is healing, we have had more time to spend with our loved ones and people of the world have become more creative, even those who are not from the world of design.

I have always been a person that sees the glass half full rather than half empty. Even in these times it's tough to remain positive, but this adjustment will make us all look at the way we consume, and it will create new possibilities. For example, alcohol distilleries around the world have shifted production to create hand sanitiser, and PPE is being created using 3D printers. "In the middle of difficulty lies opportunity" – this was one of the tenets of Albert Einstein's work, according to John Archibald Wheeler, and very relevant to remember today.

But will these changes affect packaging?

The sustainability agenda has become one of the most important issues for the packaging industry. Brands have started taking an eco-friendlier approach to packaging. Consumers are more conscious than ever about what they're buying – and very vocal when they believe that packaging is excessive and unnecessary. Minimising waste across the packaging supply chain, going plastic free, using reusable and alternative materials are approaches designers and the packaging industry have been working on.

Will COVID-19 affect the sustainability agenda? Concerns about hygiene and food safety in the context of the pandemic might become a higher priority, while sustainability performance of different packaging substrates could become a lower priority, at least in the short term. This disruption will also see supply chains having strong cost pressures, but this will bring opportunity to adapt and to digitalise business where possible.

There has been an expected acceleration of e-commerce during the pandemic. As a result of this shift, brands no longer only have to consider how good a product looks on a shelf, but how good it looks in a thumbnail online and, crucially, how it looks and feels when it arrives directly to your home. Social media channels like Instagram have become the new shopfronts. We discover products through images and videos shared by others and are purchasing them without ever touching the physical product. Many other emerging direct-to-consumer brands have successfully created instantly recognisable packaging that people want to take photos of, building brand exposure as people share images online. As a result, we have started seeing more distinctive packaging designs emerging as brands strive to create an individual presence for online-only appeal.

Where do I see packaging in 100 years' time?

In 2019, *Forbes* said, "The next decade of innovation will be the most consequential of all time". Recent events will speed this up; during times like these research shows product innovation will slow but brand innovation will increase. Thus, brands will find new ways to engage with consumers and packaging, which I believe, has never been so vital.

It doesn't matter if it's a pandemic, a political issue or an ecological matter, the power of packaging will play a huge role. One hundred years from now, businesses and brands need to ensure that their packaging will have a positive impact on the environment and there is zero waste. Advances in technology and new materials will create a better future – it's now up to all of us to make this happen.

Since 2007, more than 19,000 high-quality packaging designs have been submitted to the Pentawards. An international jury chose the winning entries, including the wonderful designs found in this book, the sixth in the series. The Pentawards showcase designs worldwide, highlighting the best innovations in packaging design from all four corners of the planet.

Every year, the entries are judged by an international jury formed by leading names in design and marketing. With more than 2,000 designs across the 59 categories, it is an arduous endeavour, but it is thrilling and rewarding at the same time. In some categories, the jury's task is made all the more difficult by the ever-increasing number of submissions each year. The jury members must also judge designs from "new" marketing countries outside Europe, the United States and Japan. Every year, there are some remarkable entries from these new countries, in particular China, Russia, the emerging nations of Eastern Europe and the large South American countries. Creativity is probably less restrained in those countries, with consumers more open to new ideas.

But what makes one design stand out from all the rest? What does the jury look for? Here are some of the factors that stood out among the winning entries in 2019 and 2020.

___

2019

1. Unity around a purpose
Xbox by Microsoft

When Microsoft unveiled the Xbox Adaptive Controller (p. 25) for gamers with limited mobility, it received huge applause from the gaming community. But when it came to inclusive design, Microsoft didn't stop with the controller, it took a hard look at the packaging, which resulted in something groundbreaking. Microsoft used loops and a hinge mechanism on a box with a low centre of gravity and even printed instructions on a part of the packaging that helps remove the product, meaning no excessive use of materials. The result is a milestone for consumer accessibility; not only is it a beautiful piece of packaging it serves a real purpose. It's truly meaningful, and this is now more important than ever.

2. Paying homage:
Lind & Lime – Contagious

Lind & Lime (p. 32) is a gin produced at the port of Leith Distillery in Edinburgh, Scotland. Leith's shores were once home to a plethora of industries, a history which inspired the design and detail applied to the bespoke bottle. The cones from the Edinburgh and Leith Glass Works used to be seen rising above sea level. The strong, elegant long-necked bottle pays them homage with its unique shape and embossed tribute to the factory stamped firmly at its base. Half white glass with its translucent light green hue epitomises the citrus tones of the gin.

3. Playfulness:
Stonebrick – Established

Stonebrick is a new line of makeup for South Korea's largest retailer, Emart (part of Shinsegae Group). The idea behind the line is to allow the customer to buy a tailor-made set of cosmetics in a playful, fun and joyful way (p. 259). This new line is the first fully customisable makeup range with individual components that magnetise together to create personalised collections with endless possibilities.

4. A new constructive form:
Riceman – Backbone Branding

Tired of the same old plain designs used for rice packaging, Riceman (p. 144) decided it needed something to make it stand out from its competitors. Riceman honours the hard work of farmers with faces that show different emotions; the packaging conveys a human message and is functional at the same time. This is a charming new constructive form of traditional packaging, something many designers will search for in the future to strengthen brands and the storytelling of a product.

5. Juxtaposition:
Perfeccionista – Robert Núñez

Imperfections add distinguishing elements and make for something truly unique. Perfeccionista is a limited-edition single-estate wine with a limited production of only 697 units. In order to connect emotionally with the consumer, value is given to the idea of imperfection. The wooden tags for each bottle were broken by hand, without a die cutter, and numbered with an ink stamp, making every piece of packaging distinctive (p. 318).

6. Being memorable:
Data Xmas – Auriga

In a world saturated by Christmas gift options, Spanish design agency Auriga wanted to create a gift that also promoted their business and services in a non-traditional way. XMAS Data is a set of four chocolate boxes with edible infographics (p. 398), using design to turn data into something pleasing to the eyes and to the taste buds. The minimalist design, clean typography, various flavours of chocolates and a user-friendly unboxing experience make this promotional item interactive and memorable.

2020

1. Sustainability at the core
Air Vodka by Air Company

The Air Company mission is to be the most sustainable alcohol brand in the world, resulting in reusable and 100% sustainable packaging for the world's first carbon negative vodka brand. To reflect the purity of the alcohol, a novel yet beautiful and thoughtful bottle design was created (p. 24). With a custom-made, natural, non-toxic label that can be removed easily, the glass bottle can be used for other purposes, such as a water bottle, flower vase or candle holder. Air Company's vodka remains the star – there is ample space for the display of the spirit as opposed to the usual method of centring the label on the bottle. By placing the label lower, the vodka itself is the first thing to meet the eye.

2. Personality personified
Pridem's Gin – Enpedra Estudio

Pridem's Gin celebrates freedom as the most essential principle of human beings by creating a bottle that represents a sailor, a classic symbol of freedom (p. 31). The stopper shaped like a sailor's hat gives the product real personality, and the label, made up of four separate parts that completely wrap around the bottle, creates a distinctive pattern reminiscent of a sailor's uniform. The result is something truly original, memorable and timeless.

3. Capturing the zeitgeist
Chioture – Shanghai Nianxiang Brand Design & Consulting Co., Ltd.

Chioture is a makeup brand that is vibrant and youthful. This makeup kit is in the form of an adorable camera (p. 258). The use of pastel pink, subtle detailing and clean lines makes this a very collectable piece of packaging. As an object to covet, it is sure to be shared across social media platforms and excite its target audience.

4. A simple idea
Nongfu Wangtian – ShenZhen BOB Design

Nongfu Wangtian is a chilli sauce brand that brings an unconventional approach to the supermarket shelf. With this collection of chilli sauce flavours, the designers represent each variety with a bold bright use of colour and packaging in the shape of a chilli pepper (p. 145). The cap of the sauce takes the form of a chilli stem, which curves naturally and can easily hang in a store display. This makes the consumer feel like they are actually picking a chilli from the field.

5. Collaboration
Hennessy – Felipe Pantone – Appartement 103

Hennessy is a French cognac that sells over 50 million bottles a year worldwide. The brand, design agency Appartement 103 and world-renowned pioneer street artist Felipe Pantone collaborated on the latest Collector's Edition (p. 319), and the result is stunning. Pantone is known for his use of colour, which is seen through a prism of graphical elements and textures for this project. Released globally at a limited quantity of 70 pieces, the exclusive bottle stands on a pedestal in the centre of a grid of moiré-finished rods that consumers themselves can place, move and interchange to alter the bottle's optics. This piece of packaging turns into a configurable artwork, and the consumer can change its form, shifting its perspective and shaping its narrative.

6. Perfect Execution
Hema – Magnet Design firm

Hema is a well-known Dutch brand that has a chain of stores selling a variety of everyday housewares. This charming range of inflatable pool toys by the Dutch retailer shows a number of "mini swimming pools" on the packaging (p. 399). A perfect use of photography makes all the inflatables look three dimensional, comfortable and fun, and allows consumers to envisage using them at a holiday destination. Real care and attention to detail have been dedicated to this project, when in most cases this type of product doesn't get the love it deserves.

I hope that you thoroughly enjoy looking through this book and discovering the winning packaging designs from the 2019 and 2020 Pentawards.

VERPACKEN 2020

Adam Ryan
Leiter von Pentawards

Es ist Dezember 2020 und eines ist sicher, niemand hätte vorhersagen können, dass die Welt mit so viel Unsicherheit konfrontiert sein würde. Die letzten neun Monate haben alles verändert und gleich zwei Krisen auf einmal mit sich gebracht: COVID-19 und seine wirtschaftlichen Folgen. Es fühlt sich an wie ein Traum, aber dies ist das wirkliche Leben, und wir alle passen uns an eine neue Lebensweise an.

Diese Zeiten hatten aber auch einen positiven Effekt auf die Menschheit. Wir haben Solidarität erlebt, die Natur heilt, wir hatten mehr Zeit für unsere Liebsten und die Menschen in der Welt sind kreativer geworden, selbst die, die nicht aus der Designwelt kommen.

Ich sehe das Glas eigentlich immer halb voll. Obwohl es in diesen Zeiten schwer ist, positiv zu bleiben, wird die Umstellung uns dazu bringen, genauer hinzusehen, wie wir konsumieren, und sie wird neue Möglichkeiten schaffen. Zum Beispiel produzieren Alkoholbrennereien nun Desinfektionsmittel, und bei der Herstellung von Schutzkleidung werden 3-D-Drucker eingesetzt. „Inmitten der Schwierigkeiten liegt die Möglichkeit" – das war laut John Archibald Wheeler einer von Albert Einsteins Grundsätzen, den es zu erinnern gilt.

Aber werden sich diese Veränderungen auf Verpackungen auswirken?

Die Nachhaltigkeitsagenda ist zu einem der wichtigsten Themen der Verpackungsindustrie geworden. Die Marken haben begonnen, einen umweltfreundlicheren Ansatz für Verpackungen zu verfolgen. Konsumenten sind sich mehr als denn je dessen bewusst, was sie kaufen – und sprechen deutlich aus, wenn sie glauben, dass eine Verpackung exzessiv und unnötig ist. In der Verpackungsindustrie wurde an Konzepten der Minimierung von Abfall in der gesamten Lieferkette, der Verzicht auf Plastik und die Verwendung von wiederverwendbaren und alternativen Materialien gearbeitet.

Wird COVID-19 die Nachhaltigkeitsagenda beeinflussen? Bedenken bezüglich Hygiene und Lebensmittelsicherheit könnten im Kontext der Pandemie eine höhere Priorität bekommen, während die Nachhaltigkeitsleistung von verschiedenen Verpackungssubstraten zumindest kurzzeitig weniger wichtig werden könnte. Diese Unterbrechung wird auch dazu führen, dass die Lieferkette unter starken Kostendruck gerät, aber das wird die Gelegenheit mit sich bringen, sich anzupassen und die Unternehmen wo immer möglich zu digitalisieren.

Wie erwartet hat sich der Onlinehandel beschleunigt. Viele von uns kaufen über Social-Media-Kanäle wie Instagram ein. Durch Bilder und Videos entdecken wir Neues und kaufen, ohne das physische Produkt auch nur zu berühren. Viele aufstrebende, direkt an die Konsumenten gerichtete Marken, sind sehr erfolgreich geworden, indem sie Verpackungen entworfen haben, von denen die Menschen gerne Fotos machen. Die Designs haben einen großen Wiedererkennungswert, was die Markenpräsenz erhöht, auch wenn die Leute die Bilder nur online sehen. Infolgedessen sehen wir vermehrt einzigartige Verpackungsdesigns, die als Marken nach einer individuellen Präsenz streben.

Wo sehe ich Verpackungen in 100 Jahren?

2019 sagte *Forbes*: „Das nächste Jahrzehnt der Innovation wird das folgenreichste aller Zeiten sein." Jüngste Ereignisse werden das beschleunigen. In Zeiten wie diesen zeigt die Forschung, dass sich die Produktinnovation verlangsamen, die Markeninnovation jedoch zunehmen wird. So werden die Marken neue Wege finden, um sich mit den Verbrauchern in Kontakt zu treten, was meiner Meinung nach nie wichtiger war.

Es spielt keine Rolle, ob es sich um eine Pandemie, ein politisches oder ein ökologisches Problem handelt, Verpackungen stehen in der Pflicht. In hundert Jahren dürfen sie die Umwelt nich mehr belasten und müssen „abfallfrei" sein. Neue Technologien und Materialien werden das ermöglichen – es liegt an uns allen, es umzusetzen. Seit 2007 wurden mehr als 19.000 Verpackungsdesigns bei den Pentawards eingereicht. Eine internationale Jury hat die Gewinner ausgewählt, darunter auch die starken Designs, die in diesem Buch, dem sechsten der Reihe, enthalten sind. Die Pentawards stellen Designs aus aller Welt vor und heben die besten Innovationen im Verpackungsdesign hervor.

Jedes Jahr werden die Beiträge von einer internationalen Jury bewertet, die sich aus den führenden Namen in Design und Marketing zusammensetzt. Mit mehr als 2000 Entwürfen in den 59 Kategorien ist das ein schwieriges Unterfangen, aber es ist zugleich aufregend und bereichernd. In einigen Kategorien wird die Aufgabe der Jury durch die jährlich ansteigende Zahl an Einreichungen noch schwieriger. Die Jurymitglieder müssen auch Designs aus „neuen" Vermarktungsländern außerhalb Europas, aus den Vereinigten Staaten und aus Japan bewerten. Es gibt jedes Jahr beeindruckende Beiträge aus diesen Ländern, insbesondere aus China, Russland und die aufstrebenden Länder Osteuropas und Südamerikas. Die Kreativität ist in diesen Ländern wahrscheinlich weniger zurückhaltend und die Verbraucher sind offener für neue Ideen.

Aber wie sticht ein Design aus allen anderen heraus? Wonach sucht die Jury? Hier sind einige Faktoren, die bei den Gewinnern von den Beiträgen 2019 und 2020 besonders auffällig waren.

2019

1. Einheit durch einen Zweck
Xbox von Microsoft

Als Microsoft den Xbox Adaptive Controller (S. 25) für Gamer mit Mobilitätseinschränkung vorstellte, bekamen sie viel Zuspruch von der Gaming-Community. Doch für ein barrierefreies Design hörte Microsoft nicht beim Controller auf, sondern schauten sich auch die Verpackung genau an. Das Resultat ist bahnbrechend. Microsoft verwendete Schlaufen und einen Scharniermechanismus an einer Box mit niedrigem Schwerpunkt und druckte sogar eine Anleitung auf die Verpackung, was einerseits hilft und dazu noch überflüssige Materialien einspart. Das Produkt ist ein Meilenstein für Barrierefreiheit in der Verpackungsindustrie. Es ist nicht nur ein hübsches Stück Verpackung, sondern erfüllt auch einen echten Zweck – und das ist jetzt wichtiger als je zuvor.

2. Ehre erweisen
Lind & Lime – Contagious

Lind & Lime (S. 33) ist ein Gin, der am Hafen der Leith Distillery in Edinburgh hergestellt wird. Die Ufer von Leith waren einst die Heimat einer Vielzahl von Industrien, eine Geschichte, die das Design und die Details der maßgeschneiderten Flasche inspirierte. Die trichterförmigen Glasöfen der Edinburgh und Leith Glass Works Fabrik konnten einst über dem Meeresspiegel gesehen werden. Die Flasche mit dem starken, eleganten langen Hals zollt ihnen mit ihrer einzigartigen Form und der Hommage an die Fabrik, die in den Boden eingraviert ist, Tribut. Das halbweiße Glas mit durchscheinendem hellgrünen Farbton verkörpert die Zitrusnuance des Getränks.

3. Verspieltheit
Stonebrick – Established

Stonebrick (S. 259) ist eine neue Make-up-Linie für Südkoreas größten Emart-Händler (Teil der Shinsegae Group). Die Idee hinter der Linie ist es, dem Kunden die Möglichkeit zu geben, ein maßgeschneidertes Kosmetikset auf spielerische Art zusammenzustellen. Diese neue Linie ist das erste komplett individualisierbare Make-up-Sortiment mit einzelnen magnetischen Komponenten, um personalisierte Kollektionen mit endlosen Möglichkeiten zu kreieren.

4. Eine neue konstruktive Form
Riceman – Backbone Branding

Müde von den immer gleichen einfachen Designs für Reisverpackungen, entschied Riceman (S. 144), dass sie etwas tun mussten, um sich von den Mitbewerbern abzuheben. Sie würdigen die harte Arbeit der Bauern mit Gesichtern, die verschiedene Emotionen zeigen. Die Verpackung vermittelt eine humane Botschaft und ist gleichzeitig funktional. Das ist eine charmante neue konstruktive Form von traditioneller Verpackung, etwas, wonach viele Designer in der Zukunft suchen werden, um Marken und das Storytelling eines Produkts zu stärken.

5. Nebeneinanderstellung
Perfeccionista – Robert Nuñez

Unvollkommenheit ergänzt einzigartige Elemente und schafft etwas wahrhaft Einzigartiges. Perfeccionista ist ein Wein aus der limitierten Produktion von nur 697 Flaschen eines Weinguts (S. 318). Um sich emotional mit dem Kunden zu verbinden, wird der Idee der Unvollkommenheit Wert beigemessen. Die Holzschilder wurden von Hand, ohne Stanze, gebrochen und mit einem Stempel nummeriert. So wird jede Verpackung einzigartig.

6. Denkwürdig sein
Xmas Data – Auriga

In einer Welt, die von potenziellen Weihnachtsgeschenken überflutet ist, wollte die spanische Designagentur Auriga ein Geschenk entwickeln, das ihr Geschäft und ihre Dienstleistungen auf eine unkonventionelle Art und Weise bewirbt. XMAS Data (S. 398) ist ein Set von vier Schokoladenschachteln mit essbaren Infografiken, die den Augen und Geschmacksnerven schmeicheln. Das minimalistische Design, die saubere Typografie, die verschiedene Schokoladensorten und ein benutzerfreundliches Auspacken machen dieses Werbestück interaktiv und unvergesslich.

2020

1. Nachhaltigkeit im Kern
Air Vodka von Air Company

Die Mission der Air Company ist es, die weltweit nachhaltigste Alkohol-Marke der Welt zu sein, was zu einer wiederverwendbaren und zu 100 % nachhaltigen Verpackung für die emissionsfreie Wodka-Marke führte. Um die Reinheit des Alkohols widerzuspiegeln, wurde ein durchdachtes Flaschendesign entwickelt (S. 24). Durch das natürliche und schadstofffreie Etikett kann die Glasflasche später auch für andere Zwecke genutzt werden – beispielsweise als Blumenvase. In der Erstnutzung bleibt der Wodka aber der Star, durch das niedrig platzierte Etikett ist er das Erste, was ins Auge sticht.

2. Personifizierte Persönlichkeit
Pridems Gin – Enpedra Estudio

Pridems Gin feiert Freiheit als das wesentlichste Prinzip des Menschen, indem sie eine Flasche entwarfen, die einen Seefahrer darstellt, ein klassisches Freiheitssymbol (S. 31). Der Verschluss in Form einer Matrosenmütze verleiht dem Produkt wahre Persönlichkeit und das Etikett, das aus vier einzelnen Teilen besteht, die sich vollständig um die Flasche wickeln, erzeugt ein einzigartiges Muster, das an die Uniform eines Matrosen erinnert. Das Resultat ist wirklich originell, denkwürdig und zeitlos.

3. Den Zeitgeist einfangen
Chioture – Shanghai Nianxiang Brand Design & Consulting Co., Ltd.

Chioture ist eine Make-up-Marke, die lebhaft und jugendlich ist. Ihr Schminkset hat die Form einer Kamera (S. 258). Die Verwendung von Pastellrosa, subtilen Details und sauberen Linien macht es zu einem sammelswerten Stück Verpackung. Als begehrenswertes Objekt wird es bestimmt auf Social-Media-Plattformen geteilt und seine Zielgruppe begeistern.

4. Eine einfache Idee
Nongfu Wangtian – ShenZhen BOB Design

Nongfu Wangtian (S. 145) ist eine Marke für Chilisoßen, die eine unkonventionelle Herangehensweise in die Supermarktregale bringt. Mit seiner Kollektion aus verschiedenen Geschmackssorten repräsentieren die Designer jede Sorte mit frecher leuchtender Farbe und der Verpackungen in Form einer Chilischote. Der Deckel der Soße hat die Form eines natürlich gebogenen Chilistiels, die so einfach im Laden aufgehängt und präsentiert werden kann. Dadurch fühlt sich der Kunde so, als ob er tatsächlich eine Chili vom Feld pflücken würde.

5. Zusammenarbeit
Hennessy – Felipe Pantone – Appartement 103

Hennessy ist ein französischer Cognac, von dem jährlich 50 Millionen Flaschen in der ganzen Welt verkauft werden. Die Marke, Designagentur Appartement 103 und der weltbekannte Straßenkünstler Felipe Pantone, haben für die neueste Collector's Edition (S. 319) zusammengearbeitet und das Resultat ist beeindruckend. Pantone ist bekannt für seinen Einsatz von Farbe, die bei diesem Projekt durch ein Prisma von grafischen Elementen und Texturen betrachtet werden kann. Der exklusive Flakon, der mit einer limitierten Auflage von 70 Stück auf den Markt gebracht wurde, steht auf einem Sockel im Zentrum eines Gitters aus Stäben mit Moiré-Muster, die der Konsument selbst positionieren, bewegen und austauschen kann, um die Optik der Flasche zu verändern. Dieses Verpackungsstück wird zu einem konfigurierbaren Kunstwerk und der Verbraucher kann seine Form verändern, die Perspektive wechseln und so ein Narrativ formen.

6. Perfekte Ausführung
Hema – Magnet Design firm

Hema ist eine bekannte niederländische Ladenkette, die eine Vielzahl von Haushaltswaren verkauft. Dieses charmante Sortiment von aufblasbaren Pool-Spielzeugen (S. 399) des Einzelhändlers zeigt verschiedene „Minischwimmbecken" auf der Verpackung. Der perfekte Einsatz der Fotografie lässt die Spielzeuge dreidimensional, bequem und spaßig wirken und macht es dem Konsumenten leicht, sie sich bei der Benutzung am Urlaubsort vorzustellen. Diesem Projekt wurden große Sorgfalt und Detailgenauigkeit zuteil, obwohl diese Art von Produkt in den meisten Fällen nicht die Liebe erfährt, die ihm gebührt.

Ich hoffe, Sie haben viel Freude beim Durchblättern und beim Entdecken der siegreichen Verpackungsdesigns der Pentawards von 2019 und 2020.

LE PACKAGING EN 2020

Adam Ryan
Directeur des Pentawards

J'écris ces lignes en décembre 2020 et si une chose est sûre, c'est que personne n'aurait pu prévoir que le monde allait plonger dans une telle incertitude. Tout a changé au cours des neuf derniers mois et entraîné deux crises simultanées : la COVID-19 et son impact sur l'économie. Tout ceci semble onirique mais est cependant bien réel, et nous sommes tous en train de faire un exercice d'adaptation à ce nouveau mode de vie.

Cette époque n'est pourtant pas sans effet positif sur l'humanité. Nous avons été témoins de merveilleux actes d'amour et de solidarité, la nature respire, nous avons plus de temps pour nos proches et le monde est devenu plus créatif, y compris des personnes n'appartenant pas à l'univers du design.

J'ai toujours été quelqu'un voyant plutôt le verre moitié plein que moitié vide. Il n'est pas évident de rester positif dernièrement, mais cette adaptation nous fera reconsidérer nos habitudes de consommation et ouvrira la porte à de nouvelles possibilités. Par exemple, les distilleries à divers coins du globe ont réorienté leur production pour fabriquer du désinfectant pour les mains, et des équipements de protection individuelle sont conçus à l'aide d'imprimantes 3D. Aux dires de John Archibald Wheeler, l'un des principes d'Albert Einstein était : « Au centre de la difficulté se trouve l'opportunité ». Tellement pertinent à l'heure actuelle.

Ces changements auront-ils alors une incidence sur le packaging ?

Le développement durable est devenu un aspect crucial pour le secteur des emballages, et les marques ont commencé à adopter une approche plus écoresponsable envers le packaging. Les consommateurs sont pour leur part plus conscients que jamais de ce qu'ils achètent et ils n'hésitent pas à se faire entendre si un emballage leur semble excessif et superflu. La réduction des déchets au fil de la chaîne de conditionnement, l'élimination du plastique et l'emploi de matériaux réutilisables sont autant de points sur lesquels travaillent dernièrement les designers et l'industrie des emballages.

La COVID-19 va-t-elle pour autant altérer cette approche de développement durable ? Dans le contexte de la pandémie, il se peut que les préoccupations en matière d'hygiène et de sécurité alimentaire prennent le dessus, et que la performance de certains substrats issus d'emballages en termes de développement durable voie, du moins à court terme, son importance diminuer. Ce bouleversement supposera également une pression accrue sur les coûts des lignes de conditionnement, mais aussi l'occasion d'adapter et de numériser l'activité chaque fois que possible.

Le commerce en ligne a pendant ce temps enregistré l'accélération attendue. Nombre d'entre nous consommons à travers des réseaux sociaux comme Instagram : nous découvrons des produits grâce aux images et vidéos que d'autres partagent et nous les achetons sans même les avoir physiquement touchés. Beaucoup de marques montantes de vente directe ont remporté un énorme succès en créant des packagings que les gens aiment photographier. Qui plus est, de nombreux designs sont reconnaissables à l'instant, ce qui offre aux marques une visibilité même lorsque leur public doit se contenter de photos en ligne. C'est pourquoi ont commencé à circuler des packagings plus singuliers car les marques s'efforcent de faire leur trou.

Comment je vois le packaging dans 100 ans ?

En 2019, *Forbes* déclarait : « La prochaine décennie d'innovation sera la plus importante de tous les temps ». Les récents événements ne feront qu'accélérer le processus, car à des époques comme celle que nous vivons aujourd'hui, on sait que l'innovation de produits diminue mais que celle de marques augmente. De nouvelles techniques verront par conséquent le jour pour que les marques interagissent avec les consommateurs et s'impliquent dans le packaging, qui n'a, à mon sens, jamais été aussi vital.

Qu'importe s'il s'agit d'une pandémie, d'un enjeu politique ou d'une question écologique : le packaging jouera dans tous les cas un rôle fondamental. Dans un siècle, nous devrons garantir le zéro déchets, et les emballages devront avoir un impact positif sur l'environnement. Les matériaux qui le permettront n'ont pas encore été inventés, et il nous revient à tous de parvenir à cette réalité.

Depuis 2007, plus de 19 000 designs de packagings de grande qualité ont été proposés aux Pentawards. Un jury international a choisi les lauréats, dont vous verrez les superbes créations dans cet ouvrage, sixième de la série. Les Pentawards sont la vitrine de ces designs et montrent les meilleures innovations en matière de packaging au niveau mondial.

Chaque année, les créations retenues sont jugées par un jury international formé de grands noms dans le monde du design et du marketing. Avec plus de 2 000 designs dans 59 catégories, la tâche est complexe, mais également passionnante et gratifiante. Dans certaines catégories, la sélection par le jury est d'autant plus difficile que le nombre de participants croît chaque année. Les membres doivent par ailleurs juger des créations provenant de « nouveaux » marchés en dehors de l'Europe, des États-Unis et du Japon. Tous les ans, un nombre conséquent de candidats proviennent de ces nouveaux pays, tels que la Chine, la Russie, les nations émergentes d'Europe de l'Est et les pays d'Amérique du Sud. La créativité est probablement moins limitée dans ces pays, et les consommateurs plus ouverts aux nouveautés.

Mais en quoi un design se distingue-t-il des autres ? Que recherche le jury ? Voici quelques aspects qui sont sortis du lot parmi les lauréats de 2019 et 2020.

2019

1. Unité autour d'un objectif
Xbox par Microsoft

Quand Microsoft a dévoilé sa manette Xbox Adaptive Controller (p. 25) pour les joueurs à mobilité réduite, elle a été largement applaudie par la communauté des gamers. En matière de design inclusif, Microsoft ne s'en est toutefois pas tenu à sa manette : le packaging a été soigneusement étudié et s'est avéré révolutionnaire. Dotée d'anses et d'un mécanisme de charnière, la boîte a un centre de gravité bas et les instructions sont imprimées sur la partie de l'emballage qui aide à retirer le produit, ce qui évite l'emploi excessif de matières. Le résultat marque un tournant en matière d'accessibilité pour les consommateurs, car le packaging n'est pas seulement superbe, il sert aussi un objectif. Sa pertinence compte aujourd'hui plus que jamais.

2. Rendre hommage
Lind & Lime – Contagious

Lind & Lime (p. 32) est un gin produit dans la distillerie écossaise du port de Leith à Édimbourg. Le littoral de Leith accueillait dans le passé une pléthore d'industries, et cette histoire a inspiré le design et les détails de cette bouteille sur mesure. Il fut un temps où le profil de la fabrique de verre Edinburgh and Leith Glass Works se dessinait au-dessus du niveau de la mer. Avec sa forme unique, l'élégante bouteille au long col lui rend hommage, tout comme l'inscription en relief sur son culot. La teinte vert clair du verre translucide vient symboliser les notes citronnées du gin.

3. Jovialité
Stonebrick – Established

Stonebrick est une nouvelle ligne de maquillage proposée par Emart (du groupe Shinsegae), le plus grand détaillant de Corée du Sud, avec l'idée de permettre au consommateur d'acheter des produits cosmétiques d'une manière amusante et originale (p. 259). Grâce à des éléments aimantés, la ligne est totalement personnalisable pour créer des collections aux combinaisons infinies.

4. Une nouvelle forme constructive
Riceman – Backbone Branding

Lassé des habituels designs ordinaires pour les emballages de riz, la marque Riceman (p. 144) a décidé qu'elle devait se démarquer de ses concurrents. Et pour ce faire, elle honore le dur labeur des exploitants grâce aux illustrations de visages exprimant divers sentiments ; le packaging humanise ainsi le produit tout en étant fonctionnel. Cette charmante réinterprétation de l'emballage traditionnel est une forme constructive que nombre de concepteurs rechercheront à l'avenir pour renforcer les marques et l'accroche narrative des produits.

5. Juxtaposition
Perfeccionista – Robert Nuñez

Les imperfections rajoutent des éléments distinctifs et confèrent un caractère unique. Perfeccionista est le vin d'un domaine viticole dont la production est limitée à seulement 697 bouteilles. Afin de nouer un lien émotionnel avec le consommateur, le packaging donne de la valeur à l'idée d'imperfection. Les étiquettes en bois ont été cassées à la main, sans emporte-pièce, et estampillées à l'encre pour que chaque emballage soit exclusif (p. 318).

6. Être mémorable
Xmas Data – Auriga

Dans un monde saturé d'options pour les cadeaux de Noël, l'agence de design espagnole Auriga a souhaité créer un cadeau original pour vanter son activité et ses services. XMAS Data est un lot de quatre boîtes de chocolats aux infographies comestibles (p. 398), un design qui organise les données en une composition aussi plaisante pour les yeux que pour les papilles. La création minimaliste, la typographie épurée, les divers parfums des chocolats et une expérience de déballage conviviale rendent cet article promotionnel à la fois interactif et mémorable.

2020

1. Durable par essence
Air Vodka par Air Company

Servant l'objectif d'Air Company d'être la marque d'alcool la plus écoresponsable au monde, le packaging de la première vodka à bilan carbone négatif est 100 % durable. La pureté du spiritueux est reflétée par la magnifique bouteille novatrice et soignée (p.24). L'étiquette est personnalisée, non toxique et facilement amovible pour réutiliser la bouteille comme récipient à eau, vase ou bougeoir. La vodka d'Air Company garde la vedette : au lieu de l'habituel emplacement au centre de la bouteille, l'étiquette se trouve au bas et dégage ainsi une généreuse surface pour exhiber la vodka, qui retient alors toute l'attention.

2. Personnalité personnifiée
Gin Pridem's – Enpedra Estudio

En créant une bouteille à l'image d'un matelot, Pridem's transmet avec son gin l'idée de liberté tellement essentielle pour l'être humain (p.31). Le bouchon en forme de béret de marin dote le produit de personnalité, alors que l'étiquette est faite de quatre bandes qui enveloppent totalement la bouteille pour rappeler le motif de l'uniforme. La bouteille obtenue est aussi originale que mémorable et intemporelle.

3. Capturer le zeitgeist
Chioture – Shanghai Nianxiang Brand Design & Consulting Co., Ltd.

Chioture est une marque de maquillage jeune et dynamique qui propose un kit prenant la forme d'un adorable appareil photo (p.258). Le choix du rose pastel, de détails subtils et de lignes épurées font de ce packaging un collector. Objet de convoitise, il garantit son partage sur les réseaux sociaux pour le plaisir de son public cible.

4. Une idée simple
Nongfu Wangtian – ShenZhen BOB Design

Nongfu Wangtian est une marque de sauce au chili qui offre une expérience originale au supermarché. À travers une collection de goûts, les designers représentent chaque variété en recourant à des couleurs franches et un packaging en forme de piment (p.145). Le bouchon du tube rappelle une tige dont l'arrondi permet de le pendre facilement dans un présentoir, ce qui donne au consommateur l'impression de cueillir réellement un piment.

5. Collaboration
Hennessy – Felipe Pantone – Appartement 103

Hennessy est une entreprise française de Cognac qui vend à travers le monde plus de 50 millions de bouteilles par an. Le résultat de la collaboration entre la marque, l'agence de design Appartement 103 et le célèbre artiste de rue innovateur Felipe Pantone sur la dernière édition Collector (p.319) est tout simplement sensationnel. Pantone est célèbre pour son utilisation de la couleur qui se retrouve dans ce projet avec un prisme d'élément graphiques et de textures. Avec un lancement mondial limité à 70 unités, la carafe de luxe repose sur un piédestal au centre d'une grille de tiges moirées que le consommateur peut insérer, déplacer ou permuter afin de changer le visuel de la bouteille. Ce packaging devient une création évolutive dont le consommateur peut changer la forme et en modifier ainsi la perspective et la mise en récit.

6. Exécution parfaite
Hema – Magnet Design

Hema est une célèbre chaîne de magasins néerlandaise qui vend toute une gamme d'articles ménagers. Le packaging de cette charmante collection de jouets gonflables est illustré de mini-piscines 8p. 399), et les prises de vue les font paraître en 3 dimensions, confortables et amusants, autant d'attraits pour que les consommateurs les imaginent pour leurs vacances. Ce projet dénote un souci tout particulier du détail, sachant que ce type de produit ne reçoit le plus souvent pas toute l'attention qu'il mérite.

Je vous souhaite infiniment de plaisir à parcourir cet ouvrage et à découvrir les packagings gagnants des Pentawards 2019 et 2020.

pentawards

LOVE PACKAGING DESIGN?

Find out how you can enter our competition,
attend our live events and join our global network at:

pentawards.com

diamond

Best of show

COMBINING THE ART AND SCIENCE OF LABEL DESIGN

Consumers do not just buy a product – they want to feel it with all their senses. When a consumer looks at the product on the shelf, it is the **first opportunity for a brand to make a lasting impression**. The label is the most influential element in the decision-making process – consumers need to be attracted to its look and feel. Therefore, the label sells the first product.

The label is the silent salesman, and thus, brands must work hard to create eye-catching designs that speak to the consumer and are part of the experience. If the bottle forms the body of the wine, the label is its face. Label materials help to tell the story and **enable the experience of elegance, authenticity and environmental awareness**. They play a crucial role in showing the quality and might need to survive in demanding conditions like ice buckets or refrigerated storage.

Successful label design is a collaborative process. **UPM Raflatac** works closely with designers, brand managers and printers from around the world to create product label designs that tell a story without compromising sustainability or functionality.

Climate change is the greatest challenge of our times, and sustainable packaging is a step in the right direction. For UPM Raflatac, supporting brand owners in their transformation is a natural part of the business. Even though labels are a small part of the packaging, they **play an important role in keeping the environmental footprint as small as possible** and in enhancing recyclability.

In the world of packaging, labels matter. Design is the starting point for sustainable packaging, and **labels are a part of sustainable packaging design**. As one of the world's leading producers of self-adhesive label materials, UPM Raflatac has taken up the task of labelling a smarter future beyond fossil resources.

KUNST UND WISSENSCHAFT BEIM ETTIKETTENDESIGN VEREINEN

Konsumenten kaufen ein Produkt nicht einfach – sie möchten es mit all ihren Sinnen erleben. Wenn ein Konsument das Produkt in den Regalen sieht, ist das die **erste Möglichkeit für eine Marke, einen bleibenden Eindruck zu hinterlassen**. Das Etikett ist in diesem Entscheidungsprozess am einflussreichsten – Konsumenten müssen von dessen Aussehen und Haptik angezogen werden. Deswegen verkauft das Etikett das erste Produkt.

Das Etikett ist ein stiller Verkäufer und deswegen müssen Marken hart arbeiten, um auffällige Designs zu schaffen, die den Konsumenten ansprechen und Teil des Verkaufserlebnisses sind. Wenn die Flasche der Körper des Weins ist, so ist das Etikett sein Gesicht. Die Materialien der Etiketten helfen, die Geschichte zu erzählen und **ermöglichen die Erfahrung von Eleganz, Authentizität und Umweltbewusstsein**. Sie spielen eine entscheidende Rolle, wenn es darum geht, die Qualität zu zeigen und müssen unter Umständen unter anspruchsvollen Bedingungen überleben wie in Eiskübeln oder dem Kühllager.

Das erfolgreiche Design eines Etiketts ist ein gemeinsamer Prozess. **UPM Raflatac** arbeitet eng mit Designern, Markenmanagern und Druckereien aus der ganzen Welt zusammen, um Produktetikettendesigns zu entwerfen, die eine Geschichte erzählen, ohne Kompromisse einzugehen, wenn es um Nachhaltigkeit oder Funktionalität geht.

Der Klimawandel ist die größte Herausforderung unserer Zeit und nachhaltige Verpackungen sind ein Schritt in die richtige Richtung. Für UPM Raflatac ist die Unterstützung der Markeninhaber bei dieser Transformation ein natürlicher Teil des Geschäfts. Auch wenn Etiketten nur ein kleiner Teil der Verpackung sind, **spielen sie eine wichtige Rolle, um den ökologischen Fußabdruck so klein wie möglich zu halten** und die Wiederverwertbarkeit zu verbessern.

In der Verpackungswelt spielen Etiketten eine wichtige Rolle. Das Design ist der Anfangspunkt für nachhaltige Verpackungen, und **Etiketten sind ein Teil des nachhaltigen Verpackungsdesigns**. Als einer der weltweit führenden Produzenten von selbstklebenden Etikettenmaterialien hat sich UPM Raflatac der Aufgabe angenommen, eine intelligentere Zukunft jenseits von fossilen Rohstoffen anzugehen.

LE MARIAGE DE L'ART ET DE LA SCIENCE DU DESIGN D'ÉTIQUETTES

Les consommateurs ne se contentent pas d'acheter un produit : ils veulent le sentir à travers tous leurs sens. Et quand ils le voient en rayon, c'est la **première occasion pour la marque de laisser une impression durable**. L'étiquette est donc l'élément ayant le plus de poids dans le processus de prise de décision, car le client doit être attiré par son apparence. Elle est par conséquent le premier argument de vente.

L'étiquette est un vendeur silencieux, et les marques doivent s'efforcer de créer des designs accrocheurs parlant aux clients et contribuant à leur expérience. Si la bouteille forme le corps du vin, l'étiquette en est le visage. Les matériaux des étiquettes aident à la mise en récit et **offrent une expérience d'élégance, d'authenticité et de conscience environnementale**. Ils sont déterminants car vecteurs de qualité, et ils doivent parfois survivre dans des conditions difficiles telles que seaux à glace ou chambres réfrigérées.

Une conception réussie d'étiquette est un processus collaboratif. **UPM Raflatac** travaille en étroite collaboration avec les concepteurs, les directeurs de marque et les imprimeurs du monde entier pour réaliser des designs d'étiquettes de produits racontant une histoire sans en compromettre la durabilité ou la fonctionnalité.

Le changement climatique est le défi le plus important de notre époque, et un packaging écoresponsable marque un pas dans la bonne direction. Pour UPM Raflatac, il est tout naturel d'aider les marques à évoluer. Et même si les étiquettes sont un petit élément de l'emballage, elles **jouent un rôle majeur pour limiter le plus possible l'empreinte écologique** et améliorer la recyclabilité.

Dans l'univers du packaging, les étiquettes comptent. La conception est le point de départ de tout emballage écoresponsable, et les **étiquettes font partie intégrante du design de cet emballage**. En tant que l'un des principaux fabricants au monde de matériaux pour étiquettes auto-adhésives, UPM Raflatac prépare l'étiquetage d'un futur plus intelligent affranchi des énergies fossiles.

PENTAWARDS' DIAMOND

Our international jury is composed of members from 18 countries, across three continents, including first-time representatives from India, Denmark, Armenia, Switzerland and Brazil. In 2020 we expanded our jury to include a wide mix of design agencies, brands and cooperations, which include Lego, Nestlé, Amazon, Microsoft, Shiseido and Facebook. Having more jury members has helped with an ever-growing number of competition entries, allowing each jury member more time to dedicate to each entry they vote on.

Each of the 30 jury members brings their own expertise, cultural perspective and energy, creating an incredible formula that is just unparalleled across the globe. Each member is a part of the jury for a minimum of three years, showing how dedicated they are, even in such busy times.

The mix of different cultures on the jury is extremely important, especially when it comes to comparing work from China to work from Spain, Russia or the Nordic countries, just as there are clear cultural distinctions between work coming out of the UK and that coming from South America.

As our competition becomes more competitive year after year, the eclectic group of individuals collectively referred to as the International Pentawards Jury are faced with the task of reaching a unanimous decision on which packaging designs have truly universal appeal. Consensus is essential but not always easy. However, when the jury meet to cast their votes, they are invariably united over the Best of Show Diamond winner.

Since its conception in 2007, Pentawards has consistently awarded the top accolade to designs that cut through the unnecessary and leave only the necessary, making simplicity the defining criterion of the Diamond Pentaward winner. In 2019, it was the groundbreaking Xbox Adaptive Controller; in 2020, it was the unmistakable perfection of the packaging for world's first carbon negative vodka, Air Vodka.

Unsere internationale Jury setzt sich aus Mitgliedern aus 18 verschiedenen Ländern verteilt auf drei Kontinente zusammen. Dazu gehören Vertreter aus Indien, Dänemark, Armenien, der Schweiz und Brasilien. Im Jahr 2020 haben wir unsere Jury erweitert, die jetzt aus einer vielfältigen Mischung aus Designagenturen, Markenvertretern und Kooperationspartnern besteht, zu denen unter anderem Lego, Nestlé, Amazon, Microsoft, Shiseido und Facebook gehören. Durch die größere Anzahl an Jurymitgliedern war es einfacher, die stetig wachsende Zahl an Wettbewerbsbeiträgen zu bewältigen, denn so hatte jedes Jurymitglied mehr Zeit, sich einem Beitrag zu widmen, über den es abstimmt.

Jedes der 30 Jurymitglieder bringt seine eigene Expertise, seine eigene kulturelle Sichtweise und Energie ein, wodurch eine unglaubliche Formel entsteht, die weltweit ihresgleichen sucht. Die Mitglieder gehören der Jury mindestens drei Jahre lang an, was zeigt, wie engagiert sie sind, selbst in so turbulenten Zeiten.

Die Mischung verschiedener Kulturen in der Jury ist unheimlich wichtig, besonders wenn es darum geht, Arbeiten aus China mit Arbeiten aus Spanien, Russland oder den nordischen Ländern zu vergleichen. Genauso wie es auch klare kulturelle Unterschiede zwischen der Arbeit aus dem Vereinigten Königreich und der aus Südamerika gibt.

Da unser Wettbewerb von Jahr zu Jahr konkurrenzstärker wird, steht die vielfältige Gruppe aus Einzelpersonen, die gemeinsam als „International Pentawards Jury" bezeichnet wird, vor der Aufgabe, eine einstimmige Entscheidung darüber zu treffen, welche Verpackungsdesigns wirklich universell ansprechend sind. Ein Konsens ist dabei essenziell wichtig, aber nicht immer einfach zu finden. Über die Wahl des „Best of Show Diamond"-Gewinners sind sich die Jurymitglieder jedoch jedes Jahr einig.

Seit seiner Gründung im Jahr 2007, hat Pentawards die höchste Auszeichnung stets an Designs verliehen, die Unnötiges ausmerzen und das Nötige herausarbeiten. Schlicht und einfach – das sind die ausschlaggebenden Kriterien für den „Diamond Pentaward". Im Jahr 2019 hat das der bahnbrechende Xbox Adaptive Controller erfüllt; 2020 überzeugte die unverkennbare Perfektion der Flasche des ersten emissionsfreien Wodkas, Air Vodka.

Notre jury international est composé de membres originaires de 18 pays et trois continents, intégrant pour la première fois des représentants de l'Inde, du Danemark, de l'Arménie, de la Suisse et du Brésil. Il a en 2020 pris de l'ampleur pour inclure un large éventail d'agences de design, de marques et de collaborations, dont Lego, Nestlé, Amazon, Microsoft, Shiseido et Facebook. Un plus grand jury s'est avéré opportun face au volume toujours croissant de contributions à la compétition, les membres ayant pu consacrer plus de temps à chaque candidature avant d'émettre leur vote.

Chacun des 30 membres du jury apporte sa propre expertise, sa perspective culturelle et son énergie, ce qui donne lieu à une incroyable formule sans pareille dans le monde. Chaque membre participe au jury pour un minimum de trois ans, preuve de leur engagement y compris en ces temps mouvementés.

La diversité culturelle du jury est essentielle, notamment lorsqu'il s'agit de comparer des créations de Chine à d'autres d'Espagne, de Russie ou des pays nordiques ; de la même façon, les contrastes culturels sont évidents entre un design du Royaume-Uni et un d'Amérique du Sud.

La compétition s'intensifiant avec les années, le groupe éclectique de personnes qui forment le jury international des Pentawards a la rude mission de choisir à l'unanimité les packagings possédant un attrait réellement universel. Le consensus n'est pas toujours simple à atteindre mais lorsque le jury se réunit pour voter, il finit toujours par s'entendre sur le lauréat du Best of Show Diamond.

Depuis leur création en 2007, les Pentawards décernent la plus prestigieuse récompense aux designs qui savent éliminer le superflu pour ne conserver que le nécessaire, faisant de la simplicité le critère principal pour élire le lauréat d'un Diamond Pentaward. En 2019, le prix est allé à la manette révolutionnaire Xbox Adaptive Controller ; en 2020, il a récompensé la perfection manifeste du packaging pour Air Vodka, la première vodka au monde à bilan carbone négatif.

AIR VODKA

Co-Founder and CEO: Gregory Constantine
(Air Company)
Co-Founder and CTO: Dr. Stafford Sheehan
(Air Company)
Graphic and Packaging Design: Joe Doucet,
Chris Thorpe (Joe Doucet x Partners)
Logo Design: Mythology
Company: Air Company
Country: USA
Category: Spirits (clear)

DIAMOND PENTAWARD 2020

With a mission to be the most sustainable alcohol brand in the world, the packaging for **Air Company**, the world's first carbon negative vodka brand, is both reusable and 100% sustainable. Keeping the vodka as the star, the label is split in two parts, with one placed at the neck of the bottle and the other at the bottom, giving ample space to display the spirit. The label itself is simple, custom-made, natural and non-toxic and can be removed easily so the bottle can be used for other purposes, such as a water bottle, flower vase or candle holder. This packaging and design is as forward-thinking, modern and transformative as the approach to creating the Air Company brand.

Mit der Mission, der nachhaltigste Alkohol-hersteller der Welt zu sein, entwirft die erste emissions-freie Wodka-Marke **Air Company** eine Flasche, die sowohl wiederverwendbar als auch 100 % nachhaltig ist. Damit der Wodka der Star bleibt, ist das Etikett in zwei Teile geteilt, eine Hälfte ist auf dem Flaschenhals platziert, die andere auf dem Boden. So bleibt genügend Platz, um die Spirituose zu präsentieren. Das Etikett selbst ist schlicht, handgefertigt, schadstofffrei und kann leicht entfernt werden. So kann die Flasche für andere Zwecke genutzt werden, etwa als Blumenvase oder Kerzenhalter. Diese Verpackung ist zukunftsorientiert, modern und wandelbar, genau wie die Marke.

Servant l'objectif d'être la marque d'alcool la plus écoresponsable de la planète, l'emballage pour **Air Company**, première marque de vodka au monde à bilan carbone négatif, est à la fois réutilisable et 100 % durable. La vodka reste la vedette et l'étiquette compte deux parties : l'une sur le goulot et l'autre au bas de la bouteille, laissant un grand espace pour exhiber le spiritueux. L'étiquette en soi est simple, sur mesure, non toxique mais aussi amovible, ce qui permet d'utiliser ensuite la bouteille comme récipient à eau, vase ou bougeoir. Packaging et design s'avèrent être aussi visionnaires, modernes et transformateurs que l'approche créative de la marque Air Company.

What made this Diamond winning piece stand out was its unique customer experience. Designed for gamers with limited mobility, the **Xbox Adaptive Controller** perfected the out-of-box experience with its accessible packaging. Using insights gleaned from beta testers and UX respondents, each element of the packaging and unboxing had accessibility first in mind. Key elements that were incorporated include loops, which are highly proven to assist in accessibility, and an open area under the controller, making it easier to remove it from the box. This packaging design was a milestone for accessible packaging, one which Microsoft should be proud of.

Dieser Diamant-Gewinner stach vor allem durch seine einzigartige Verbrauchernähe heraus. Entworfen für Gamer mit eingeschränkter Beweglichkeit bietet der **Xbox Adaptive Controller** mit seiner barrierefreien Verpackung ein ganzheitliches Auspackerlebnis. Die Erfahrungen von Beta-Testern und Erkenntnisse aus einer Verbraucherumfrage flossen in das Design ein, damit jedes Element der Verpackung in der Praxis funktioniert. Schlüsselelemente, sind Schlaufen, die sich gut greifen lassen, sowie ein offener Bereich unterhalb des Controllers, der das Herausnehmen aus der Box erleichtert. Das Verpackungsdesign ist ein Meilenstein für barrierefreie Verpackung, auf das Microsoft stolz sein sollte.

La raison pour laquelle cette création lauréate d'un Diamond s'est distinguée est l'expérience unique qu'elle garantit au consommateur. Conçue pour les joueurs à mobilité réduite, la manette **Xbox Adaptive Controller** atteint la perfection de l'expérience immédiate grâce à son packaging accessible. À partir des informations obtenues de testeurs bêta et de personnes interrogées sur l'UX, chaque élément de l'emballage et son unboxing privilégient l'accessibilité. Des aspects clés ont été incorporés, comme des anses à l'utilité prouvée en matière d'accessibilité, et un espace ouvert sous la manette pour en simplifier l'extraction de la boîte. Le design de ce packaging a fait date dans l'histoire des emballages accessibles, et Microsoft peut en être fier.

XBOX

Packaging Design: Mark Weiser
Creative Direction: Kevin Marshall
Company: Microsoft
Country: USA
Category: Electronic

DIAMOND PENTAWARD 2019

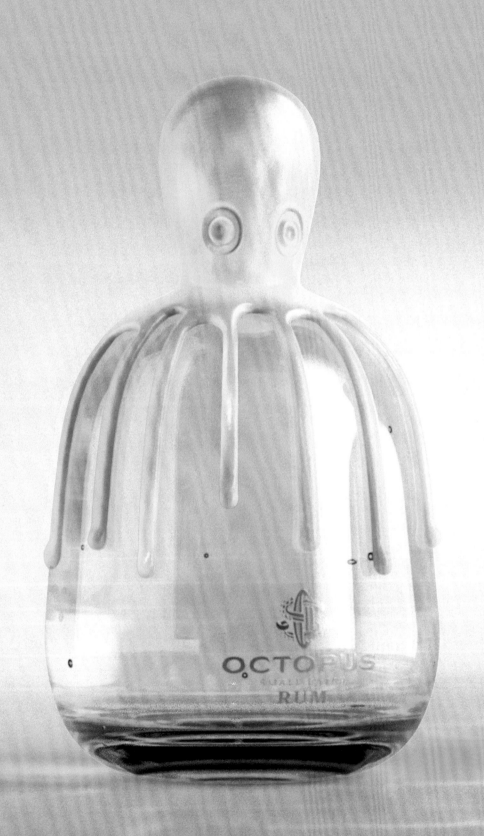

Best of the category

Water

Soft drinks, juices

Tea and coffee

Functional beverages

Beer

Ciders and low-alcohol drinks

beverages

Aperitifs

Wines

Spirits

Limited editions, limited series, event creations

Distributors'/retailers' own brands/private labels

Packaging concept

Sponsored by

THE GOLD AMBASSADOR

Luxoro is the exclusive Italian partner of the KURZ Group, a global player and international flagship for hot and cold stamping technologies. Luxoro inspirations are meant to spread a new form of packaging experience for brand identity, finishing solutions of remarkable beauty and high-quality materials to create unique designs.

Whether it be **packaging, labels, bookbinding, high security, brand protection, cosmetics, automotive or fashion industry**, Luxoro products and ideas are always avant-garde and surprising. Luxoro finishing products can also protect surfaces and prevent counterfeiting. Moreover, the huge product portfolio includes optical elements with digital functions, linking the visual to the virtual world. Luxoro provides complete solutions that include project consultancy plus machine and die technology. Thanks to rigorous corporate policies for environmental sustainability, Luxoro has long been a **carbon neutral and fully renewable energy** company.

Why Luxoro special wine labels? The wine label is like a business card, which tells the product history and expresses its value. It is necessary to pay attention to the sensations, to make the label no longer just a means of information, but **a life experience, a story that remains**. Luxoro wine label projects are studied to obtain an innovative packaging by creating infinite combinations with the best finishing technologies, in order to make the label not only attractive but also a work of art.

Luxoro likes to be known as the Gold Ambassador; gold is the most important eye-catcher. An element that is historically a **symbol of value and beauty**. Through the hot stamping of precious and structured effects, the label is able to emerge and make a difference, arousing emotions and sensations.

DER GOLD-BOTSCHAFTER

Luxoro ist der exklusive italienische Partner der KURZ-Gruppe, einem Weltkonzern und internationalen Flaggschiff für Heiß- und Kaltprägetechnologien. Luxoros Inspirationen sollen eine neue Form des Verpackungserlebnisses für die Markenidentität, Veredelungslösungen von bemerkenswerter Schönheit und Materialien mit hoher Qualität verbreiten, um einzigartige Designs zu erschaffen.

Ob es um **Verpackung, Etiketten, Buchbindung, Hochsicherheit, Markenschutz, Kosmetik, die Automobil- oder Modeindustrie** geht, die Produkte und Ideen von Luxoro sind immer fortschrittlich und überraschend. Luxoros Veredelungsprodukte können auch Oberflächen schützen und Produktfälschung verhindern. Außerdem umfasst das große Produktportfolio optische Elemente mit digitalen Funktionen, die die visuelle mit der virtuellen Welt verbinden. Luxoro bietet Komplettlösungen, die Projektberatung sowie Maschinen- und Werkzeugtechnologie beinhalten. Dank der rigorosen Unternehmenspolitik für Umweltverträglichkeit ist Luxoro seit langem ein **emissionsfreies und komplett mit erneuerbaren** Energien betriebenes Unternehmen.

Warum spezielle Weinetiketten von Luxoro? Das Weinetikett ist wie eine Visitenkarte, die die Produktgeschichte erzählt und seinen Wert zum Ausdruck bringt. Es ist notwendig, auf die Empfindungen zu achten, um das Etikett nicht mehr länger ein Informationsmittel sein zu lassen, sondern **eine Lebenserfahrung, eine Geschichte, die bleibt**. Weinetiketten-Projekte von Luxoro werden analysiert, um eine innovative Verpackung zu erhalten, indem unendliche Kombinationsmöglichkeiten mit den besten Veredelungstechnologien geschaffen werden, um das Etikett nicht nur attraktiv, sondern auch zu einem Kunstwerk zu machen.

Luxoro ist gerne als Goldbotschafter bekannt; Gold ist der wichtigste Blickfang. Ein Element, das historisch gesehen ein **Symbol von Wert und Schönheit ist**. Durch die Heißprägung von besonderen und strukturierten Effekten ist das Etikett in der Lage hervorzustechen und einen Unterschied zu machen, um Emotionen und Gefühle zu erregen.

L'AMBASSADEUR DE L'OR

Luxoro est le distributeur italien exclusif du groupe KURZ, leader mondial des technologies d'estampage à chaud et à froid. L'inspiration créative de Luxoro s'attache à diffuser une nouvelle forme d'expérience de packaging concernant l'identité des marques, des solutions de finition d'une extrême beauté et des matériaux de grande qualité, le tout dans le but de créer des designs uniques.

Packaging, étiquettes, reliure, haute sécurité, protection de marques, cosmétiques, automobile ou mode : quel que soit le secteur, les produits et les idées de Luxoro sont toujours avant-gardistes et surprenants. Les produits de finition Luxoro permettent également de protéger les surfaces et d'éviter les contrefaçons. Son large éventail de produits compte par ailleurs des éléments optiques dotés de fonctions numériques qui connectent le monde réel au monde virtuel. Luxoro offre des solutions complètes allant de l'étude de projets aux machines et aux technologies de découpe. Grâce à des politiques strictes en matière de viabilité environnementale, Luxoro est depuis longtemps une entreprise opérant avec des **énergies entièrement renouvelables, à neutralité carbone.**

Alors pourquoi les étiquettes de vin Luxoro ? Pour un vin, l'étiquette est sa carte de visite, elle transmet son histoire et sa valeur. Il ne faut pas négliger les sensations et l'étiquette ne doit pas être uniquement informative, mais **une expérience de vie, une histoire qui reste en mémoire**. Les projets d'étiquettes de vin Luxoro sont conçus pour procurer un packaging innovant à l'aide de combinaisons infinies et des meilleures technologies de finition. Plus qu'attrayante, l'étiquette devient une œuvre d'art.

Luxoro aime être considéré comme l'Ambassadeur de l'Or. L'or est accrocheur, il est de tout temps un élément **symbole de valeur et de beauté**. Avec l'estampage à chaud d'effets précieux et structurés, l'étiquette se révèle et fait toute la différence en suscitant des émotions et des sensations.

LUXORO

This conceptual piece for **Happy Ghost** is based on the iconic image of a ghost in a white shroud, which made its first appearance in 1916. Today this eerie spirit can be seen haunting the shelves of off-licences. To create this character, the design uses a deep indentation at the bottom of the bottle, along with a pair of spooky eyes, whilst the colouring of the glass creates a dark fog and mystical atmosphere.

Dieses konzeptionelle Stück für **Happy Ghost** basiert auf dem Bild eines Geists im weißen Laken, das 1916 das erste Mal auftauchte. Heute kann man dieses schaurige Gespenst auf den Regalen von Wein- und Spirituosenhändlern spuken sehen. Das Design nutzt die Wölbung am Boden der Flasche. In Kombination mit einem Paar gespenstischer Augen bildet die Vertiefung den Charakter des Geists, während die Farbe des Glases dunklen Nebel und eine mystische Atmosphäre erzeugt.

Cette création pour le rhum **Happy Ghost** s'inspire de la typique image du fantôme sous un voile blanc, dont la première apparition remonte à 1916. Cet esprit surnaturel se retrouve aujourd'hui à hanter les rayons des débits de boissons. Le personnage prend vie grâce à la forme du profond renfoncement à la base de la bouteille et à une paire d'yeux lugubres, sans compter la teinte du verre qui crée une brume obscure et une atmosphère mystique.

HAPPY GHOST

Design: Pavla Chuykina
Company: Pavla Chuykina
Country: Australia
Category: Packaging concept (professional)
PLATINUM PENTAWARD 2020

PRIDEM'S GIN

Design and Art Direction: Jose Vila
Company: Enpedra Estudio
Country: Spain
Category: Spirits (clear)

PLATINUM PENTAWARD 2020

The design concept for **Pridem's** premium gin centres around the idea of a sailor, to represent and celebrate freedom. The design is made up of two complex elements: a striking stopper shaped like a sailor's hat that gives the product personality and emphasises its uniqueness, and a label that is made up of four separate parts that wrap completely around the frustoconical bottle.

Im Mittelpunkt des Konzepts für den Premium Gin von **Pridem** steht das Bild eines freeheitsliebenden Seefahrers. Das Design besteht aus zwei komplexen Elementen: Einem auffälligen Verschluss in Form einer Matrosenmütze, der dem Produkt Persönlichkeit verleiht und seine Einzigartigkeit unterstreicht, und einem Etikett, das aus vier einzelnen Teilen besteht, die sich um die kegelstumpfförmige Flasche wickeln.

Le design pensé pour le gin premium de **Pridem** gravite autour de l'image du matelot afin de transmettre l'idée de liberté. Il se compose de deux éléments élaborés, que sont un bouchon impactant en forme de béret de marin, dotant le produit de personnalité et soulignant sa singularité, et une étiquette faite de quatre bandes enveloppant totalement la bouteille tronconique.

LIND & LIME

Art Direction and Design: James Hartigan
Artwork: Chris McCluskie
Account Management: Lauren Baillie
Photography: Paul Hollingworth
Printing: CCL Labels
Bottle Production: Vetro Elite
Company: Contagious
Country: UK
Category: Spirits

PLATINUM PENTAWARD 2019

Inspiration for the **Lind & Lime Gin** bottle was drawn from the histories of the people and industries of Leith in Scotland, represented by the unique intricacies of the bespoke bottle, label and name. The outline of the Edinburgh and Leith Glass Works factory could once be seen rising above sea level, which is reflected in both the strong, elegant long neck of the bottle and in the embossed depiction stamped at its base. The design also takes inspiration from the bottle contents, with the translucent light green hue of the glass epitomising the citrus tones of the gin.

Die **Lind & Lime Gin**-Flasche ist von der Geschichte der Menschen im schottischen Leith und ihrer Industrie inspiriert, die in den einzigartigen Feinheiten besagter Flasche dargestellt werden. Die Umrisse der trichterförmigen Glasbrennöfen der Edinburgh und Leith Glass Works Fabrik erhoben sich einst über dem Meeresspiegel. Die Form findet sich in dem starken, eleganten langen Hals der Flasche und in dem eingravierten Bild auf deren Boden wieder. Vom Inhalt der Flasche inspiriert, verkörpert der durchscheinende hellgrüne Farbton des Glases die Zitrusnuancen des Gins.

L'inspiration à l'origine de la bouteille **Lind & Lime Gin** se trouve dans les histoires des habitants et des industries de la ville écossaise de Leith, évoquées par les subtilités du nom, de l'étiquette et de la bouteille sur mesure. Il fut un temps où la silhouette de la fabrique de verre Edinburgh and Leith Glass Works se dressait au-dessus du niveau de la mer : le long col, à la fois robuste et élégant, et l'inscription en relief sur le culot de la bouteille font référence à ce passé. Le design s'inspire également du contenu, avec une teinte vert clair translucide qui symbolise parfaitement les notes citronnées du gin.

LUHUA MOUNTAIN SPRING WATER

Design: Shaobin Lin
Photography: Yanpeng Chen
Company: Lin Shaobin Design
Country: China
Category: Water

GOLD PENTAWARD 2020

HANSHUIXIGU

Creative Direction and Design: Xiongbo Deng
Illustration: Zhijie Liu
Client: Shaanxi Selenium Valley
Industry Development
Company: ShenZhen Lingyun Creative
Packaging Design
Country: China
Category: Water

GOLD PENTAWARD 2019

This limited edition of **HanShuiXiGu** mineral water was launched in 2018 with packaging inspired by its water source, the Qinling Mountains. The main features of the design are the drawings of four rare animals that live in these mountains: the panda, the crested ibis, the golden monkey and the antelope. Within the outline of these the local landscape of the mountains is visible. Furthermore, to help promote the importance of environmental protection, the conventional plastic water bottles were swapped with "Ooho", an edible water blob widely promoted in 2017.

Diese limitierte Edition des **HanShuiXiGu**-Mineralwassers wurde 2018 auf den Markt gebracht. Die Verpackung ist von der Quelle des Wassers, den Qinling-Bergen, inspiriert. Die Hauptmerkmale des Designs sind die Zeichnungen von vier seltenen Tieren, die in diesen Bergen leben: der Panda, der japanische Ibis, die Goldmeerkatze und die Antilope. Im Umriss der Tiere ist die Gebirgslandschaft sichtbar. Um die Wichtigkeit des Umweltschutzes zu unterstreichen, wurde eine konventionelle Plastikflasche durch „Ooho"-Wasserkugeln ersetzt. Seit 2017 sorgen diese für Aufsehen. Die Kugeln halten Flüssigkeit in einer essbaren Membran aus Pflanzen und Kalziumchlorid.

Cette édition limitée de l'eau minérale **HanShuiXiGu** a été lancée en 2018 avec un packaging inspiré de sa source naturelle, les monts Qinling. Le design se caractérise principalement par les dessins de quatre animaux rares qui vivent dans ces montagnes : le panda, l'ibis nippon, le singe doré et l'antilope. Le paysage montagneux sert de remplissage à ces illustrations. En outre, pour promouvoir la protection de l'environnement, le plastique habituel des bouteilles d'eau a été substitué par Ooho, un emballage comestible qui a connu une large diffusion en 2017.

QIZHI SPRING

Design: Xiong Hao, Kong Chengxiang, Liu Ping,
He Weisheng, Huang Weiwen, Li Jiabao
Manufacturing: Huang Qiqi
Company: Kurz Kurz Design
Country: China
Category: Water

SILVER PENTAWARD 2019

SOUROTI

Creative Direction: Konstantinos Thanasakis
Design: Thalassinos Anastasiou
Copywriting: Jason Psarras, Marialena Gousiou
Client Service: Dimitris Belecos, Manos Chelmis
Strategic Planning: Konstantinos Verveniotis
Company: The Newtons Laboratory
Country: Greece
Category: Water

SILVER PENTAWARD 2020

LOFOTEN WATER

Art Direction: Morten Throndsen
Design: Morten Throndsen, Eia Grødal,
Ida Elén Sørhaug
Strategic Advice: Susanne Munch-Rasmussen
Company: Strømme Throndsen Design
Country: Norway
Category: Water

SILVER PENTAWARD 2020

RISHI TEA & BOTANICALS

Creative Direction: Dan Olson
Art Direction and Senior Design: Christina Fischer
Photography: Brent Schoepf
Project Management: Ian Gerstl
Company: Studio MPLS
Country: USA
Category: Water

BRONZE PENTAWARD 2020

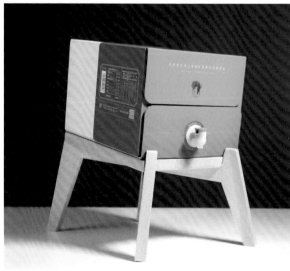

BADOIT

Creative Direction: Maud Mulder
Account Direction: Adrien Vicariot
Company: Absolut Reality
Country: France
Category: Water

BRONZE PENTAWARD 2019

LUZHUOQUAN MINERAL WATER

Design: KL&K Design
Creative Direction: Hong Ko
Design Direction: Dayong Zhang
Design: Yu Cao, Yongsheng Lu
Company: Luzhuoquan Mineral Water
Country: China
Category: Water

BRONZE PENTAWARD 2019

LIFEWTR SERIES 6:
DIVERSITY IN DESIGN

Design: PepsiCo Design & Innovation team
Artwork: Ji Won Choi,
Jamall Osterholm, Daniel Cloke
Company: PepsiCo Design & Innovation
Country: USA
Category: Water

SILVER PENTAWARD 2019

LIFEWTR SERIES 7:
ART THROUGH TECHNOLOGY

Design: PepsiCo Design & Innovation team
Artwork: Sarah Ludy, Zach Lieberman,
Andrew Benson
Company: PepsiCo Design & Innovation
Country: USA
Category: Water

BRONZE PENTAWARD 2020

LIFEWTR SERIES 4:
ARTS IN EDUCATION

Design: PepsiCo Design & Innovation team
Artwork: Luis Gonzalez, Krivvy, David Lee
Company: PepsiCo Design & Innovation
Country: USA
Category: Water

SILVER PENTAWARD 2019

LIFEWTR SERIES 5:
ART BEYOND BORDERS

Design: PepsiCo Design & Innovation team
Artwork: Aiko, Yinka Ilori, Laercio Redondo
Company: PepsiCo Design & Innovation
Country: USA
Category: Water

SILVER PENTAWARD 2019

DALSTON'S SODA CO.

Creative Direction: Shaun Bowen
Design: Elle Eveleigh
Account Direction: Kate Thomas
Company: B&B studio
Country: UK
Category: Soft drinks, juices

GOLD PENTAWARD 2020

A pioneer of the craft soda category, **Dalston's** range comprises six canned sodas, three light seltzers and two alcohol-free botanical G&Ts. The overall visual identity is centred around the iconic Dalston's "D" combined with distinctive graphic illustrations, a bold fruity colour palette and a personality-driven tone of voice. The boom-box-inspired designs celebrate the brand's community-focused ethos and reflect its music and cultural origins. The brand started its life at Passing Clouds, a culturally-rich music venue in Hackney, East London, and the design pays homage to this historic venue through a real sense of nostalgia.

Als Pionier in der Kategorie handgemachte Limonade umfasst diese Reihe von **Dalston** sechs verschiedene Sorten Dosenlimonade: drei leichte Selterswassersorten und zwei alkoholfreie pflanzliche Gin Tonics. Die visuelle Identität stützt sich auf das auffallende „D" von Dalston's. In Kombination mit markanten Illustrationen und einer gewagten, fruchtigen Farbpalette wird eine lockere Atmosphäre geschaffen. Das Design, das von Gettoblastern inspiriert wurde, zelebriert das auf die Gemeinschaft ausgerichtete Ethos der Marke und spiegelt damit auch deren musikalische und kulturelle Hintergründe wider. Die Marke wurde zuerst bei Passing Clouds vorgestellt, einem Veranstaltungsort für Musik in Hackney, im Osten Londons, der reich an kulturellen Einflüssen ist. Das Design huldigt diesem historischen Ort mit einem echten Gefühl von Nostalgie.

Dalston est un pionnier en matière de soda artisanal, avec une gamme de six sodas en cannettes, trois eaux pétillantes légères et deux gin tonics sans alcool à base de plantes. Toute l'identité visuelle tourne autour de l'emblématique « D » de Dalston, assorti d'illustrations originales, d'une palette de couleurs fruitées et d'un style personnel. Le design inspiré des radiocassettes est fidèle à la philosophie de Dalston axée sur la collectivité et renvoie à ses origines musicales et culturelles. La marque a en effet débuté à Passing Clouds, une salle de concerts d'une grande richesse culturelle située à Hackney, dans l'Est londonien ; le design cherche à rendre hommage à ce lieu historique par une touche de nostalgie.

YILI

Brand Management: Hedi Li, Yang Zhang
Graphic Design: Mousegraphics
Creative Direction Graphic: Greg Tsaknakis
Creative Direction Shape: Tiecheng Zhang,
Xiaoxiao Qiu
Shape Design: Hotdesign
Bottle Design: Fengyu Dong
Company: Inner Mongolia Yili Group
Country: China
Category: Soft drinks, juices

GOLD PENTAWARD 2019

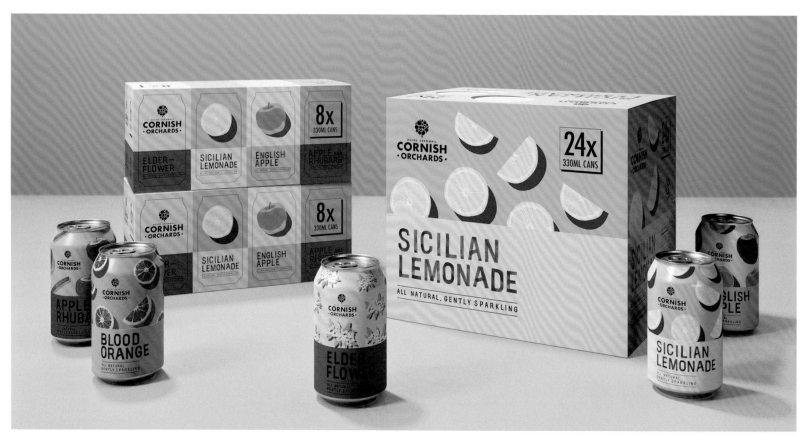

CORNISH ORCHARDS

Creative Direction: Matt Burns
Design: Rachel Porter
Company: Thirst Craft
Country: UK
Category: Soft drinks, juices

SILVER PENTAWARD 2020

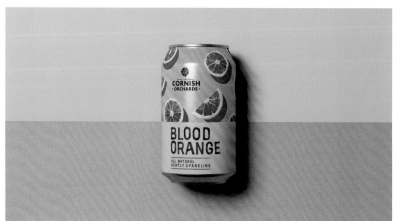

YASNAYA POLYANA

Design: Transformer Studio
Creative Direction: Nikita Melnikov
Photography: Stas Savin
Company: Transformer Studio
Country: Russian Federation
Category: Soft drinks, juices
BRONZE PENTAWARD 2020

SOMERSAULT

Creative Direction: Margaret Nolan
Design: Ben Galbraith
Finished Artwork: Peter Bradley
Company: Denomination
Country: Australia
Category: Soft drinks, juices
BRONZE PENTAWARD 2019

FANTOLA

Creative Direction: Andrey Kugaevskikh
Design: Yaroslav Zheleznyakov
Company: Svoe Mnenie
Country: Russian Federation
Category: Soft drinks, juices

SILVER PENTAWARD 2020

VEIVI

Creative Direction: Alexey Fadeev,
Anastasia Tretyakova
Art Direction: Anastasia Tsyrkina
Design: Anastasia Tsyrkina, Jane Struk
Copywriting: Sasha Fedoseeva
Project Management: Alena Baklikova
Strategic Direction: Farhad Kuchkarov
Strategic Management: Roman Frolov
CEO: Alexey Andreev
Executive Direction: Ksenia Parkhomenko
Company: Depot Branding Agency
Country: Russian Federation
Category: Soft drinks, juices

BRONZE PENTAWARD 2020

Sepoy&Co Tonic Water makes a nod to Indian history with a name inspired by the legacy of the Sepoy warriors who have deep roots in Indian culture and are an integral part of the story of gin and tonic itself. The visual strategy is based on colour codes and patterns that communicate the different taste profiles, whilst the typography is a combination of sans serif and script creating a contrast between heritage and contemporary brand identity. The structured vertical pattern of the bottle design borrows inspiration from spirits and soda water bottles from the 19th century and is another nod to the brotherhood of the Sepoys and their mantra "stronger together".

Das Design von Sepoy&Co Tonic Water ist eine Hommage an die indische Geschichte. Mit einem Namen, der von dem Vermächtnis der Sepoy-Krieger inspiriert ist, die tief in der indischen Kultur verwurzelt und ein bedeutender Teil der Geschichte von Gin und Tonic selbst sind. Die visuelle Strategie basiert auf einem Farbsystem und Mustern, die die verschiedenen Geschmackssorten widerspiegeln, während die Typografie, eine Kombination aus Sans Serif und Script, einen Kontrast zwischen Erbe und zeitgemäßer Markenidentität schafft. Das vertikale Muster des Flaschendesigns zieht seine Inspiration von Spirituosen- und Sodaflaschen des 19. Jahrhunderts und verweist außerdem auf die Bruderschaft der Sepoy und deren Mantra: „Gemeinsam sind wir stärker".

L'eau tonique Sepoy&Co Tonic Water fait un clin d'œil à l'histoire de l'Inde avec un nom inspiré de l'héritage des soldats cipayes, dont les racines sont profondément ancrées dans la culture indienne et qui font partie intégrante de l'histoire du gin et de l'eau tonique à proprement parler. La stratégie visuelle repose sur des codes chromatiques et des motifs distinguant différents goûts. Pour sa part, la combinaison typographique Sans serif et Script crée un contraste entre cet héritage et l'identité contemporaine de la marque. Le motif vertical du design de la bouteille puise son inspiration dans les bouteilles de spiritueux et de sodas du XIXᵉ siècle, avec une claire référence à la confraternité des cipayes et à leur devise « Plus forts ensemble ».

SEPOY&CO

Creative Direction: Erika Barbieri
Brand and Bottle Design: Erika Barbieri, Henrik Olsson
Client: Sepoy&Co
CAD Development: Hansson Design
Company: OlssønBarbieri
Country: Norway
Category: Soft drinks, juices

SILVER PENTAWARD 2019

BÆRBAR JUICE

Creative Direction: Garrick Hamm
Client Services Direction: Wybe Magermans
Account Management: Faye Pulleyn
Design Direction: Mark Nichols
Design: Christopher Ribét, Thomas Monsen
Artwork: Emma Udell
Production Management: Mark Tosey
Client: Magne Hareide, Andre Luca W. Bruvold,
Co-Founders of Bærbar Juice
Company: Williams Murray Hamm (London)
Country: UK
Category: Soft drinks, juices
BRONZE PENTAWARD 2019

URBAN CORDIAL

Creative Direction: Amanda Jackson
Illustration: Hannah George, Ana Seixas, Ron Yee
Copywriting: Francesca Tenenbaum
Photography: Scott Kimble
Company: Jackdaw Design
Country: UK
Category: Soft drinks, juices
SILVER PENTAWARD 2019

4U

Design: Bendito Design Team
Company: Bendito Design
Country: Brazil
Category: Tea and coffee (ready-to-drink)

GOLD PENTAWARD 2019

ANCIENT FOG PAVILION TEA

Creative Direction: Shi Changhong
Art Direction: Li Mingdeng
Design: Wang Zhong
Illustration: Wang Zhong
Company: Guizhou Uplink Creative Brand Design
Country: China
Category: Tea and coffee (ready-to-drink)

GOLD PENTAWARD 2020

Ancient Fog Pavilion Tea comes from deep in the mountains, picked from ancient trees surrounded by clouds and mist. On the outer packaging, illustrations of ancient trees and forest foothills are used, whilst on the inside, the container is made up of six separate triangular boxes that are imprinted with the words "viewing the clouds, hunting the mountains, guarding the trees, moistening the soil, habitat water, and tea". These concepts highlight the product's key selling points, a belief in environmental protection and respect for the ancient trees that are the source of the tea.

Ancient Fog Pavilion Tea kommt tief aus dem Gebirge und wurde von alten Bäumen gepflückt, die von Wolken und Nebel umgeben sind. Auf der äußeren Verpackung wurden Illustrationen von Bäumen, Wäldern und dem Fuß des Gebirges verwendet, während der Innenbehälter aus sechs separaten dreieckigen Schachteln besteht, auf denen die Worte „Die Wolken sehend, die Berge jagend, die Bäume bewachend, den Boden befeuchtend, Lebensraum Wasser und Tee" zu lesen sind. Diese Konzepte unterstreichen die wichtigsten Verkaufsargumente des Produkts, den Glauben an den Umweltschutz und den Respekt für die alten Bäume, von denen der Tee stammt.

Au creux des montagnes, le thé **Ancient Fog Pavilion Tea** est récolté sur des arbres séculaires baignés par les nuages et la brume. L'extérieur du packaging affiche des illustrations de ces arbres anciens et des contreforts de forêts, alors que l'intérieur compte six boîtes triangulaires sur lesquelles on peut lire « observer les nuages, arpenter les montagnes, protéger les arbres, humidifier le sol, préserver l'habitat, l'eau et le thé ». Ces concepts mettent en valeur les arguments de vente du produit, à savoir la protection de l'environnement et le respect des arbres séculaires produisant le thé.

WORKAHOLIC

Strategy and Copywriting:
Aleksandr Bozhko, Ivan Dergachev
Art Direction: Lidiya Kapysh
Design: Anna Pazyuk, Albert Safin,
Alexandra Chushkina
Illustration: Viktor Khomenko,
Alexandra Chushkina
3D: Albert Safin
Motion: Alexandra Chushkina
Company: The Clients
Country: Russian Federation
Category: Tea and coffee (ready-to-drink)

GOLD PENTAWARD 2020

A coffee for workaholics, designed by workaholics. The **Workaholic** cold coffee brew packaging design project begun with just one wine bottle and one beer can. But this quickly evolved into a true workaholics project with the team developing 10 logos and 10 label design variations based on the 'workaholics' concept, to use across multiple containers and items including coffee bean bags, coasters, stickers, wine bottles, beer cans, gift boxes, flasks, posters and even Telegram sticker packs.

Ein Kaffee für Workaholics, entworfen von Workaholics. Das Designprojekt für den Cold Brew **Workaholic** Kaffee begann mit einer Flasche Wein und einer Bierdose. Daraus entwickelte sich sehr schnell ein wahres Workaholic-Projekt, im Zuge dessen das Team auf Grundlage des Konzepts „Arbeitsmensch" zehn Logos und zehn Etiketten entwarf, die auf verschiedenen Behältern und Artikeln zum Einsatz kommen sollten, darunter Kaffeebohnensäcke, Untersetzer, Weinflaschen, Bierdosen, Geschenkboxen, Flachmänner, Poster und sogar Sticker für den Messenger-Dienst Telegram.

Un café pour accros du travail conçu par des accros du travail. Le projet de design du packaging pour **Workaholic**, qui propose un café à consommer froid, se limitait au début à une bouteille de vin et une cannette de bière. Le projet s'est toutefois vite intensifié et l'équipe a mis au point 10 logos et 10 variantes d'étiquettes à partir du concept « accros du travail ». On les retrouve sur divers emballages et articles, tels que paquets de café en grains, sous-verres, adhésifs, bouteilles de vin, cannettes de bière, coffrets-cadeaux, gourdes, posters, et même des packs d'autocollants Telegram.

MADRE MONTE

Strategic Branding: Miguel Ángel del Baño,
Beatriz Suárez
Design: Miguel Ángel del Baño
Company: Estudio Maba
Country: Spain
Category: Tea and coffee (ready-to-drink)

SILVER PENTAWARD 2019

DELAFFE

Design Direction: Sangyun Shin, Dongcheong Kang
Design: Hongchul Bae, Mia Lim, Soyeon Park,
Sunny Yusun Moon
Company: BGF Retail
Country: Republic of Korea
Category: Tea and coffee (ready-to-drink)

BRONZE PENTAWARD 2019

COOLBREW

Creative Direction: Alexey Fadeev,
Anastasia Tretyakova
Design Direction: Nikita Ivanov
Art Direction: Tatiana Mikolaevskaya
Design: Tatiana Mikolaevskaya, Stanislav Neretin
Project Management: Anastasia Fedorova
Strategic Management: Maxim Babakaev
Company: Depot Branding Agency
Country: Russian Federation
Category: Tea and coffee (ready-to-drink)

SILVER PENTAWARD 2019

ROSA ROXBUNGHII
TEA WITH FRUIT JUICE

Creative Direction: Zhiji Dong
Design: Lu Gu
Company: Guangzhou Cheung Ying Design
Country: China
Category: Tea and coffee (ready-to-drink)

BRONZE PENTAWARD 2020

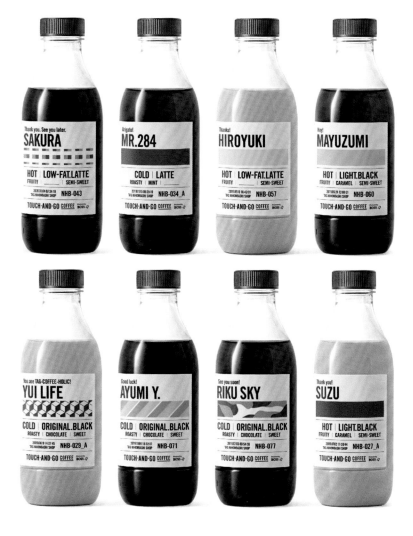

BOSS TOUCH-AND-GO COFFEE

Creative Direction: Hiroyuki Ishiura, Satoshi Abe
Art Direction: Satoshi Abe
Design: Satoshi Abe, Ayano Yamagishi
Company: Suntory
Country: Japan
Category: Tea and coffee (ready-to-drink)

SILVER PENTAWARD 2020

TYPE-FACES PROJECT

Art Direction: Jimmi Tuan
Design: Si Tran, Alex Dang, Nguyễn X. Hoàng
Account Direction: Hien Nguyen
Company: Bratus Agency
Country: Vietnam
Category: Tea and coffee (ready-to-drink)

SILVER PENTAWARD 2020

SUNSU

Design: Phakhawan Sarakit,
Pannaporn Thasak, Monnapat Saikaew
Company: Yindee Design
Country: Thailand
Category: Tea and coffee (ready-to-drink)
BRONZE PENTAWARD 2020

BALLE IRIS COFFEE

Project Direction: Haishan Li
Project Management: Chi Zou
General Design Guidance: Ji Chen
Design: Ji Chen, Zhiguang Huang
Company: Shenzhen Jinye Wannyuan R&D
Country: China
Category: Tea and coffee (ready-to-drink)
SILVER PENTAWARD 2020

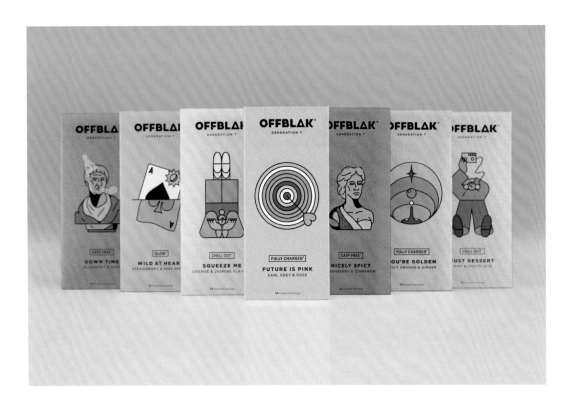

OFFBLAK

Creative Partner: Dan Bernstein
Design Direction: Susan Jamieson
Design: Sam Kang
Company: & Smith
Country: UK
Category: Tea and coffee (ready-to-drink)
BRONZE PENTAWARD 2020

IYEMON LABEL-LESS

Creative Direction: Akiko Kirimoto
Art Direction: Kei Nishikawa
Design: Keiko Genkaku
Bottle Design: Yoji Minakuchi
Company: Suntory
Country: Japan
Category: Tea and coffee (ready-to-drink)
SILVER PENTAWARD 2020

FENGWEI TEA

General Management and Chief Design: Xu NanFu
Company: Xiamen Jiangshan Design
Country: China
Category: Tea and coffee (ready-to-drink)

BRONZE PENTAWARD 2020

TRUESTART

Chief Creative Officer: Paul Taylor
Creative Direction: Ellen Munro
Design: Claire Hamblen, Maddie Freestone
Company: BrandOpus
Country: UK
Category: Tea and coffee (ready-to-drink)

BRONZE PENTAWARD 2019

The three colours of packaging for **Song Chinese Cuisine Mountain Tea** reflect the different concentrations of the charcoal-baked tea and the mountainous area in which the tea is grown. The burn mark effect on the packaging was copied from real burnt paper and folded to highlight the charcoal-baked nature of the tea, and to create the effect of layer upon layer of mountains. The products are placed in a gift box, which when opened shows abstract paintings of flying cranes, high mountains and the moon.

Die drei Farbtöne der Verpackung des **Song Chinese Cuisine Gebirgstees** spiegeln die Nuancen des über Holzkohle gerösteten Tees und der Gebirgsgegend, in der er angebaut wurde, wider. Die Brandspuren wurden echtem verbranntem Papier nachempfunden, das gefaltet wurde, um die Charakteristik des gerösteten Tees darzustellen. So entsteht ein Effekt, der den vielschichtigen Bergen gleicht. Die Produkte befinden sich in einer Geschenkbox, die beim Öffnen abstrakte Bilder von fliegenden Kranichen, hohen Bergen und dem Mond zeigt.

Les trois couleurs du packaging de **Song Chinese Cuisine Mountain Tea** sont à l'image des différentes concentrations de ce thé cuit au charbon, et de la région montagneuse où il est cultivé. L'effet de trace de brûlure sur l'emballage est la reproduction d'un véritable papier brûlé et plié pour évoquer la cuisson au charbon du thé et créer l'effet de superposition de couches de montagnes. Les produits sont logés dans un coffret-cadeau : à son ouverture, il révèle des peintures abstraites de grues en vol, de hauts massifs et de la lune.

SONG CHINESE CUISINE

Design: Shaobin Lin
Client: Haiyang Song
Photography: Yanpeng Chen
Company: Lin Shaobin Design
Country: China
Category: Tea and coffee (dry and capsules)

GOLD PENTAWARD 2019

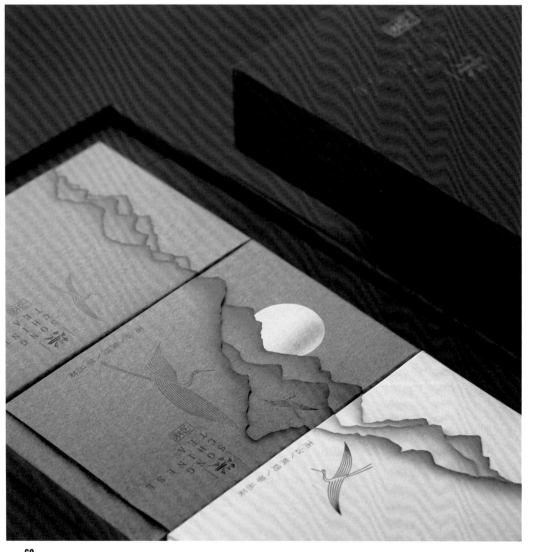

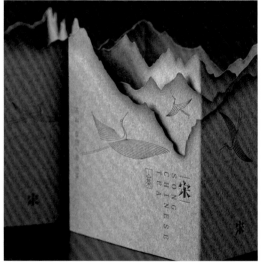

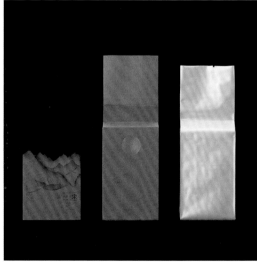

JINGYANG BRICK TEA

Creative Direction: Langcer Lee
Design: Jie Yang, Linwei Guo, Riso Guo, Limo Pan
Illustration: Fan Zhang
Photography: Tao Jiang
Company: Litete Brand Design
Country: China
Category: Tea and coffee (dry and capsules)

SILVER PENTAWARD 2019

FIKA COFFEE

Creative Direction: Dan Olson
Design: Brent Schoepf
Company: Studio MPLS
Country: USA
Category: Tea and coffee (dry and capsules)

BRONZE PENTAWARD 2019

AMADO COFFEE

Art Direction: Katya Mushkina
Project Management: Alyona Trifonova,
Evgenia Nefedova
CG Artwork: Aleksey Shelukho
Copywriting: Aleksey Kalyan
Company: Katya Mushkina
Country: Russian Federation
Category: Tea and coffee (dry and capsules)

BRONZE PENTAWARD 2019

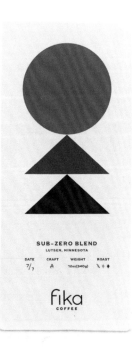

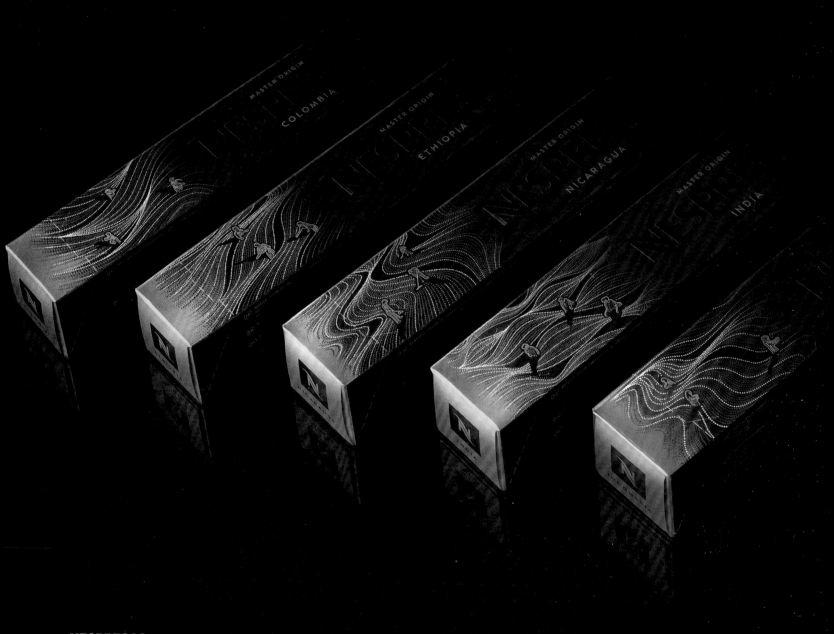

NESPRESSO

Design: Becki Sewell
Senior Design: Sam Hall
Design Direction: Kevin Lan
Creative Direction: David Roberts
Account Management: Andrew Webster
Company: Superunion
Country: UK
Category: Tea and coffee (dry and capsules)
SILVER PENTAWARD 2019

CANSI FRUIT GROUP

Design: Zhangyong Hou
Company: Zhongshihuanmei (Dalian) Advertising
Country: China
Category: Functional beverages

GOLD PENTAWARD 2019

SENSER SPIRITS: LIFT YOUR MIND & MOOD

Creative Direction: David Azurdia
Creative Direction: Ben Christie
Design: Heidi Shepherd, John Randall
Project Management: Alice Thompson
Illustration: Jessica Benhar,
David Azurdia, Heidi Shepherd
Copywriting: Joe Coleman, David Azurdia,
We All Need Words
Client: Vanessa Jacoby, James Jacoby
Company: Magpie Studio
Country: UK
Category: Functional beverages

GOLD PENTAWARD 2020

U GO

Design: Jordy Huisman,
Monique Gaillard
Brand Creation: Loes Altena,
Lena Knörzer, Annemart Tielens
Company: SHIOK
Country: Netherlands
Category: Functional beverages

BRONZE PENTAWARD 2019

ANCIENT & BRAVE

Creative Direction: Scott Wotherspoon,
Jem Egerton
Design: Ranulph Horne, Harry Ives
Artwork: Steve Morphy
Company: Liquid Studio
Country: UK
Category: Functional beverages

SILVER PENTAWARD 2020

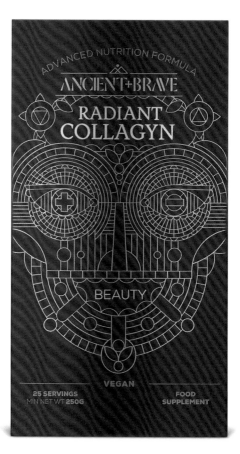

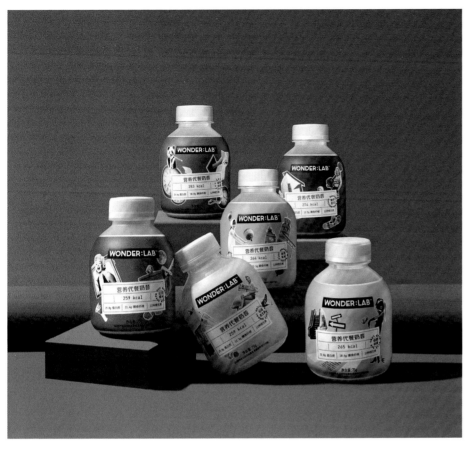

WONDERLAB

Strategy Direction: Yi (Yisa) He
Strategy Consultation: Jundai (Claire) Qian
Art Direction: Qiurong Ji
Design: Li Shao
Design Assistance: Chen (Haru) Yang
Client: Shenzhen Precision Health Food Technology
Brand Management: Shuqian (Sure) Huang
Company: Shanghai Wuyi Brand Management
Country: China
Category: Functional beverages

BRONZE PENTAWARD 2020

SAPSUCKER

Creative Direction: Julie Vander Herberg,
Anna Vander Herberg
Art Direction: Melanie Hong
Design: Olivier Rohner
Company: Vanderbrand
Country: Canada
Category: Functional beverages

SILVER PENTAWARD 2020

FOODSPA

Creative Direction: Nadie Parshina
Design: Ann Burlakina
Company: Ohmybrand
Country: Russian Federation
Category: Functional beverages

BRONZE PENTAWARD 2019

SYNGJA BEVERAGES

Creative Direction: Mikael Tonning
Design: Jonathan Faust
Strategy Direction: Christian Halsted
Photography: Martin Højer Kofod
Company: Everland
Country: Denmark
Category: Functional beverages

SILVER PENTAWARD 2019

MOO DRINKABLE YOGURT

Design: Mousegraphics
Industrial Design: Nikos Kastanakis
Company: Mousegraphics
Country: Greece
Category: Functional beverages

BRONZE PENTAWARD 2020

SMEAL

CEO: Peng Cao
Creative Direction: Zhengda Li
Company: Smeal Limited
Country: China
Category: Functional beverages

SILVER PENTAWARD 2019

HEINEKEN

Design Direction: Peter Eisen
Brand Direction: Elseline Ploem
Client: Heineken Global Design
Senior Packaging and Identity
Design Management: Ramses Dingenouts
Company: VBAT
Country: Netherlands
Category: Beer

GOLD PENTAWARD 2019

DONG YOU JI

Design: Wen Liu, Weijie Kang, Shuanglong Wang
Company: Shenzhen Oracle Creative Design
Country: China
Category: Beer
GOLD PENTAWARD 2020

Wanting to harmonise their visual identity across their global portfolio, **Carlsberg** revisited all elements of their product, from the 100-year-old logo to the colour of the glass bottle. As part of the rebrand, each element was redrawn by hand, a new typeface was created and a more eco-friendly "greener green" signature colour was developed, inspired by the natural green of the buds and the mature leaves of the hop plant. The team were guided by three design principles from the founder's devotion to "the constant pursuit of better beer": Crafted Authenticity, Danish By Nature and Progressive Ingenuity, all of which were reflected in the packaging redesign.

Weil **Carlsberg** die visuelle Identität seines globalen Portfolios harmonischer gestalten wollte, wurden alle Elemente des Produkts überarbeitet – von dem 100 Jahre alten Logo bis hin zur Farbe der Glasflasche. Als Teil des Rebrandings wurde jedes Element neu von Hand entworfen, eine Schriftype wurde konzipiert und ein umweltfreundliches „grüneres Grün" entwickelt, inspiriert von der natürlichen Farbe der Knospen und den reifen Blättern der Hopfenpflanze. Das Team ließ sich dabei von den drei Designprinzipien des Gründers und seiner Hingabe für ein „konstantes Streben nach dem besseren Bier" leiten: handgemachte Authentizität, „Danish by nature" und fortschrittlicher Einfallsreichtum. All das spiegelte sich im Verpackungsdesign wider.

Dans l'optique d'harmoniser son identité visuelle pour l'ensemble de sa gamme, **Carlsberg** a repensé tous les éléments de son produit, du logo centenaire à la couleur de la bouteille en verre. Pour cette nouvelle image, chaque élément a été dessiné à la main, une nouvelle police a été créée et une couleur de signature d'un « vert plus vert » a été conçue à partir de la couleur naturelle des boutons et des feuilles matures du houblon. L'équipe de design a obéi à trois principes basés sur l'attachement du fondateur de la marque à « la quête incessante d'une bière meilleure » : authenticité artisanale, nature danoise et ingéniosité. La refonte du packaging reflète parfaitement ces lignes directrices.

CARLSBERG

Creative Partner: Spencer Buck
Associate Creative Direction: Jonathan Rogers
Senior Creative Strategy: Rob Wynn-Jones
Account Direction: Laura Lancaster,
Hannah Bartholomew
Design Direction: Jonathan Ferriday
Senior Account Management: Lottie Pettinger
Senior Design: Ali Bartlett, Dave Badock
Design: Jasmine Rees
Junior Design: Liv Beresford-Evans
Client: Carlsberg
Chief Commercial Officer: Jessica Spence (Carlsberg)
Global Design Direction: Jessica Felby (Carlsberg)
Head of Marketing: Richard Whitty (Carlsberg)
Global Brand Direction: Julian Marsili (Carlsberg)
VP Marketing: Russell Jones (Carlsberg)
Design-to-print Management: Rob Martin (Carlsberg)
Design Management: Benjamin Hoffmann (Carlsberg)
Company: Taxi Studio
Country: UK
Category: Beer
GOLD PENTAWARD 2019

AMSTEL KARGO IPA

Brand: Paris Mexis
Photography Packshots: Theodosis Georgiadis,
Konstantinos Gikas
Sampling kit, Printing and Production:
La Petite Jumelle
Company: Caparo Design Crew
Country: Greece
Category: Beer
SILVER PENTAWARD 2020

OMORI SANNO BREWERY

Creative Direction: Yohei Murakoshi
Design: Yuka Chiba
Company: Seesaw
Country: Japan
Category: Beer
BRONZE PENTAWARD 2020

TROKYA BEER

Art Direction: Cem Hasimi
Company: Pata Studio
Country: UK
Category: Beer

BRONZE PENTAWARD 2020

PILSENER

Creative Direction and Design: Adrian Pierini
Company: Pierini Partners
Country: Argentina
Category: Beer

SILVER PENTAWARD 2019

The design of **Wiseman Beer** is inspired by the images of alien and myths, using a one-eyed wise man who controls the prophecy, wisdom, poetry and aesthetics of life. Aimed at a younger audience, the figure on the front of the bottle creates a strong visual identity and impact that connects with the consumer. This is done through a three-dimensional image that is simple and playful, creating a unique effect that looks like a piece of art. All of the product information for Wiseman Beer is then printed on the bottleneck label.

Das Design von **Wiseman Bier** wurde von Aliens und Mythen inspiriert und sein Hauptmotiv ist ein einäugiger, weiser Mann, der mit der Prophezeiung, Weisheit, Poesie und Ästhetik des Lebens im Einklang ist. Ausgerichtet auf eine jüngere Kundschaft, kreiert die Figur auf der Vorderseite der Flasche eine starke visuelle Identität und Wirkung, mit der sich der Verbraucher verbunden fühlt. Dieses dreidimensionale Bild ist einfach und spielerisch und kreiert einen einzigartigen Effekt gleich einem Kunstwerk. Alle Produktinformationen zum Wiseman Bier finden sich auf dem Etikett am Flaschenhals.

Le design de **Wiseman Beer** s'inspire d'images d'extraterrestres et de mythes, avec pour seule illustration un cyclope avisé quant à la prophétie, aux croyances, à la poésie et à l'esthétique de la vie. S'adressant à un public jeune, ce personnage à l'avant de la bouteille crée une forte identité visuelle et un lien avec le consommateur. À la fois simple et ludique, son image tridimensionnelle provoque un effet unique, comme une œuvre d'art. Toutes les informations sur la bière Wiseman Beer figurent sur l'étiquette autour du goulot.

WISEMAN BEER

Design: Wen Liu, Henghong Yang, Weijie Kang
Company: Shenzhen Oracle Creative Design
Country: China
Category: Beer

SILVER PENTAWARD 2020

GOTLANDS BRYGGERI

Creative Direction: Mattias Lindstedt
Design: Nils Lilja
Project Management: Anna Stenmark
Artwork: Nico Paredes
Illustration: Siri Carlén
Company: Neumeister Strategic Design
Country: Sweden
Category: Beer

BRONZE PENTAWARD 2019

MEANTIME LONDON

Creative Direction: Brett Stabler
Strategy Direction: Elissa O'Brien
Senior Design: Alex Rexworthy
Company: OUTLAW
Country: UK
Category: Beer

SILVER PENTAWARD 2019

SWEDISH TONIC

Client Direction: Johanna Augustin
Production Management: Niclas Hemlin
Senior Design: Viktoria Hamberger
Design: Robin Boström
Final Art: Anna Johansson
Copywriting: Malin Strinnhed
Company: Pond Design
Country: Sweden
Category: Ciders and low-alcohol drinks

GOLD PENTAWARD 2020

SEEDLIP RANGE

Founder and CCO: Jonathan Ford
Founder and CEO: Mike Branson
Creative Direction: Hamish Campbell
Head of Realization: Brandi Parker
Senior Digital Artwork: Stephen Kwartler
Senior Visualization: Liviu Dimulescu
Company: Pearlfisher
Country: USA
Category: Ciders and low-alcohol drinks

SILVER PENTAWARD 2019

Drawing on the strategic brand essence of "the art of nature," the design for the **Seedlip Range** was inspired by botanical illustrations. For Spice 94, the illustration takes the form of a subtle "S" which reveals itself as the profile of the native red fox – a creature indigenous to the English countryside. Garden 108 and Grove 42 follow suit, leading with illustrations of a hare and a squirrel on the face of each bottle as a nod to the disruptive nature of these non-alcoholic spirits and acknowledgement of the power of the ingredients within. A pharmaceutical-style bottle reinforces the spirit's medicinal roots, while a copper cap and copper detailing elevate the brand and reference the copper stills used to create it.

Basierend auf dem strategischen Markenkern „die Kunst der Natur", wurde das Design der **Seedlip-Range** von botanischen Zeichnungen inspiriert. Für Spice 94 nimmt die Illustration die Form eines einfachen „S" an, das sich als das Profil eines Rotfuchses – einer einheimischen Tierart der englischen Landschaft – herausstellt. Garden 108 und Grove 42 tun es ihm gleich mit Illustrationen eines Hasen und eines Eichhörnchens auf dem Etikett der Flasche, als Hinweis auf die disruptive Natur dieser alkoholfreien Spirituosen und als Anerkennung der Kraft der Inhaltsstoffe. Die pharmazeutische Flasche bestärkt die medizinischen Wurzeln, während der Kupferdeckel und kupferfarbenen Details die Marke hervorheben und eine Referenz auf die Kolben sind, die für die Herstellung der Spirituose verwendet wurden.

S'appuyant sur l'essence de la marque de « l'art de la nature », le design pour **Seedlip Range** s'est inspiré d'illustrations botaniques. Pour Spice 94, l'illustration a la forme d'un subtil « S » qui se devine dans le profil du renard roux, espèce indigène dans la campagne anglaise. L'approche est identique pour Garden 108 et Grove 42, avec des illustrations de lièvre et d'écureuil à l'avant de chaque bouteille, en référence au caractère décalé de ces spiritueux non alcoolisés et en reconnaissance du pouvoir de leurs ingrédients. D'allure pharmaceutique, la bouteille vient consolider les racines médicinales du spiritueux, alors que le bouchon et les détails cuivrés évoquent les alambics de cuivre employés pour son élaboration.

EL TAMAL

Design: Gonzalo Jaen
3D Rendering: Marco Silva
Company: Digital Fish
Country: Spain
Category: Ciders and low-alcohol drinks

SILVER PENTAWARD 2019

NIIGATA SAKE
WITH FURUMACHI GEIGI

Art Direction: Ryuta Ishikawa
Design: Kiyokazu Shimizu
Company: Niigata Chamber of Commerce & Industry
Country: Japan
Category: Ciders and low-alcohol drinks

BRONZE PENTAWARD 2020

CROWMOOR

Creative Direction: Katie Eaton
Executive Strategy Direction: Dan Monteith
Senior Account Management: Charlie Spiers
Senior Visualisation: Simon Thomas
Artwork and Realisation: Steve Gordon
Company: Bluemarlin
Country: UK
Category: Ciders and low-alcohol drinks
BRONZE PENTAWARD 2019

TAILS COCKTAILS

Boundless Founder and Creative Direction:
Hamish Shand
Design: Sean O'Donovan
Client: Nick Wall and Christina Bertram
Company: Boundless Brand Design
Country: UK
Category: Ciders and low-alcohol drinks
BRONZE PENTAWARD 2020

Abrogatto 18 is a brand of premium, ready-to-drink bottled cocktails. As a small company, they chose to create collections of small batches of classic cocktails, the first one being Negroni. The visual identity of Abrogatto 18 is versatile and neutral so that it can adapt to each of the collections without losing the essence of the brand, whilst the design was inspired by the name of the brand and history of alcoholic drinks around the world. It's sophisticated and classic but contemporary, and in line with the values of the brand: premium and meticulous.

Abrogatto 18 ist eine Marke trinkfertiger Premium-Cocktails in der Flasche. Als kleines Unternehmen entschieden sie sich, Kollektionen mit kleinen Chargen klassischer Cocktails herzustellen, der erste war ein Negroni. Die visuelle Identität von Abrogatto 18 ist vielseitig und neutral, sodass sie sich an jede Flasche der Kollektion anpassen kann, ohne die Essenz der Marke zu verlieren. Das Design wurde dabei von dem Namen der Marke und der Geschichte von alkoholischen Getränken aus der ganzen Welt inspiriert. Es ist raffiniert und klassisch, aber zeitgemäß und auf einer Linie mit den Werten der Marke: hochwertig und akribisch.

Abrogatto 18 est une marque de cocktails en bouteille prêts à boire. De petite taille, l'entreprise a opté pour lancer des collections limitées de cocktails classiques, en commençant par le Negroni. L'identité visuelle d'Abrogatto 18 est à la fois neutre et versatile, s'adaptant ainsi à chaque collection sans perdre l'essence de la marque. Le design s'est inspiré quant à lui du nom de la marque et de l'histoire des boissons alcoolisées du monde entier. Il est sophistiqué, classique mais aussi contemporain, en phase avec les valeurs de cette marque haut de gamme et soignée.

ABROGATTO 18

3D: Oscar Gómez
Company: Alejandro Gavancho
Country: Peru
Category: Ciders and low-alcohol drinks

SILVER PENTAWARD 2020

Creative Direction: Davide Mosconi
Design: Miriam Frescura
Company: Auge Design
Country: Italy
Category: Aperitifs

GOLD PENTAWARD 2020

The brand of wine **Uovo**, Italian for "egg", was born when Larry Cherubino imported individual special clay cement ovoid tanks – or giant "eggs" – to age his wines. The egg name was incorporated into the creative solution, from the shape of the label and paper stock with its eggshell-like texture, to the touch of the gift box with its egg-carton-like shape and feel. Similar to the stripped-back nature of the winemaking, the label for the wine was stripped of any branding, copy or graphics, letting the shape alone become the unique identifier of the brand.

Die Weinmarke **Uovo**, italienisch für „Ei", wurde ins Leben gerufen, als Larry Cherubino eiförmige Spezialtanks – oder gigantische „Eier" – aus Tonzement importierte, um darin seinen Wein altern zu lassen. Der Ei-Name wurde Teil der kreativen Lösung, von der Form des Etiketts über das Papier mit seiner ei-ähnlichen Textur bis hin zur Haptik der Geschenkbox, die die Form und Beschaffenheit eines Eierkartons hat. Der einfachen Art der Weinproduktion entsprechend, wurde das Etikett des Weins von jeglicher Markenerkennung, Schrift oder Grafik befreit und macht damit die Form zum einzigartigen Alleinstellungsmerkmal der Marke.

La marque de vin **Uovo**, mot italien signifiant « œuf », a vu le jour quand Larry Cherubino a importé des cuves ovoïdes en ciment d'argile, sorte d'œufs géants, pour faire vieillir ses vins. Le concept d'œuf a été intégré à la solution créative, de la forme de l'étiquette (dont la texture rappelle celle d'une coquille) à l'aspect et au toucher du coffret-cadeau, tel une boîte d'œufs. À l'image de la nature dépouillée de la vinification, l'étiquette a été débarrassée de tout marquage ou illustration, ce qui fait de la forme la seule identification de la marque.

UOVO

Creative Direction and Design: Margaret Nolan
Finished Artwork: Lloyd Richards
Company: Denomination
Country: Australia
Category: Wine
GOLD PENTAWARD 2019

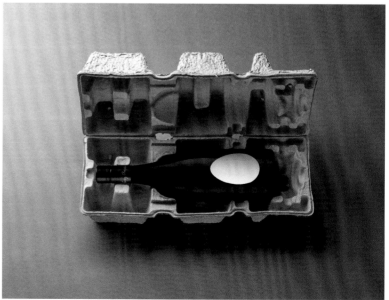

CÓDICE

Strategy Direction: Beatriz Suárez
Creative Direction: Miguel Ángel del Baño
Design: Miguel Ángel del Baño
Design Assistance: Manel Quílez, Jose Lorente
Illustration: Borja Torres
Company: Estudio Maba
Country: Spain
Category: Wine

GOLD PENTAWARD 2020

TREAD SOFTLY

Creative Direction and Design: Margaret Nolan
Finished Artwork: Lloyd Richards
Strategy: Rowena Curlewis
Company: Denomination
Country: Australia
Category: Wine

SILVER PENTAWARD 2020

PEACOCK

Creation Direction: Rui Niu
Design: Zhen Shen
Photography: Wei Hong
Manufacturing: Swan Wine Group
Company: I'mnext Communications
Country: China
Category: Wine

BRONZE PENTAWARD 2019

ADARAS

Art Direction: Miguel Ángel del Baño
Project Management: Beatriz Suárez
Company: Estudio Maba
Country: Spain
Category: Wine

BRONZE PENTAWARD 2019

BRAVO CARMEN

Strategy: Beatriz Suárez
Art Direction and Design: Manel Quílez
Photography: La Industrial
Company: Estudio Maba
Country: Spain
Category: Wine
BRONZE PENTAWARD 2020

PARANORMAL

Creative Direction: Miguel Ángel del Baño,
Beatriz Suárez
Design: Miguel Ángel del Baño
Illustration: Miguel Ángel González,
Borja Torres
Photography: La Industrial
Company: Estudio Maba
Country: Spain
Category: Wine
BRONZE PENTAWARD 2020

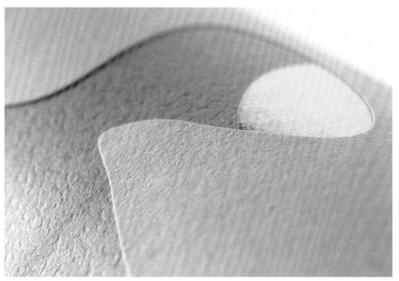

VELENOSI

Design: Mario Di Paolo
Company: Spazio Di Paolo
Country: Italy
Category: Wine

SILVER PENTAWARD 2019

BOUQUET WINE

Design: Wei Peng
Company: LionPeng Packaging Design Studio
Country: China
Category: Wine

SILVER PENTAWARD 2019

BRAND BREEDER

Design: Mario Di Paolo
Company: Spazio Di Paolo
Country: Italy
Category: Wine

BRONZE PENTAWARD 2020

HEGAN

Creative Direction: Xiongbo Deng
Design: Xiongbo Deng, Min Lin
Client: Shaanxi Tianmu Industry
Company: ShenZhen Lingyun
Creative Packaging Design
Country: China
Category: Spirits (clear)

GOLD PENTAWARD 2020

HUANG DI NEI JING

Creative Direction: Zhang Xiaoming
Design Direction: Chen Yue
Design: Liu Danhua, Huang Renqiang,
Xie Shijun, Liao Fenfen, Xu Hanxin
Company: Unidea Bank
Country: China
Category: Spirits

GOLD PENTAWARD 2019

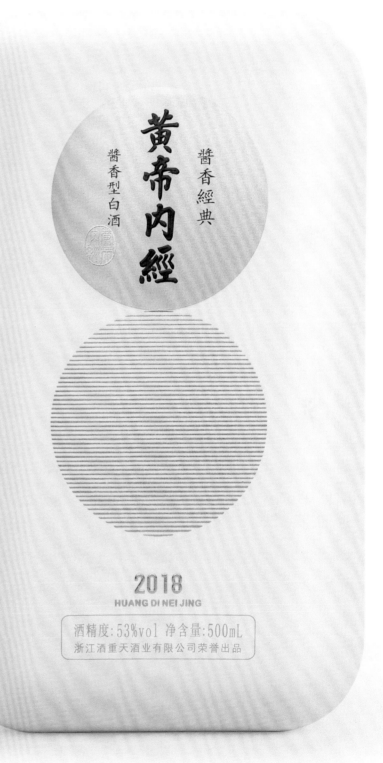

ISLAND GIN

Bottle Design: Andi Ross (Island Gin),
Tanja Ledwich (Tanja Ledwich Design), Gavin Wong
(OI NPD & Innovation Management)
Branding and Label Design: David Macdonald,
Rachel Doherty, Casey King (One Design)
Manufacturing: O-I APAC
Strategic Marketing Direction: Bayard Sinemma
Asia Pacific (O-I APAC)
Company: Madame Distiller Limited
Country: New Zealand
Category: Spirits (clear)

SILVER PENTAWARD 2020

El Rayo, 'The Lightning', is designed to challenge traditional perceptions of tequila. Gone are the days of lime, salt and lazy stereotypes of sombreros – this identity does nothing to reflect the incredible vibrancy and depth of Mexico. The idea of the brand is to reinvent how you think about tequila by opening up the idea of a more modern, tasteful Mexican culture. The intention is to create a balance between heritage, progress and endless possibility - something that speaks about Mexico today. It's a twist on a classic product, to attract a new generation of drinkers.

El Rayo, „der Blitz", wurde entworfen, um die traditionelle Wahrnehmung von Tequila in Frage zu stellen. Die Tage von Limette und Salz und dem Klischee fauler Sombreros sind vorüber – diese Zuschreibung wird der unglaublichen Lebendigkeit und Tiefe Mexikos nicht gerecht. Die Absicht der Marke ist es, Tequila neu zu erfinden, indem eine moderne, anspruchsvolle mexikanische Kultur erschlossen wird. So soll ein Gleichgewicht zwischen Erbe, Fortschritt und unendlichen Möglichkeiten geschaffen werden – etwas, das vom heutigen Mexiko erzählt. Es ist ein klassisches Produkt mit modernem Twist, um eine neue Generation von Kunden anzuziehen.

La bouteille El Rayo, « L'éclair », est pensée pour révolutionner l'image traditionnelle de la tequila. Fuyant les citrons verts, le sel et les clichés de sombreros, l'identité visuelle ne cherche en rien à refléter la vitalité et l'intensité du Mexique. L'idée de la marque est de réinventer la perception de la tequila en révélant une culture mexicaine plus moderne et sophistiquée. Son objectif est de trouver l'équilibre entre héritage, progrès et possibilités infinies pour parler du Mexique actuel. Cette remise au goût d'un produit classique vise à séduire une nouvelle génération d'amateurs de cette boisson.

EL RAYO TEQUILA

Art Direction: Mario Hgno
Design: Mario Hgno, Nubia Fernández
Copywriting: Olga Villegas,
Karen Vizcarra, Jack Vereker
Photography: Fredy "el gato" Morfín,
The Clerkenwell Brothers, Elliott Lacey
Company: Toro Pinto
Country: Mexico
Category: Spirits (clear)

SILVER PENTAWARD 2020

HEGAN

Creative Direction: Xiongbo Deng
Design: Xiongbo Deng
Client: Shanxi Tianmu Industrial
Company: ShenZhen Lingyun
Creative Packaging Design
Country: China
Category: Spirits

SILVER PENTAWARD 2019

TOISON

Creative Direction, Graphic Design and
Structural Design: Juraj Demovic
Technical Support: Anton Bendis, Vojtech Varga
Photography: Marco Balaz
Company: Pergamen s.r.o.
Country: Slovakia
Category: Spirits (clear)
BRONZE PENTAWARD 2020

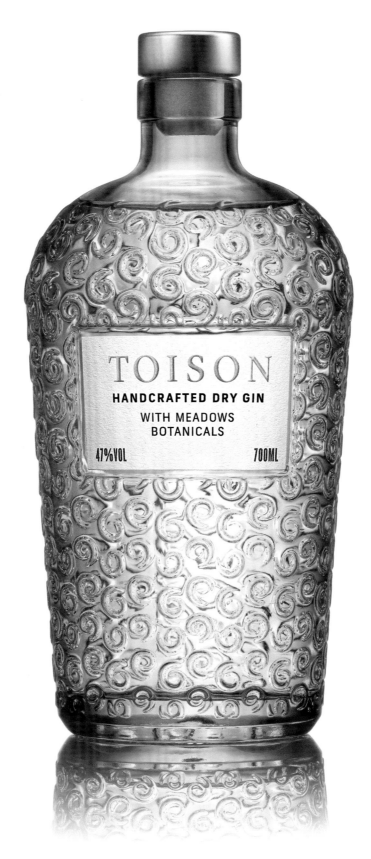

TOISON

HANDCRAFTED DRY GIN

WITH MEADOWS
BOTANICALS

47%VOL   700ML

ABSOLUT VODKA

CCO: Mårten Knutsson
EDC: John Lagerqvist
Art Direction: Fredrik Lindquist
Design: Anna-Karin Rosén
Copywriting: Anna Perrolf
Planning: Annika Rehn-Frobell
Account Direction: Johan Lundgren
Production Management: Sara Kindbom
Industrial Design: Ardagh Group
Company: Drama Queen
Country: Sweden
Category: Spirits (clear)
BRONZE PENTAWARD 2020

PALO TÚNEL

Creatives: Pep Bernat Vizcaya,
Ainhoa Nicolau Salas
Client: Destilleries Antonio Nadal
Company: Simil
Country: UK
Category: Spirits
BRONZE PENTAWARD 2019

GRACIAS A DIOS AGAVE GIN

Photography: Francisco de Deus
Production Assistance: Natalia Auza
Client Representation: Xaime Niembro
Company: Work by Lule
Country: USA
Category: Spirits

SILVER PENTAWARD 2019

Goji Wine is a trendy "health" wine for young Chinese people which uses goji berries as its main ingredient. As goji is recognised for its strong health-giving effects, one of the challenges was to make a healthy drink seem more exciting. For this, the brand image of a "health care punk" was created. This is embodied in the external packaging of the wine which features characters from Chinese culture in trendy illustrations, as well as the small goji-coloured block-like containers which can be piled one on top of the other.

Goji Wine ist ein trendiger „gesunder" Wein für junge Chinesen mit Goji-Beeren als Hauptzutat. Da die Goji-Beere für ihre starken gesundheitsfördernden Effekte bekannt ist, war es eine der größten Herausforderungen, aus dem gesunden Getränk etwas Aufregendes zu machen. Dafür wurde das Markenimage des „Gesundheitspunks" entworfen. Das spiegelt sich auch in der Verpackung wider, die Charaktere aus der chinesischen Kultur in trendigen Illustrationen zeigt sowie in den kleinen gojifarbenen blockartigen Behältern, die übereinander gestapelt werden können.

Goji Wine est un vin « santé » en vogue chez les jeunes Chinois et dont les baies de goji sont le principal ingrédient. Les bienfaits du goji pour la santé sont reconnus, mais tout le défi était de créer une boisson saine plus attrayante. Pour ce faire, l'image de la marque s'est basée sur une sorte de « punk sanitaire » qui se matérialise dans le packaging externe du vin : des personnages de la culture chinoise y sont représentés dans des illustrations sophistiquées, et les petits flacons cubiques couleur goji sont empilables.

GOJI WINE

Creative Direction: Guozheng Jiang, Dan Chen
Graphic Design: Qiurong Ji, Sijie Pei
Illustration: Jing Peng
Industrial Design: Zilei Jiao
Company: Shanghai Nianxiang
Brand Design & Consulting
Country: China
Category: Spirits

BRONZE PENTAWARD 2019

WE LOVE

Design: Onfire Design
Creative Direction: Matt Grantham
Design and Illustration: Georgina Brothers
Design: Michelle Maude
Company: Onfire Design
Country: New Zealand
Category: Spirits

BRONZE PENTAWARD 2019

CHARLES MERSER & CO

Design: Stranger & Stranger team
Company: Stranger & Stranger
Country: UK
Category: Spirits (dark)

GOLD PENTAWARD 2020

YUXINLONG

Creative Direction and Design: Xiongbo Deng
Company: ShenZhen Lingyun
Creative Packaging Design
Country: China
Category: Spirits (dark)

SILVER PENTAWARD 2020

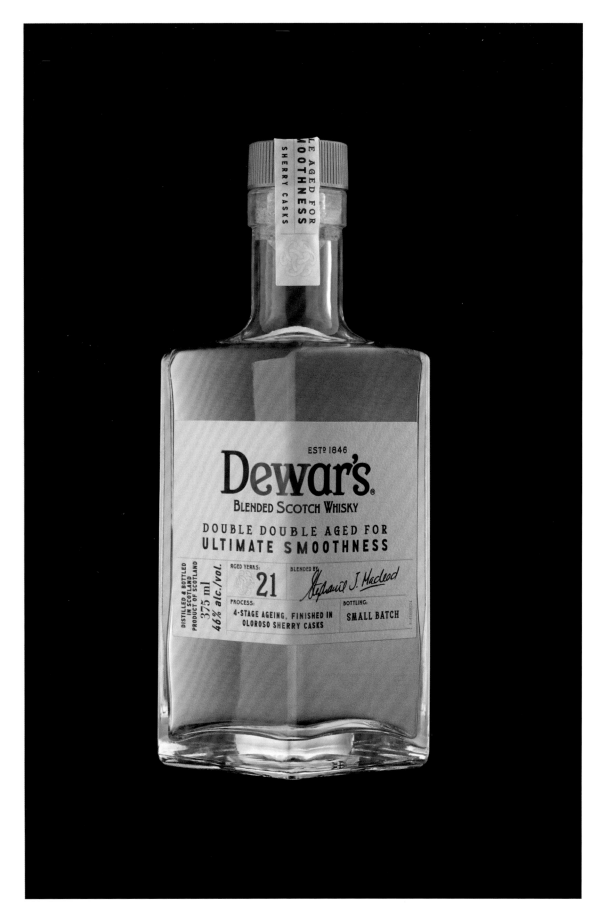

DEWAR'S DOUBLE DOUBLE

Design: Stranger & Stranger team
Company: Stranger & Stranger
Country: UK
Category: Spirits (dark)

SILVER PENTAWARD 2020

SOUTHWESTERN DISTILLERY

Design: Buddy team
Company: Buddy
Country: UK
Category: Spirits (dark)

BRONZE PENTAWARD 2020

ZUI JIN JIU

Design: Shenzhen Excel Brand Design Consultant team
Company: Shenzhen Excel Brand Design Consultant
Country: China
Category: Spirits (dark)

BRONZE PENTAWARD 2020

The **Pepsi/NFL Laces Can and Influencer Kit** was created to celebrate 16 years of partnership between Pepsi and the NFL for Super Bowl LIII. The Influencer Kit was launched the week leading up to the big game in Atlanta and included a decorative Pepsi-blue can enthroned in a specially-designed custom carton. Inspired by the form and feel of a football, the Pepsi/NFL Laces can is heavily textured and formed to mimic the laces on an actual football, creating excitement and enhancing the recipient's sensory experience of the product.

Das **Pepsi/NFL Laces Can und Influencer Kit** wurde entworfen, um 16 Jahre Partnerschaft zwischen Pepsi und der NFL (US-amerikanische Football-Profiliga) zum 58. Superbowl zu feiern. Das Influencer Kit wurde in der Woche vor dem großen Spiel in Atlanta vorgestellt und beinhaltete eine dekorative Dose Pepsi Blue, die in einem eigens entworfenen Karton prominent präsentiert wurde. Inspiriert von der Form und der Haptik eines Footballs, ist die Pepsi/NFL Dose stark strukturiert und so geformt, dass sie die Schnüre eines echten Footballs nachahmt, Begeisterung erzeugen und die sensorische Produkterfahrung des Kunden verstärken soll.

Le **Pepsi/NFL Laces Can and Influencer Kit** a été créé pour fêter les 16 ans de partenariat entre Pepsi et la NFL pour le Super Bowl LIII. Lancé la semaine précédant le grand match à Atlanta, cet Influencer Kit incluait une cannette bleue Pepsi décorative et présentée dans une boîte spécialement conçue. La cannette Pepsi/NFL Laces, qui évoque la forme et le toucher d'un ballon de football américain, est texturée et imite le lacet d'un vrai ballon. Le produit résulte attrayant et améliore l'expérience sensorielle du consommateur.

PEPSI

Design: PepsiCo Design & Innovation,
PepsiCo Global Beverage R&D
Company: PepsiCo Design & Innovation
Country: USA
Category: Limited editions, limited series, event creations
GOLD PENTAWARD 2019

BECK'S

CCO: Alexander Schill
Executive Creative Direction: Michael Wilk
Photography: Johann Cohrs
Motion Design: Dennis Fritz
Copywriting: Joy Chakravorty
Management Supervision: Lars Holling
Senior Account Management: Sabrina Schwarz
Marketing Management: Susanne Koop
(Anheuser Busch AB InBev)
Company: Serviceplan
Country: Germany
Category: Limited editions, limited series,
event creations

GOLD PENTAWARD 2020

TWENTY STORIES, LIDL

Photography: Theodosis Georgiadis
Styling: Stavroula Foutsa
Copywriting: Yorgos Garefalakis
Company: Caparo Design Crew

RHUM CLÉMENT

Design and Illustration: Linea Team
Company: Linea – The Spirit Valley Designers
Country: France
Category: Limited editions, limited series,
event creations

SILVER PENTAWARD 2019

THE PRISONER WINERY
EXCLUSIVES RANGE

Design: Stranger & Stranger team
Company: Stranger & Stranger
Country: UK
Category: Limited editions, limited series,
event creations

SILVER PENTAWARD 2019

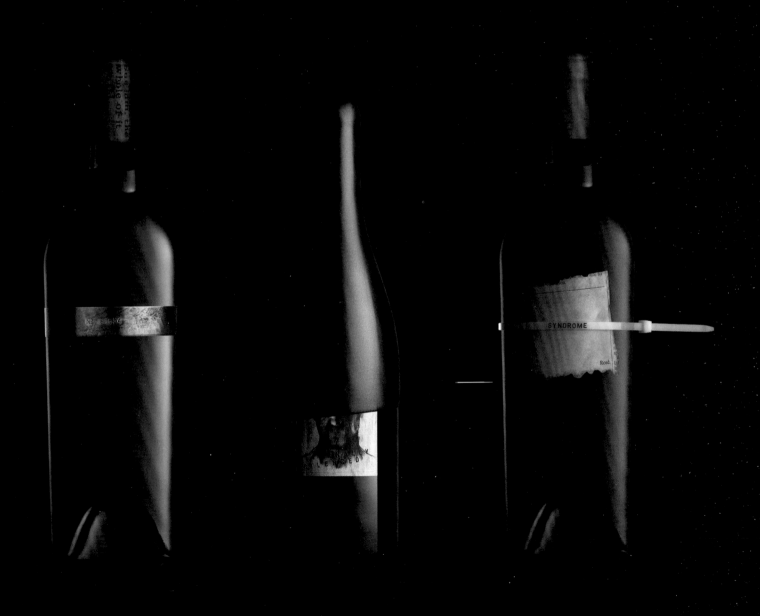

ZAMORA GROUP

Creative Direction: Enric Batlle
Design Direction: Chema Sánchez
Storytelling: Anna Muni, Marcel Batlle
Account Direction: Marisol Sopena
Artwork: Esther Martín
Company: Enric Batlle Group
Country: Spain
Category: Limited editions, limited series, event creations

BRONZE PENTAWARD 2020

COCA-COLA CHINA
40TH ANNIVERSARY SPECIAL EDITION

Creative Direction: Guanru Li
Design: Jiahui Xing
Illustration: Jing Xie
Company: L3 Branding
Country: China
Category: Limited editions, limited series, event creations

BRONZE PENTAWARD 2019

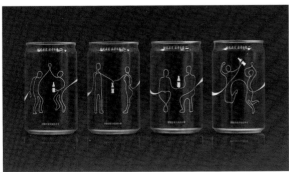

BUDWEISER

Partner and Managing Direction: René Chen
Partner and Creative Direction: Yolanda Tang
Senior Design: Woei Yang Fang
Company: Jones Knowles Richie
Country: China
Category: Limited editions, limited series, event creations

BRONZE PENTAWARD 2019

NIULANSHAN

Design: Tiger Pan, Julie Xia, Lawrence Liu
Illustration: Min Li
Pictures: Kelin Tan
Technician: Zhangkun Xie
Project Management: Krystal You
Company: Shenzhen Tigerpan Packaging Design
Country: China
Category: Limited editions, limited series, event creations

BRONZE PENTAWARD 2020

SMIRNOFF

Group Account Direction: Samuel Fowler
Creative Direction: Leigh Chandler
Associate Design Direction: Tom MacPherson
Company: Vault49
Country: USA
Category: Limited editions, limited series,
event creations

SILVER PENTAWARD 2020

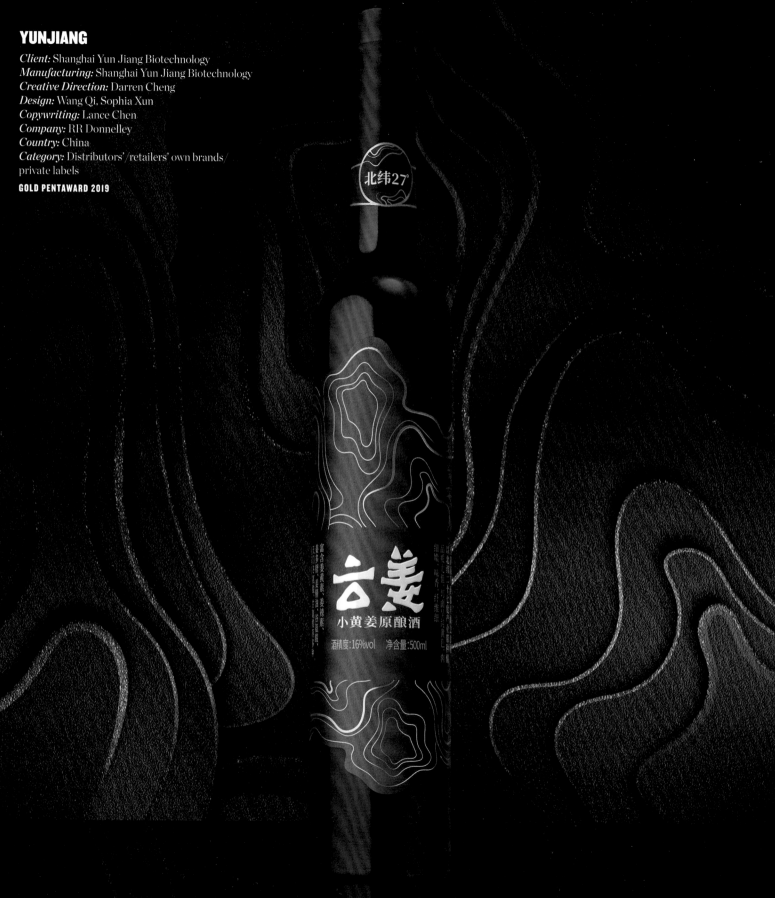

YUNJIANG

Client: Shanghai Yun Jiang Biotechnology
Manufacturing: Shanghai Yun Jiang Biotechnology
Creative Direction: Darren Cheng
Design: Wang Qi, Sophia Xun
Copywriting: Lance Chen
Company: RR Donnelley
Country: China
Category: Distributors'/retailers' own brands/
private labels

GOLD PENTAWARD 2019

ΦILOSOΦ

Brand Strategy: Lusie Grigoryan
Creative Direction, Design Idea and Graphic Design:
Stepan Azaryan
Art Direction and Illustration: Mariam Stepanyan
Project Management: Marianna Atshemyan
Copywriting: Grace Jerejian
Company: Backbone Branding
Country: Armenia
Category: Distributors'/retailers' own brands/
private labels

GOLD PENTAWARD 2020

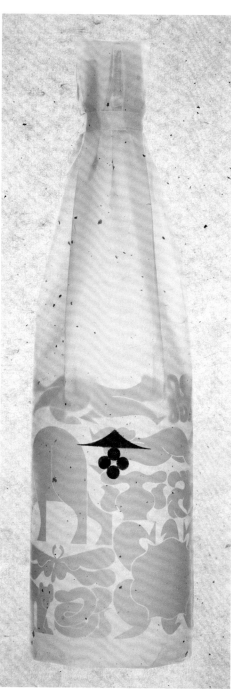

HIKAMI YONMARU –
JUNMAI DAIGINJO

Creative Direction: Naomi Yamamoto
Package Art Direction: Maria Hirokawa
Graphic Art Direction: Ikki Kobayashi
Production: Sachiko Takamine
Bottle: Seieido Printing
Wrapping Paper: Tozan Washi
Client: Suisen Shuzo
Company: Shiseido
Country: Japan
Category: Distributors'/retailers' own brands/
private labels

SILVER PENTAWARD 2019

MONUMENTO

Creative Direction: Paco Adín
Account Direction: Lourdes Morillas
Account Management: Susana Seijas
Company: Supperstudio
Country: Spain
Category: Distributors'/retailers' own brands/
private labels

SILVER PENTAWARD 2019

PREMIERE OF TASTE

Creative Direction: Alexey Fadeev,
Anastasia Tretyakova
Art Direction: Stas Neretin, Nikita Ivanov
Design: Elena Ratner, Stas Neretin
Strategic Direction: Farhad Kuchkarov
Project Management: Alena Baklikova
CEO: Alexey Andreev
Photography: Irina Zavyalova
Executive Direction: Ksenia Parkhomenko
Company: Depot Branding Agency
Country: Russian Federation
Category: Distributors'/retailers' own brands/
private labels

SILVER PENTAWARD 2020

THE ENERGY DRINK

Creative Direction: Michelle Romeo-Wiegman
Design: Tamas Paszto
Illustration: Willemijn de Lint
Manufacturing: Action, Refresco Benelux
Company: Yellow Dress Retail
Country: Netherlands
Category: Distributors'/retailers' own brands/
private labels

BRONZE PENTAWARD 2019

CHIARO

Creative Direction: Annette Harcus
Design: Jaimee-Lee Field
Stock: Spicers Manter Cotone Extra Bianco Ultra
Label Printing: Labelhouse Victoria
Bottle Photography: Stephen Clarke
Company: Harcus Design
Country: Australia
Category: Distributors'/retailers' own brands/
private labels

BRONZE PENTAWARD 2019

SHAOXING YELLOW WINE

Creative, Design and Illustration: Guanzi
Copywriting: Cherry Lu
Company: Beijing ChiZha Company
Country: China
Category: Distributors'/
retailers' own brands/private labels
SILVER PENTAWARD 2020

RETSINA WINE, LIDL

Photography: Konstantinos Gikas
Company: Caparo Design Crew
Country: Greece
Category: Distributors'/
retailers' own brands/private labels
BRONZE PENTAWARD 2020

TIGRE BLANC

President: Mareva Essia
Creative Direction: Marc Ramos
Head of Development: Agathe Vincent-Läy
Photography: Louis Gantiez
Company: Tigre Blanc Paris
Country: France
Category: Distributors'/
retailers' own brands/private labels
BRONZE PENTAWARD 2020

INDIEBREWERIE

Art Direction: Paul Roeters, Jeroen Hoedjes
Design: Jeroen Hoedjes
Company: Studio Kluif
Country: Netherlands
Category: Packaging concept (professional)

GOLD PENTAWARD 2020

OCTOPUS

Design: Pavla Chuykina
Company: Pavla Chuykina
Country: Russian Federation
Category: Packaging concept (professional)

GOLD PENTAWARD 2019

The elegance of the **Octopus Rum** bottle shifts toward a playful dimension with this conceptual idea that transforms the traditional look of a wax seal flowing down a bottle to create the head and tentacles of an octopus. Looking every bit the sentry, the wax sea creature guards the contents of the bottle from errant oxygen or prying hands. With the simple addition of two embossed eyes, the designer brings Billy the octopus to life, creating an emotional connection between consumer and brand.

Die Eleganz der **Octopus Rum**-Flasche spielt mit der Idee, das Aussehen eines die Flasche herunterfließenden Wachssiegels so zu transformieren, dass es zu einem Oktopus wird. Wie ein Wachposten beschützt das Seeungeheuer den Inhalt der Flasche vor Sauerstoff oder spitzen Fingern. Durch die zwei eingeprägten Augen lässt der Designer Oktopus Billy lebendig wirken und schafft so eine emotionale Bindung zwischen Konsument und Marke.

L'originalité de la bouteille **Octopus Rum** tient à son aspect ludique, l'habituel cachet de cire dégoulinant sur les côtés pour créer la tête et les tentacules d'un poulpe. Telle une sentinelle, la créature marine en cire garde le contenu de la bouteille à l'abri de l'oxygène ambient ou de mains fureteuses. En ajoutant deux yeux en relief, le designer donne vie à Billy le poulpe et crée un lien émotionnel entre le consommateur et la marque.

OTHER WIDOWS

Creative Direction and Design: Jason Kempen
Illustration: Max Baitinger
Visualisation: Frankie Forzoni
Company: Studio Kempen
Country: Netherlands
Category: Packaging concept (professional)

SILVER PENTAWARD 2020

EL ORO

Creative Direction: Alexey Astakhov
Design and Illustration: Polina Tikhonenko
Company: Uprise Branding Agency
Country: Russian Federation
Category: Packaging concept (professional)

BRONZE PENTAWARD 2019

SECOND LIFE TEA

Design: Lauren Fillols
Company: SGK Anthem – Amsterdam
Country: Netherlands
Category: Packaging concept (professional)

BRONZE PENTAWARD 2020

RECYCLICK

Design: Maciej Gil, Paweł Frej
Company: Hi Brands
Country: Poland
Category: Packaging concept (professional)

BRONZE PENTAWARD 2020

21º

Design: Pavla Chuykina
Company: Pavla Chuykina
Country: Russian Federation
Category: Packaging concept
(professional)

SILVER PENTAWARD 2019

SOAR "LEVITATING" PREMIUM VODKA 88%

Design: Dean Brodie
Creative Direction: Dimitri Castrique
Company: Mona Lisa
Country: Belgium
Category: Packaging concept (professional)

SILVER PENTAWARD 2019

XIAOHUTUXIAN

Creative Direction: Xiongbo Deng
Design: Xing Liu
Illustration: Xing Liu
Company: ShenZhen Lingyun Creative
Packaging Design
Country: China
Category: Packaging concept (professional)

SILVER PENTAWARD 2020

CORN WHISKY

Creative Direction: Yoshio Kato
Art Direction: Yoshio Kato, Eijiro Kuniyoshi
Design: Kenji Takahashi
Company: Kotobuki Seihan Printing
Country: Japan
Category: Packaging concept (professional)

BRONZE PENTAWARD 2019

The packaging for **Corn Whiskey** was designed to look like the product's main ingredient: corn. The "husks" that form the outer packaging are not just for aesthetics; they also help protect the bottle from damage. This conceptual piece is a great example of how package design can be straightforward, fun and effective.

Die Verpackung von **Corn Whiskey** wurde so entworfen, dass sie genau wie die Hauptzutat des Produkts aussieht: Mais. Die „Hülsen", die die äußere Verpackung bilden, sind nicht nur ästhetisch, sie helfen außerdem, die Flasche vor Bruch zu schützen. Dieses konzeptionelle Stück ist ein tolles Beispiel dafür, wie Verpackungsdesign unkompliziert, lustig und effektiv sein kann.

Le packaging pour **Corn Whiskey** a été conçu pour simuler le principal ingrédient du produit, à savoir le maïs. Les « feuilles » qui forment le packaging externe ne sont pas simplement esthétiques, elles servent aussi à protéger la bouteille. Cette création conceptuelle illustre bien comment un emballage peut être à la fois simple, amusant et utile.

MOOD COFFEE PACKAGING

Design: David Hovhannisyan
Company: Hello-agency Moscow
Country: Russian Federation
Category: Packaging concept (student)

GOLD PENTAWARD 2019

PURE
JUICED WATER

Design: Ethan Brown,
Ben Chamberlain, Ella Flood
School: Norwich University of the Arts
Country: UK
Category: Packaging concept (student)

GOLD PENTAWARD 2020

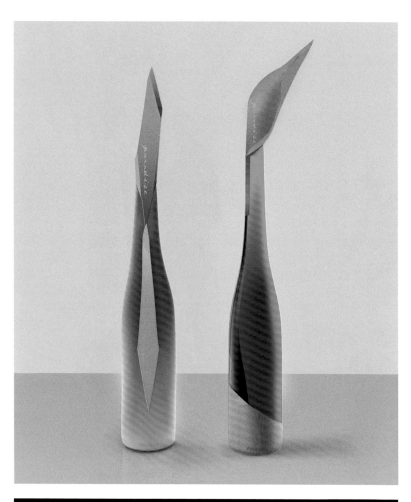

PARADISE

Design: Siyu Yu
Supervision: Hu Ji-Jun
School: Shanghai Institute of Visual Arts (SIVA)
Country: China
Category: Packaging concept (student)

BRONZE PENTAWARD 2020

PU'ER TEA CUBE

Design: Yongzhou Ma, Boxuan Yu, Shilei Niu, Hao Zhu
School: Changsha University of Science and Technology
Country: China
Category: Packaging concept (student)

BRONZE PENTAWARD 2020

BODEGAS VÉRTIGO 27

Creative Direction, Design and Photography:
Alba Albelda Puras, Lucía Fernández Arozamena
Instruction: Gracia de Prado, Silvia Cerrolaza
Advising: Daniel Morales, Javier Euba
School: Escuela Superior de Diseño de La Rioja (Esdir)
Country: Spain
Category: Packaging concept (student)
SILVER PENTAWARD 2020

TWIST

Design: Huang Jiayin
Supervision: Hu Jijun
School: Shanghai Institute of Visual Arts (SIVA)
Country: China
Category: Packaging concept (student)

SILVER PENTAWARD 2019

LINGYUN, GUIZHOU AND SICHUAN

Supervision: Lu Jun
Design: Liu Xiaoyan
School: Yunnan Minzu University
Country: China
Category: Packaging concept (student)

SILVER PENTAWARD 2019

SERÉ BREVE

Creative Direction and Design:
Carlota Carrillo, Mercè Puig
School: Escuela Superior
de Diseño de La Rioja (Esdir)
Country: Spain
Category: Packaging concept (student)

BRONZE PENTAWARD 2019

PIPE

Design: Xiangxin Li
Supervision: Gu Chuan-Xi
School: Shanghai Institute of Visual Arts (SIVA)
Country: China
Category: Packaging concept (student)

SILVER PENTAWARD 2020

MAETI

Design: Mercè Puig
School: Escuela Superior
de Diseño de La Rioja (Esdir)
Country: Spain
Category: Packaging concept (student)
BRONZE PENTAWARD 2019

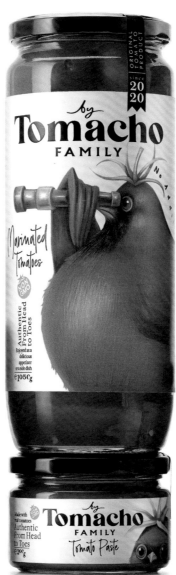

Best of the category
Bread, cereals and pasta
Dairy or soya-based products
Spices, oils and sauces
Fish, meat, poultry
Fruit and vegetables
Soups, ready-to-eat dishes, fast food

food

Confectionery and sweet snacks
Savory snacks
Desserts, sweet foods and confection dishes
Food trends
Limited editions, limited series, event creations
Distributors'/retailers' own brands/private labels
Packaging concept

Sponsored by

 Proof+

GIVING LIFE TO CREATIVITY

Imagine a space where real like-for-like prototyping connects creative design and the final printing of packaging. A disconnect once existed between the digital world and the real world at the point of brand execution in the final phase of the creative process.

For **Proof**+, the **theory of design thinking** and the value of accurate prototyping are fundamental in the innovation and pursuit of features and functions of any product. Prototyping is the last crucial step in design innovation and achievement. Creativity no longer needs to be limited to the digital space alone. Prototyping gives you the opportunity to explore, uncover the potential of design and thereby close the loop on the final output.

The ability to **fuse the virtual and real worlds** together, whilst harnessing the power to see, touch and feel is extremely important to actually perceiving a brand. Proof+ allows you to breathe life into any creative idea. This concept enables designers to interpret the script and to judge the efficiency of their designs, and reduces the risk of failure. The jump from the digital world to the real world gives reassurance on-shelf, market analysis for consumer engagement, cost control evaluation, defect detection and the sensory experience. Harnessing decades of print knowledge and expertise, using our unique "Colour Guardian" colour management technology, and in collaboration with market leading raw material suppliers, Proof+ was born.

By bringing design to life from a digital to a physical format, all of the design criteria come into play when accessing a product. The majority of product engagement is through sight, and the crucial last part is through **touch and feel**. This allows that all-important **connection to a product**, which contributes to the biggest part of the impulse to buy. With the physical proof you are able to evaluate the packaging through engagement with the consumer in mind to create an emotional connection. This is something that you can only generate physically. Proof+ is 100% accurate for colour, materials and embellishments, which are true representations of the final product. **Proof+, "Real-Life Prototyping"**.

KREATIVITÄT ERSCHAFFEN

Stellen Sie sich einen Ort vor, der echte vergleichbare Prototypenentwicklung, kreatives Design und das abschließende Bedrucken der Verpackungen miteinander verbindet. Früher gab es eine Trennung zwischen der digitalen und der realen Welt am Punkt der Markenausführung in der letzten Phase des kreativen Prozesses.

Für **Proof**+ sind die **Theorie des Design Thinking** und der Wert von akkuraten Prototypen fundamental für die Innovation und das Streben nach Merkmalen und Funktionen jedes Produkts. Die Entwicklung von Prototypen ist der letzte entscheidende Schritt bei der Designinnovation und -leistung. Kreativität muss nicht mehr länger auf den digitalen Raum beschränkt sein. Das Erstellen von Prototypen ermöglicht es Ihnen, das Potenzial des Designs zu erforschen und aufzudecken und so den Kreis für das Endprodukt zu schließen, das auf den Markt gebracht wird.

Die Fähigkeit, die **virtuelle und die reale Welt miteinander zu verschmelzen** während man gleichzeitig die Kraft des Sehens, Fühlens und Tastens nutzt, ist für die tatsächliche Wahrnehmung einer Marke äußerst wichtig. Proof+ ermöglicht es Ihnen, jeder kreativen Idee Leben einzuhauchen. Dieses Konzept ermöglicht es den Designern, das Skript zu interpretieren und die Effizienz ihrer Entwürfe zu beurteilen und somit das Risiko eines Misserfolgs verringern. Der Sprung von der digitalen zur realen Welt gibt Sicherheit über das fertige Produkt in den Regalen, Marktanalysen für die Konsumentenbindung, Evaluationen der Kostenkontrollen, Fehlererkennung und das sensorische Erlebnis. Durch unsere jahrzehntelange Erfahrung im Bereich des Drucks und unsere Fachkompetenz können wir unsere einzigartige „Colour Guardian"-Farbmanagement-Technologie anwenden, wodurch Proof+ in Zusammenarbeit mit führenden Rohstofflieferanten auf dem Markt gegründet wurde.

Indem das Design von einem digitalen in ein physisches Format überführt wird, kommen alle Designkriterien mit ins Spiel, wenn das Produkt beurteilt wird. Die Auseinandersetzung mit dem Produkt geschieht hauptsächlich durch das Ansehen, aber der wesentliche letzte Teil, ist das **Anfassen und Fühlen**. Das ermöglicht die so wichtige **Verbindung zu einem Produkt**, die den größten Teil des Kaufimpulses ausmacht. Mit der physischen Bestätigung sind Sie in der Lage, die Verpackung durch die Auseinandersetzung mit dem Kunden im Hinterkopf zu beurteilen, um eine emotionale Verbindung herzustellen. Das ist etwas, das Sie nur physisch schaffen werden. Proof+ ist zu 100 % akkurat, was Farbe, Material und Verzierungen betrifft, die die wahre Repräsentation des Endprodukts ausmachen. **Proof+, „lebensechte Prototypenentwicklung"**.

DONNER VIE À LA CRÉATIVITÉ

Imaginez un espace dans lequel un prototypage réellement à l'identique matérialise la rencontre entre la conception créative et l'impression finale du packaging. Il fut un temps où le monde numérique et le monde réel se découplaient au point de mise en œuvre de la marque, lors de la phase finale du processus de création.

Pour **Proof**+, la **théorie du design thinking** et la valeur d'un prototypage fidèle sont fondamentales pour l'innovation et la recherche de caractéristiques et de fonctions pour un produit. Le prototypage est l'ultime étape clé pour innover et réaliser une conception. La créativité ne doit plus se cantonner au seul espace numérique, car les prototypes offrent la chance de découvrir et d'explorer tout le potentiel du design, et ainsi de boucler la boucle avec le résultat final.

La possibilité de **fusionner ensemble les mondes réel et virtuel**, et donc de voir, toucher et sentir, est extrêmement importante pour comprendre réellement une marque. Proof+ vous permet d'insuffler la vie à une idée créative, concept grâce auquel les concepteurs peuvent interpréter le script et évaluer l'efficacité de leurs designs, ce qui réduit par là même le risque d'échec. Le passage du monde numérique au monde réel rassure pour la mise en rayon et fournit une analyse de marché quant à l'engagement des consommateurs, une évaluation du contrôle des coûts, une détection des défauts, ainsi qu'une expérience sensorielle. Proof+ est né des connaissances et compétences mobilisées durant des décennies dans le domaine de l'impression, de notre technologie unique de gestion des couleurs « Colour Guardian » et de la collaboration avec les principaux fournisseurs de matières premières du marché.

En donnant vie à une conception, de son format numérique à sa forme physique, tous les critères de design entrent en jeu pour réussir un produit. Le plus souvent, l'engagement produit se fait par la vue, et la dernière étape, cruciale, à travers **le toucher et les sensations**. De cette façon s'établit ce **lien capital avec le produit qui** contribue dans une très large mesure à l'impulsion d'achat. L'épreuve physique vous permet d'évaluer le packaging par la participation, avec le consommateur à l'esprit pour nouer un lien émotionnel, et cette mesure n'est possible que physiquement. Proof+ offre des prototypes d'une précision à 100 % en termes de couleurs, de matériaux et de décorations pour proposer des représentations fidèles au produit final. **Proof+, « Real-Life Prototyping »**.

RICEMAN

Brand Strategy Direction: Stepan Avanesyan
Creative Direction: Stepan Azaryan
Project Management: Meri Sargsyan
Design: Stepan Azaryan, Eliza Malkhasyan
Modelling Design: Armenuhi Avagyan
Illustration: Marieta Arzumanyan, Elina Barseghyan
Company: Backbone Branding
Country: Armenia
Category: Bread, cereals and pasta

PLATINUM PENTAWARD 2019

The brand idea for **Riceman** was based on humanising the rice-growing process, so the name and the packaging were developed to symbolise intensive human labour and the identity of the farmer. Illustrations of the farmers' diverse emotional expressions like self-confidence, satisfaction and empathy were used to reflect their daily lives, whilst the lid of the bag is in the form of the traditional Asian farmer's hat, marked inside with measurements. With tall and short size bags containing either the long grain or short grain rice, the overall design and packaging elements express the idea of human involvement, closeness to nature and the regional origin of the product.

Die Markenidee für **Riceman** basiert auf dem Anspruch auf einen fairen Reisanbau – der Name und die Verpackung wurden entwickelt, um die intensive menschliche Arbeit und die Identität der Bauern zu symbolisieren. Illustrationen von verschiedenen Gesichtsausdrücken der Bauern wie Selbstbewusstsein, Zufriedenheit und Empathie wurden benutzt, um das tägliche Leben abzubilden, während der Deckel die Form eines asiatischen Bauernhuts hat, der gleichzeitig als Messbecher für Reis genutzt werden kann. Die Beutel enthalten entweder Langkorn- oder Rundkornreis. Das Gesamtdesign und die Verpackungselemente drücken die Idee der menschlichen Beteiligung, die Nähe zur Natur und die regionale Herkunft des Produkts aus.

L'idée de la marque **Riceman** était d'humaniser la culture du riz : le nom et le packaging ont ainsi été pensés pour symboliser le travail humain intensif et l'identité du producteur. En représentant plusieurs sentiments des exploitants, comme la confiance en soi, la satisfaction et l'empathie, les illustrations reflètent leur quotidien, alors qu'un cache de la forme du traditionnel chapeau du paysan asiatique repose sur le haut avec les mesures de riz inscrites à l'intérieur. Les sacs de diverses tailles renferment du riz à grain court ou long, et tant le design global que les éléments du packaging transmettent l'intervention de l'homme, la proximité avec la nature et l'origine locale du produit.

The philosophy of **Nongfu Wangtian** is that plants are cultivated naturally without any human intervention. They respect the rules of nature and reject any additives. The creative idea of this product packaging is that by transferring the shape of the chilli pepper to the container, it brings the experience of picking chillies directly to the customer. Its distinctive and fun design will make it the first to be noticed on the shelves, enticing consumers to buy it and try it out, and to share with friends and family.

Die Philosophie von **Nongfu Wangtian** ist, dass Pflanzen auf natürliche Weise und ohne menschliche Trickserei angebaut werden. Die Regeln der Natur werden respektiert und jegliche Zusatzstoffe abgelehnt. Durch das Übertragen der Chiliform auf die Verpackung wird die Erfahrung des Pflückens mit dem Kunden geteilt. Mit seinem unverwechselbaren und spielerischen Design fällt diese Soße in den Regalen auf und sorgt für Freude — ein Produkt, das man gerne weiterempfiehlt.

Selon la philosophie de **Nongfu Wangtian**, les plantes sont cultivées naturellement sans intervention de l'homme, dans le respect des règles de la nature et sans aucun additif. Pour ce produit, l'idée créative consiste à donner à l'emballage la forme d'un piment afin d'offrir au consommateur une expérience de cueillette. Grâce à son design original et amusant, il est inratable dans les rayons et motive les consommateurs à l'essayer et à le partager en famille et entre amis.

NONGFU WANGTIAN

Design: ShenZhen BOB Design team
Company: ShenZhen BOB Design
Country: China
Category: Spices, oils and sauces
PLATINUM PENTAWARD 2020

SRISANGDAO RICE

Executive Creative Direction: Somchana Kangwarnjit
Design: Rutthawitch Akkachairin, SKJ
Retouching: Pantipa Pummuang,
Thiyada Akarasinakul, Somporn Thimkhao
Company: Prompt Design
Country: Thailand
Category: Bread, cereals and pasta

GOLD PENTAWARD 2020

IPPO'N was established as the new name in the rebranding of a Japanese noodle brand. Inaniwa udon are made in the Inaniwa area in Akita prefecture in Japan and are hand-stretched dried noodles that are slightly thinner than regular udon. The word ippon refers to a single line in Japanese, reflecting the character of the straight, beautiful udon, whilst *ippo* also means "the first step", perfect for launching a rebranded product.

IPPO'N ist der neue Name einer japanischen Nudelfirma. Inaniwa Udon werden in Inaniw in der Akita Region Japans hergestellt und sind handgeformte getrocknete Nudeln, die etwas dünner als herkömmliche Udon sind. Das Wort *ippon* bezieht sich im Japanischen auf eine einzelne Linie, die den Charakter der geraden, hübschen Udon widerspiegelt, während *ippo* auch „der erste Schritt" bedeutet, der perfekt passt, um ein Produkt nach dem Rebranding wieder auf den Markt zu bringen.

IPPO'N est le nom qui a été adopté pour le rebranding d'une marque japonaise de nouilles. Élaborées dans la région d'Inaniwa de la préfecture d'Akita au Japon, les inaniwa udon sont des nouilles sèches étirées à la main, légèrement plus fines que les udon standard. En japonais, *ippon* désigne une ligne, à l'image des belles nouilles droites, alors que le terme *ippo* signifie « le premier pas », idéal pour le lancement d'un produit à l'image revisitée.

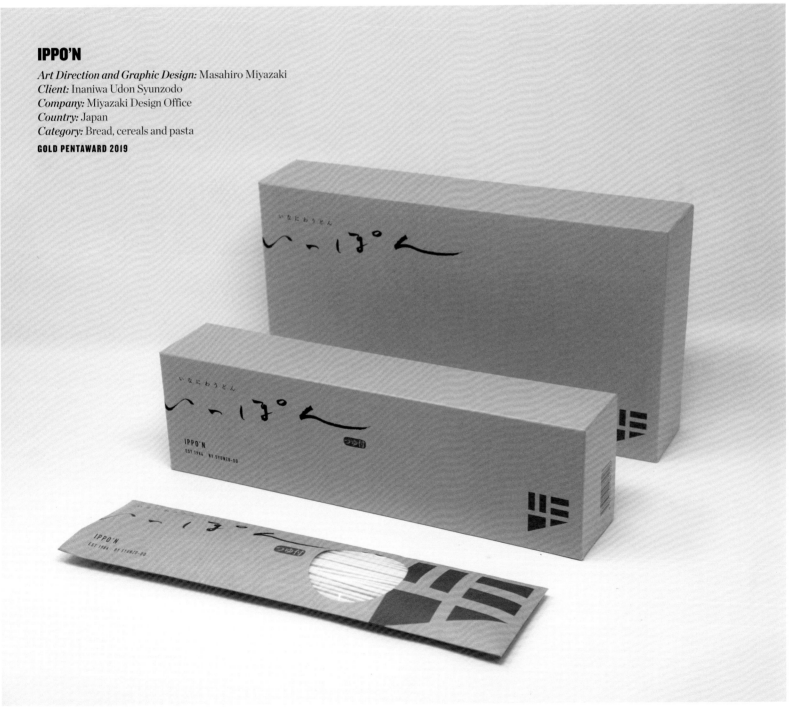

IPPO'N

Art Direction and Graphic Design: Masahiro Miyazaki
Client: Inaniwa Udon Syunzodo
Company: Miyazaki Design Office
Country: Japan
Category: Bread, cereals and pasta

GOLD PENTAWARD 2019

KELLOGG'S

Executive Creative Direction: Mark Waters
Creative Direction: Gavin Hurrell, Jason Ching
Design Direction: Chris Simpson
Design: Jessie Froggett, Jake Rimmer,
David Blakemore
Artwork: James Chilvers, James Norris, Alex Man
Retouching: Mick Connor
Account Direction: Jamie Pearce, Cyrille Ernst
Account Management: Georgia Phillips
Planning: Tim Owen, Charlie Rogers
Company: Turner Duckworth
Country: UK
Category: Bread, cereals and pasta

SILVER PENTAWARD 2020

KELLOGG'S

Design: Landor Design Team
Company: Landor
Country: UK
Category: Bread, cereals and pasta
BRONZE PENTAWARD 2019

NORTH FARM RICE

Design and Illustration: Meng Zhang
Logo Design: Lin Huang
Photography: Chao Li
Company: Meng Zhang
Country: Australia
Category: Bread, cereals and pasta
BRONZE PENTAWARD 2019

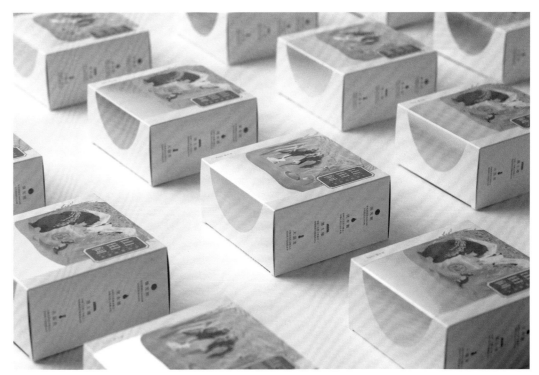

QING YI NONG NONG "LORD BAO" RYE BREAD

Design: Jingfang Mei
Company: Hangzhou Dongyun Advertising Design
Country: China
Category: Bread, cereals and pasta

BRONZE PENTAWARD 2020

JOYKO

Design: Paton
Company: Hangzhou Paton Brand Design
Country: China
Category: Bread, cereals and pasta

BRONZE PENTAWARD 2020

CHILIUXIAN

Design: The Mars Creative Team
Company: Shenzhen Baixinglong Creative Packaging
Country: China
Category: Bread, cereals and pasta

SILVER PENTAWARD 2020

AH MORE THAN PASTA

Senior Design Direction: Ditte Glebbeek
Brand Direction: Evelyn Hille
Company: VBAT
Country: Netherlands
Category: Bread, cereals and pasta

SILVER PENTAWARD 2019

ALLINSON'S

Creative Direction: Paul Williams
Design Direction: Lou Elms
Senior Design: Sophie Burt
Company: Springetts
Country: UK
Category: Bread, cereals and pasta

SILVER PENTAWARD 2019

This design for **Avgoulakia's** organic egg packaging conveys the uniqueness of the brand in a modern and playful way, enriched with vivid, bright pops of colour. The chicken/egg dilemma may ask "which came first: the chicken or the egg?" but with these cartons the chickens definitely steal the show. Enchanted by the power of stories, a visual narrative was created about chickens with interesting and unusual qualities: with Captain Machi for free-range eggs, Madame Coco for organic eggs and Miss Nelly for barn-laid eggs.

Dieses Design mit lebhaften, leuchtenden Farbhighlights für die **Avgoulakias** Bio-Ei-Verpackung übermittelt die Einzigartigkeit der Marke auf eine moderne und spielerische Art. Das Huhn/Ei-Dilemma stellt die Frage: „Wer war zuerst da: das Huhn oder das Ei?" Mit diesen Kartons stehlen definitiv die Hühner den Eiern die Show. Verzaubert von der Kraft einer Geschichte entstand eine visuelle Narrative über Hühner mit interessanten und eigenartigen Qualitäten: Captain Machi steht für Eier aus Freilandhaltung, Madame Coco für Bio-Eier und Miss Nelly für Eier aus Bodenhaltung.

Rehaussé de touches de couleurs vives, ce design moderne et amusant pour les boîtes d'œufs biologiques d'**Avgoulakia** transmet bien toute l'originalité de la marque. Le dilemme « Qui de l'œuf ou de la poule est apparu en premier ? » n'est pas résolu, mais ici c'est clairement l'animal qui vole la vedette. Le pouvoir reconnu des histoires a conduit à cette narration visuelle sur les poules, qui n'est pas sans intérêt et curiosités : on y trouve Captain Machi pour les œufs de poules élevées en liberté, Madame Coco pour les œufs biologiques et Miss Nelly pour les œufs pondus en grange.

AVGOULAKIA

Art Direction: Antonia Skarkari
Design and Illustration: Andreas Deskas
Company: A.S. Advertising
Country: Greece
Category: Dairy or soya-based products
GOLD PENTAWARD 2019

SMÖR BUTTER

Design: Mousegraphics team
Industrial Design: Nikos Kastanakis
Company: Mousegraphics
Country: Greece
Category: Dairy or soya-based products

SILVER PENTAWARD 2020

ANI DAIRY

Brand Strategy: Stepan Avanesyan
Creative Direction and Design: Stepan Azaryan
Project Management: Meri Sargsyan
Art Direction and Illustration: Mariam Stepanyan
Copywriting: Grace Jerejian
Company: Backbone Branding
Country: Armenia
Category: Dairy or soya-based products

GOLD PENTAWARD 2020

BON FROMAGE

Creative Direction: Paco Adín
Account Direction: Lourdes Morillas
Project Management: Susana Seijas
Company: Supperstudio
Country: Spain
Category: Dairy or soya-based products

SILVER PENTAWARD 2019

GENERAL MILLS

Founding Partner and CEO Americas Pearlfisher:
Mike Branson
Creative Direction: Hamish Campbell
Associate Creative Direction: Christian Bird
Strategy Direction: Lauren Koprowski
Head of Realization: Brandi Parker
Client Direction: Courtney Tight
Head of Client Management: Justine Allan
Senior Digital Artwork: Aaron Koskela,
Stephen Kwartler
Senior Visualization: Liviu Dimulescu
Design Direction: Priyanka Krishnamohan
Design: Nadia Izazi
Senior Client Management: Anne-Sophie Tomas Gautier
Company: Pearlfisher
Country: USA
Category: Dairy or soya-based products
BRONZE PENTAWARD 2019

PROVAMEL

Design: Mousegraphics team
Company: Mousegraphics
Country: Greece
Category: Dairy or soya-based products
BRONZE PENTAWARD 2020

ZUIVELLEVEN

Founding Partners and Creative Direction:
Heidi Broersma, Vincent Limburg
Company: Guts & Glorious,
Brand and Packaging Designers
Country: Netherlands
Category: Dairy or soya-based products

BRONZE PENTAWARD 2019

YO&GO

Creative Direction: Alexey Fadeev,
Anastasia Tretyakova
Art Direction: Nikita Ivanov
Design: Alexey Baiteev, Andrey Gladkov,
Tatiana Mikolaevskaya
Copywriting: Sasha Fedoseeva
Project Management: Anna Rozhnova
CEO: Alexey Andreev
Executive Direction: Ksenia Parkhomenko
Company: Depot Branding Agency
Country: Russian Federation
Category: Dairy or soya-based products

SILVER PENTAWARD 2020

JUMBO PLANTAARDIGE ZUIVEL

Design and Art Direction: Menno Mulder
Company: OD Designstudio
Country: Netherlands
Category: Dairy or soya-based products

SILVER PENTAWARD 2019

YILI

Brand Team: Bian Wu, Xi Wang, Xu Jing, Hua Wang
Account Management: Crystal Cai, Vera Ye, Benjamin Wei
Creative: Serean Tan, Vivina Li
Strategy: Minggo Li, Queenie Zhang, Orchid Pan, Hu Meng
Color Management: Leo Lai, Fone Zhang
Bottle Design: Jingyu Guo
Company: Inner Mongolia Yili Group
Country: China
Category: Dairy or soya-based products

BRONZE PENTAWARD 2020

The source of inspiration for the design of each ceramic container for the **Ahaean Land** products is the name and the history of each olive grove region, which reflect the unique culinary palette of each olive oil. In the olive groves, the crop is collected at two points in the season, with the early collection producing the fresh extra virgin green olive oil, and the later one the extra virgin olive oil. The ceramic containers distinguish between these by their colour, with white for the green olive oil and black for the mature olive oil. The Aheleon logo foil sticker on the containers highlights the sophisticated olive oil production process as well as the handmade ceramic containers.

Die Inspirationsquelle für das Design der Keramikbehälter der **Ahaean Land**-Produkte ist der Name und die Geschichte, die hinter jeder Olivenregion steckt, die die einzigartige kulinarische Palette des Olivenöls widerspiegeln. In den Olivenhainen wird die Frucht zu zwei Zeitpunkten in der Saison geerntet. Bei der frühen Ernte wird das frische grüne Olivenöl Extra Vergine hergestellt, bei der zweiten das reife Olivenöl Extra Vergine. Die Keramikbehälter unterscheiden durch ihre Farbe zwischen beiden Sorten — mit einem weißen Behälter für das grüne Olivenöl und einem schwarzen für das späte Olivenöl. Der folierte Aufkleber des Aheleon-Logos auf dem Behälter unterstreicht den anspruchsvollen Herstellungsprozess des Öls sowie der handgefertigten Keramikbehälter.

Le design de chaque récipient en céramique des produits de la marque **Ahaean Land** s'est inspiré du nom et de l'histoire de chaque région d'oliveraies, à l'image de la palette de saveurs unique de chaque huile d'olive. La récolte des olives se fait à deux moments au cours de la saison : la première collecte produit l'huile d'olive vierge extra fruité vert, la seconde l'huile d'olive vierge extra fruité mûr. Cette distinction est marquée par la couleur des récipients en céramique : le blanc pour l'huile aux accents de verdure, le noir pour l'huile maturée. L'adhésif métallisé du logo Aheleon dénote la sophistication du processus de fabrication et des récipients artisanaux en céramique.

AHAEAN LAND

Research, Design and Prototype Development: KM Creative
Art Direction: Michalis Kanonis
Ceramic Manufacturing: Attikki Keramiki
Photography: Marios Theologis
Client: Ahaean Land
Company: KM Creative
Country: Greece
Category: Spices, oils and sauces
GOLD PENTAWARD 2019

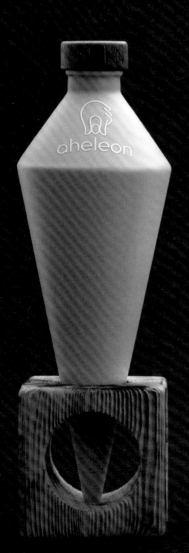

PEDRO BERNARDO

Art Direction and Graphic Design: Ana Lobo
Digital Design: Cristian Ángel
Photography: Brandrid team
Company: Brandrid
Country: Spain
Category: Spices, oils and sauces

GOLD PENTAWARD 2020

SALSUS

Design: Eia Grødal, Morten Throndsen
Creative Direction: Morten Throndsen
Account Management: Susanne Munch-Rasmussen
Company: Strømme Throndsen Design
Country: Norway
Category: Spices, oils and sauces
BRONZE PENTAWARD 2019

MARINA PALUSCI

Design: Mario Di Paolo
Company: Spazio Di Paolo
Country: Italy
Category: Spices, oils and sauces
BRONZE PENTAWARD 2019

LA MATILLA

Art Direction: Fernando Suárez
Senior Graphic Design: Jerónimo Atienza
Illustration: Jesús Barbudo
Photography: Diego Gallego
Company: Habermas Consultoría de Diseño
Country: Spain
Category: Spices, oils and sauces

SILVER PENTAWARD 2020

RAIJMAKERS HEETMAKERS

Design: Jeroen de Kok
Art Direction: Niels Alkema
Design Management: Jan-Willem Glaubitz
DTP: Sofie Manuputty
Illustration: Michael Hinkle
Company: OD Designstudio
Country: Netherlands
Category: Spices, oils and sauces

SILVER PENTAWARD 2019

LEVANTES FAMILY FARM

Creative Direction and Design: Alexandros Gavrilakis
Illustration: Virginia Andronikou
Copywriting: Olympia Aivazi
Company: AG Design Agency
Country: Greece
Category: Spices, oils and sauces

SILVER PENTAWARD 2019

TORO ALBALÁ

Design: Seriesnemo
industrial and graphic team
Company: Seriesnemo
Country: Spain
Category: Spices, oils and sauces

BRONZE PENTAWARD 2020

BRACHIA KIDS

Client: Brachia
Creative and Art Direction: Izvorka Juric
Verbal Communication, Design, Illustration and
Product Photography: Jurica Kos
Photography: Maja Danica Pecanic
Company: Design Bureau Izvorka Juric
Country: Croatia
Category: Spices, oils and sauces

SILVER PENTAWARD 2020

HENDERSON'S RELISH

Creative Direction: Paul Williams
Design Direction: Claire Ganly
Company: Springetts
Country: UK
Category: Spices, oils and sauces

BRONZE PENTAWARD 2020

LUHUA XIAOMO SESAME OIL

Design: Tiger Pan, Qian Chi, Dongwei Sun
Photography: Kelin Tan
Technician: Zhangkun Xie
Company: Shenzhen Tigerpan Packaging Design
Country: China
Category: Spices, oils and sauces

BRONZE PENTAWARD 2020

QUEEN MADE

Client: Ehime Kaisan
Art Direction and Graphic Design: Koji Matsumoto
Illustration: Aya Matsumoto
Design Studio: Grand Deluxe
Company: Grand Deluxe
Country: Japan
Category: Fish, meat, poultry
GOLD PENTAWARD 2019

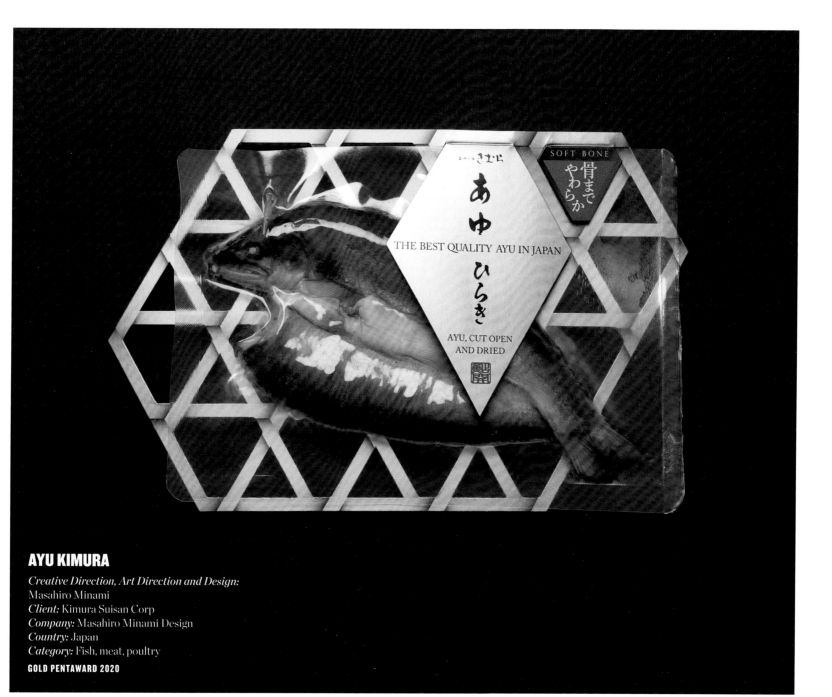

AYU KIMURA

Creative Direction, Art Direction and Design:
Masahiro Minami
Client: Kimura Suisan Corp
Company: Masahiro Minami Design
Country: Japan
Category: Fish, meat, poultry

GOLD PENTAWARD 2020

This is a packaging redesign for **AYU Kimura**, a dried sweet fish which is a very rare product in Japan. There it is common practice to cut fish in half, flay it and eat it dried – a type of processed fish called *himono*. Reducing the water content prevents the fish from spoiling and makes it more delicious. The gold paper packaging was designed to resemble the bamboo colander used in the traditional drying process. It's flat and simple, yet appears three-dimensional and woven, which adds to the high-quality feel of the product.

Das ist ein neues Verpackungsdesign für **AYU Kimura** Trockenfisch, der in Japan eine Delikatesse ist. Dort ist es üblich, den Fisch, *Himono*, in zwei Hälften zu schneiden, zu enthäuten und getrocknet zu essen. Die Reduzierung des Wassergehalts verhindert, dass der Fisch verdirbt, und macht ihn schmackhafter. Die Verpackung aus Goldpapier wurde so gestaltet, dass sie dem Bambussieb ähnelt, das für den traditionellen Trocknungsvorgang verwendet wird. Die Dreidimensionalität des scheinbar gewobenen Siebs trägt zur hochwertigen Haptik des Produkts bei.

Le packaging pour la marque **AYU Kimura** a connu une refonte. Ce poisson sucré séché est un produit extrêmement rare au Japon et se prépare selon une méthode traditionnelle : l'animal est coupé en deux moitiés, ouvert et consommé séché (himono). Sa teneur en eau étant moindre, le poisson se conserve et acquiert une saveur délicieuse. Le papier doré de l'emballage a été pensé pour rappeler la passoire en bambou employée dans le procédé de séchage traditionnel. Il est plat et simple, mais semble pourtant en trois dimensions et tressé, ce qui contribue à transmettre la grande qualité du produit.

QIDELONGDONGQIANG

Design: Yifu Pan, Han Zhen
Creative Direction: Yifu Pan
Company: IFPD Studio
Country: China
Category: Fish, meat, poultry

SILVER PENTAWARD 2020

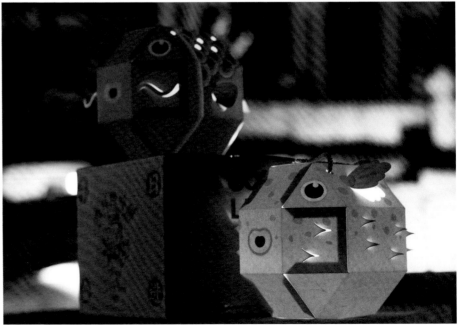

ARCTIC REIN OG VILT

Design: Eia Grødal, Morten Throndsen
Creative Direction: Morten Throndsen
Account Management: Susanne Munch-Rasmussen
Company: Strømme Throndsen Design
Country: Norway
Category: Fish, meat, poultry
BRONZE PENTAWARD 2019

LUCAS SARDINES

Art Direction and Graphic Design:
Loonatiks Design Crew
Client: Kamilaris S.A.
Company: Loonatiks Design Crew
Country: Greece
Category: Fish, meat, poultry
BRONZE PENTAWARD 2020

UNCLE PIG'S OLD BACON

Design: Zhou Jingkuan
Illustration: Hu Yunfeng
Company: Shenzhen Left and Right Packaging Design
Country: China
Category: Fish, meat, poultry
SILVER PENTAWARD 2019

JEALSA RIANXEIRA

Global Creative Direction and Founder:
Teresa Martín de la Mata
Creative Direction: Jaime García
Company: De la Mata Design
Country: Spain
Category: Fish, meat, poultry
SILVER PENTAWARD 2019

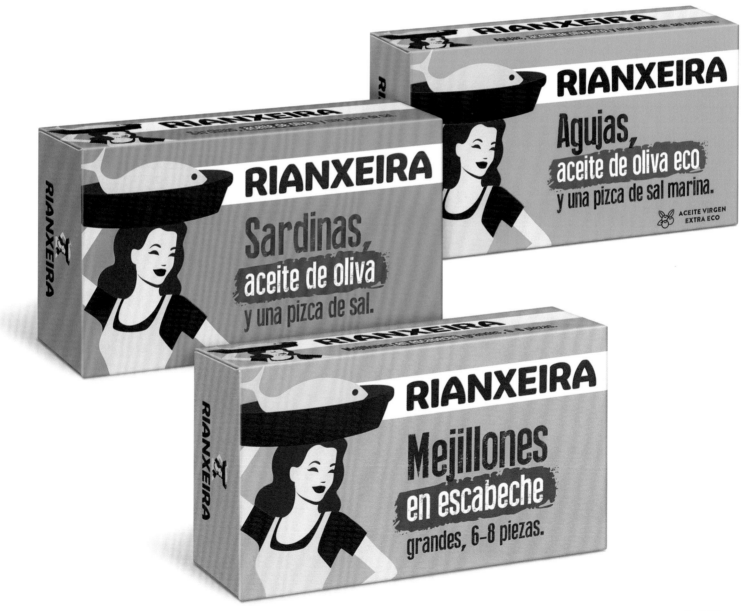

KADONAGA SEAFOODS PICKLED FISH

Creative Direction and Art Direction:
Toshiki Osada (Bespoke)
Creative Direction and Copywriting:
Kenichi Yasuda (Sakura)
Design: Shogo Seki
Illustration: Tatsuya Kobayashi
Production: Mode
Company: Sakura, Bespoke
Country: Japan
Category: Fish, meat, poultry

SILVER PENTAWARD 2020

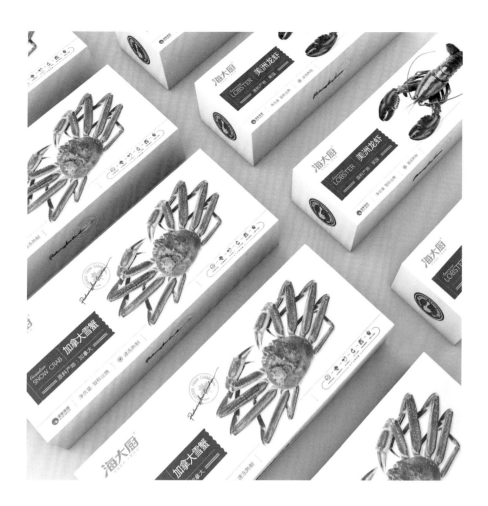

RICH GROUP

Design: Zhangyong Hou
Company: Zhongshihuanmei (Dalian) Advertising
Country: China
Category: Fish, meat, poultry
BRONZE PENTAWARD 2019

AYU KIMURA

Creative Direction, Art Direction and Design:
Masahiro Minami
Client: Kimura Suisan Corp
Company: Masahiro Minami Design
Country: Japan
Category: Fish, meat, poultry
BRONZE PENTAWARD 2020

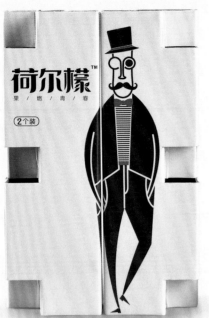

HI LEMON

Creative Direction: Bo Shen
Design: Bo Shen
Illustration: Xiaoqin Pu
Photography: Bo Shen
Client: Peng Li Lemon
Company: Beyond Brand Company
Country: China
Category: Fruit and vegetables

GOLD PENTAWARD 2019

To break out of the conventional design of produce packaging, **Hi Lemon** features a fun and clever box that protects and transports the fruit. The simple folds of the packaging materials and amusing motif help emphasise the distinguishing characteristics of the brand. The key visual image on the packaging is that of a fashionable and "cool" gentleman, whilst the main colour is a bright lemon hue, matching the product inside and creating a brand image of style and energy.

Um aus dem konventionellen Verpackungsdesign für Obst auszubrechen, bringt **Hi Lemon** eine lustige und intelligente Box heraus, welche die Frucht sowohl transportiert als auch schützt. Die einfach gefaltete Verpackung und das amüsante Motiv tragen dazu bei, die herausragenden Merkmale der Marke zu betonen. Das visuelle Hauptmerkmal der Verpackung ist ein modebewusster, „cooler" Gentleman, während die Grundfarbe ein kräftiger Zitronenton ist, der zum Produkt in der Box passt und ein Markenimage voller Stil und Energie widerspiegelt.

Pour rompre avec le design habituel des emballages de produits frais, **Hi Lemon** présente une boîte drôle et astucieuse qui protège les fruits pendant leur transport. Le pliage du carton et le motif amusant viennent souligner les caractéristiques distinguant la marque. L'image visuelle du packaging est celle d'un gentleman chic et avenant, et la couleur principale est un jaune citron vif en accord avec le produit, ce qui communique une image de marque stylisée et dynamique.

Hand-drawn birds with distinct personalities depict each of the 10 types of tomato products within the Tomacho line. Each character from the **Tomacho** family is imagined at a different stage of their lives, from the childlike cherry tomatoes to the wrinkly dried tomatoes in olive oil. Peering out confidently from the jars, the "cocky" red-blooded birds correspond well with the bright red colour that characterises tomatoes, whilst the "macho" in the brand name perfectly sums up the storylines created for each of the characters.

Handgemalte Vögel mit unterschiedlichen Persönlichkeiten zeigen die zehn Tomatenprodukte in der **Tomacho**-Reihe. Jedem Charakter der Tomacho-Familie ist eine andere Lebensphase zugedacht, von den kindlichen Cherrytomaten zu den faltigen, getrockneten Tomaten in Olivenöl. Kühn und voller Selbstvertrauen schauen die frechen blutroten Vögel von den Gläsern und passen damit gut zum Tomatenrot, während das „macho" im Markennamen die Geschichte, die für jeden Charakter geschaffen wurde, perfekt zusammenfasst.

Dessinés à la main, des oiseaux avec une personnalité propre illustrent chacun des 10 types de produits à base de tomate de la gamme **Tomacho**. Chaque personnage de la famille est imaginé à une étape distincte de sa vie, de la phase enfantine avec les tomates cherry aux tomates séchées et ridées dans l'huile d'olive. Plutôt présomptueux, les oiseaux jettent un œil en dehors des pots et arborent un plumage rouge vif en parfait accord avec la couleur caractéristique des tomates. Pour sa part, le « macho » dans le nom de la marque résume au mieux les histoires inventées pour chaque personnage.

TOMACHO

Brand Strategy Direction: Stepan Avanesyan
Assistant Brand Strategy: Lusie Grigoryan
Creative Direction: Stepan Azaryan
Art Direction: Mariam Stepanyan
Illustration: Elina Barseghyan
Project Management: Marianna Atshemyan
Graphic Design: Mane Budaghyan
Copywriting: Grace Jerejian
Company: Backbone Branding
Country: Armenia
Category: Fruit and vegetables

GOLD PENTAWARD 2020

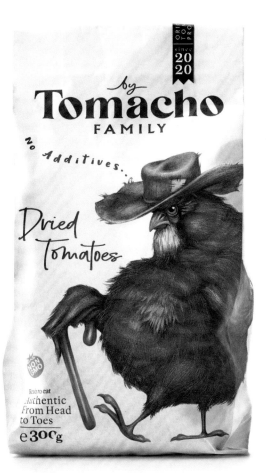

MOYO® YOUR NATURAL SWEETS

Design: Merel van Tellingen
Art Direction: Menno Mulder
Project Management: Fleur Gerritsen
DTP: Dvora Levy
Company: OD Designstudio, FLEX/design
Country: Netherlands
Category: Fruit and vegetables

SILVER PENTAWARD 2020

BOON BARIQ

Creative Direction: Stepan Azaryan
Project Management: Meri Sargsyan
Design: Stepan Azaryan, Eliza Malkhasyan
Illustration: Elina Barsegyan
Company: Backbone Branding
Country: Armenia
Category: Fruit and vegetables

SILVER PENTAWARD 2019

BEETROUTE

Owner and Creative Direction: Kevin Davis,
Kyanne Bückmann
Company: Bowler & Kimchi
Country: Netherlands
Category: Fruit and vegetables

BRONZE PENTAWARD 2019

The fresh navel oranges for **Oranginal** are picked in Zigui County, western Hubei. The cultivation of navel oranges by fruit farmers is depicted in the illustrations, whilst the packaging uses traditionally woven bamboo baskets to refer to the harvest process and the culture of traditional Chinese crafts. In addition, the label on the packaging, which is reminiscent of a pair of hands, is made of ecological materials, which are recyclable and easily decompose. Special attention and awareness to environmental protection characterise the inside and outside of the packaging.

Die frischen Navelorangen von **Oranginal** werden im Bezirk Zigui, im Westen von Hubei gepflückt. Der Anbau der Navelorangen durch Obstbauern wird in den Illustrationen dargestellt, während die Verpackung traditionell geflochtene Bambuskörbe nutzt, um auf den Ernteprozess und die Kultur des chinesischen Kunsthandwerks zu verweisen. Zusätzlich ist das Etikett, das an ein Paar Hände erinnert, aus recycelbarem Material hergestellt. Das Innere und Äußere der Verpackung charakterisieren ein besonderes Bewusstsein für den Umweltschutz.

Les oranges navel pour **Oranginal** sont cueillies dans le district de Zigui, dans l'Ouest du Hubei. Des illustrations expliquent la culture de cette variété d'oranges par des producteurs fruitiers ; le packaging prend quant à lui la forme des traditionnels paniers en bambou tressé pour évoquer la récolte et la culture de l'artisanat chinois traditionnel. L'étiquette sur l'emballage rappelle une paire de mains et est faite de matériaux écologiques recyclables et compostables. Une attention et une conscience toutes particulières portées à la protection de l'environnement se retrouvent tant à l'intérieur qu'à l'extérieur du packaging.

ORANGINAL

Design Lead: Yujie Chen
Design: Fengming Chen, Ching-Lang Chen, Jiarong Zeng, Shuzhuan Huang, Haiyong Wang, Guoxiang Zheng, Qing Yu, Mengxuan Cai
Company: inDare Design Strategy Limited
Country: China
Category: Fruit and vegetables
SILVER PENTAWARD 2020

GRIDELLI

Design and Illustration:
Mikael Selin Design Studio
Client: Gridelli
Printing: Ink N Art
Photography: Ted Olsson
Company: Mikael Selin Design Studio
Country: Sweden
Category: Fruit and vegetables

SILVER PENTAWARD 2019

QING YI NONG NONG DRIED VEGETABLES

Design: Jingfang Mei
Company: Hangzhou Dongyun Advertising Design
Country: China
Category: Fruit and vegetables

BRONZE PENTAWARD 2020

JOHANNES

Design and Illustration: Irene Ibañez
Photography: Twentyten
Company: Guts & Glorious,
Brand and Packaging Designers
Country: Netherlands
Category: Fruit and vegetables

BRONZE PENTAWARD 2020

PAOLOS

Design and Illustration:
Mikael Selin Design Studio team
Head of Marketing and Brand Paolos: Ken Nygren
Photography: Ted Olsson
Company: Mikael Selin Design Studio
Country: Sweden
Category: Fruit and vegetables

BRONZE PENTAWARD 2019

SAS SCANDINAVIAN AIRLINES

Product Design and Manufacturing:
deSter team
Branding: Bold
Company: deSter
Country: Belgium
Category: Soups, ready-to-eat dishes, fast food

GOLD PENTAWARD 2020

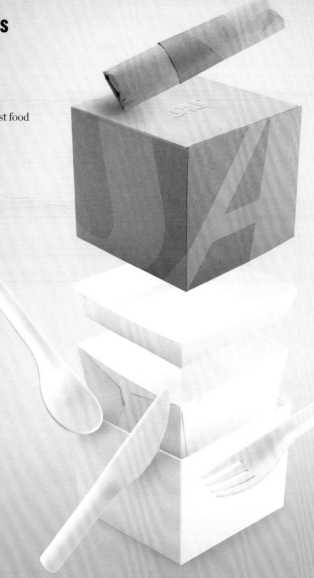

The Cube is a contemporary and sustainable in-air dining experience for **SAS Scandinavian Airlines**. Inspired by takeaway culture, the smart design saves up to 51 tons of plastic per year with FSC certified cardboard items and a PLA coating that delivers the same technical capabilities, strength and efficiency as plastic when used in a food processing environment. The cubical shape makes the content very easy to eat and leaves enough space on your table to continue to work, read or watch a movie, whilst the separately packed condiments give the passenger the freedom to customise their meal. With goals to lessen their carbon impact by 2030, this initiative towards more sustainable travel involves minimising waste and use of fossil fuel plastics through a sustainable food packaging solution.

Dieser Würfel ist das zeitgemäße und nachhaltige „Geschirr" auf den Flügen der **SAS Scandinavian Airlines**. Inspiriert von der Take-away-Kultur, spart das intelligente Design mit FSC-zertifizierten Produkten aus Karton mit PLA-Beschichtung 51 Tonnen Plastik pro Jahr ein. Es hat dieselben technischen Fähigkeiten, dieselbe Stärke und Effizienz wie Plastik, wenn es im lebensmittelverarbeitenden Umfeld eingesetzt wird. Die Würfelform macht es einfach, zu essen und gleichzeitig genug Platz auf dem Tisch zu haben, um weiter zu arbeiten, zu lesen oder einen Film zu sehen, während die einzeln verpackten Gewürze dem Passagier die Möglichkeit geben, seine Mahlzeit selbst zu würzen. Mit dem Ziel, die CO2-Bilanz bis 2030 zu senken, beinhaltet diese Initiative für nachhaltigeres Reisen die Minimierung von Verpackungsmüll und Plastik durch eine Lösung mit ressourcenschonenden Essensverpackungen.

The Cube est une expérience de repas en vol moderne et écoresponsable offerte par **SAS Scandinavian Airlines**. S'inspirant de la vente à emporter, ce design intelligent fait économiser jusqu'à 51 tonnes de plastique par an grâce aux éléments en carton certifié FSC et au revêtement PLA qui possède un potentiel, une résistance et une efficacité identiques au plastique dans un environnement agro-alimentaire. La forme cubique facilite l'accès aux plats et libère assez de place sur la tablette pour continuer à travailler, lire ou regarder un film, alors que les condiments emballés séparément offrent aux passagers la possibilité de personnaliser leur repas. L'objectif étant de réduire l'impact carbone d'ici à 2030, cette initiative en faveur de voyages plus respectueux de l'environnement passe par la réduction des déchets et de l'utilisation de plastiques d'origine fossile via une solution durable de conditionnement alimentaire.

Tteokbokki is a sweet and spicy stir-fried rice cake dish seasoned with Gochujang chili sauce. To introduce this traditional Korean street food to the Chinese market, particularly to young people with fast-paced modern lifestyles, the **Cup Tteokbokki** series was launched. The shape of the cup makes it easy to take on the go, and the contents can be microwaved in two minutes. Exaggerated cartoon faces were chosen as the main visual, with expressions that communicate the flavour and spice level of the rice cake.

Tteokbokki ist ein süß und scharf gebratenes Reiskuchengericht, das mit Gochujang-Chili-Sauce gewürzt wird. Um dieses traditionelle koreanische Streetfood auf dem chinesischen Markt einzuführen – insbesondere bei jungen Leute mit einem schnelllebigen, modernen Lebensstil – wurde die **Tteokbokki**-Reihe in Bechern auf den Markt gebracht. Diese machen es leicht, das Gericht für unterwegs mitzunehmen, und der Inhalt kann in zwei Minuten in der Mikrowelle warm gemacht werden. Als Hauptelement wurden übersteigerte Cartoon-Gesichter gewählt, die mit ihren Gesichtsausdrücken den Geschmack und den Schärfegrad des Reiskuchens vermitteln.

Tteokbokki est un gâteau de riz sucré et épicé, relevé avec la sauce au chili Gochujang. La gamme **Cup Tteokbokki** a vu le jour pour lancer sur le marché chinois ce plat traditionnel vendu dans les rues de Corée, en visant notamment la jeune génération au mode de vie moderne et accéléré. La forme du gobelet facilite sa consommation nomade et le gâteau peut se réchauffer en deux minutes au micro-ondes. Le visuel choisi est celui de visages caricaturés dont les expressions indiquent la saveur et le niveau de piment du gâteau.

CJ

Creative Direction: Byoung Yong Moon
Design: HuiNa Ran
Company: CJ (Qingdao) Foods
Country: China
Category: Soups, ready-to-eat dishes, fast food
GOLD PENTAWARD 2019

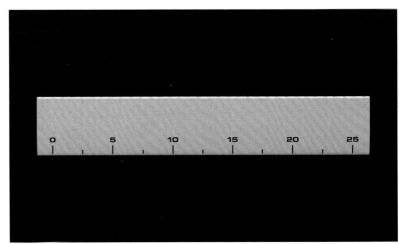

MANO PIZZA

Design: Goods team
Illustration: Samuel Nyholm
Company: Goods
Country: Norway
Category: Soups, ready-to-eat dishes, fast food

SILVER PENTAWARD 2019

OH MY GOOD!

Creative Direction: Jacob Norstedt
Senior Design: Sofia Frank Öberg
Design: Mikaela Sandström
Account Management: Sabine Price
Company: Silver
Country: Sweden
Category: Soups, ready-to-eat dishes, fast food

SILVER PENTAWARD 2020

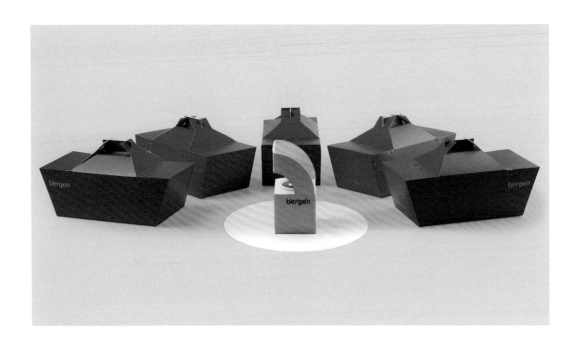

BERGEN

Creative Direction: Alexey Fadeev
Design Direction: Nikita Ivanov
Art Direction: Vera Zvereva
Design: Nikita Ivanov, Vera Zvereva
Project Management: Elena Melnik
Copywriting: Sasha Fedoseeva
Company: Depot Branding Agency
Country: Russian Federation
Category: Soups, ready-to-eat dishes, fast food

BRONZE PENTAWARD 2019

PRINCES

CCO: Paul Taylor
Creative Direction: Ellen Munro
Design Direction: Claire Marshall
Design: Jordan Taylor, Emily Myers,
Nicole Hammersley
Company: BrandOpus
Country: UK
Category: Soups, ready-to-eat dishes, fast food

BRONZE PENTAWARD 2020

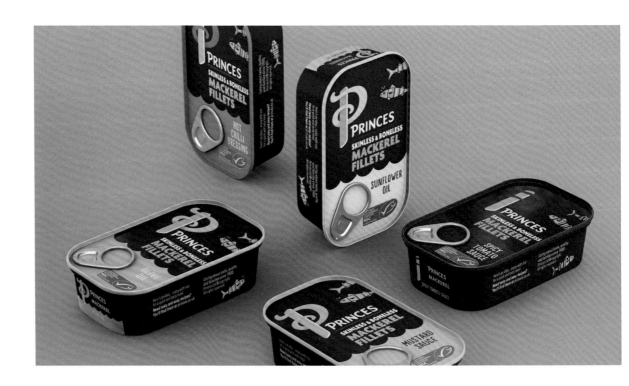

KIMCHI PLATE

Design Direction: Temur Sadi
Art Direction: Zokir Khalmatov
Design: Temur Sadi, Anastasiya Tatarchenko
Illustration: Anastasiya Tatarchenko,
Tumaris Kutlumuratova
Client Service Direction: Elina Ibragimova
Company: MA'NO Branding
Country: Uzbekistan
Category: Soups, ready-to-eat dishes, fast food

SILVER PENTAWARD 2020

UNILEVER
KNORR AMBIENT SOUPS

Design Direction: Sara Jones
Company: SGK Anthem – Amsterdam
Country: Netherlands
Category: Soups, ready-to-eat dishes, fast food

SILVER PENTAWARD 2019

GREENS&YELLOWS

Head of Design: Ioanna Drakaki
Creative Direction: Eleni Pavlaki
Senior Art Direction: Serafim Stroubis
Illustration: Kostas Kiriakakis
Strategy: Christina Apostolidi
Copywriting: Maro Tsagkaraki
Company: Lazy snail
Country: Denmark
Category: Soups, ready-to-eat dishes, fast food
BRONZE PENTAWARD 2020

TIM HORTONS

Creative Direction: Miles Marshall
Design: Rosie Hellier, Nick Cross
Artwork: James Chilvers, James Norris
Retouching: Mick Connor
Illustration: Jamie Nash
Account Management: Isabelle Erixon
Account Direction: Nicola Eager
Company: Turner Duckworth
Country: UK
Category: Soups, ready-to-eat dishes, fast food
BRONZE PENTAWARD 2019

CF 18 CHOCOLATIER

Photography: Lars Petter Pettersen (Coup)
Company: OlssønBarbieri
Country: Norway
Category: Confectionery and sweet snacks

GOLD PENTAWARD 2020

REAL HANDFUL

Design: Will Gladden
Design: Claudio Vecchio
Illustration: Call Me George(s)
Company: Midday
Country: UK
Category: Confectionery and sweet snacks
GOLD PENTAWARD 2019

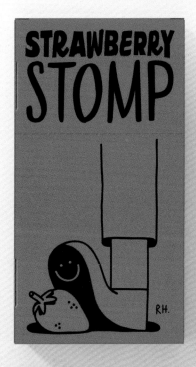

HONMIDO

Design: Bravis International team
Company: Bravis International
Country: Japan
Category: Confectionery and sweet snacks
SILVER PENTAWARD 2019

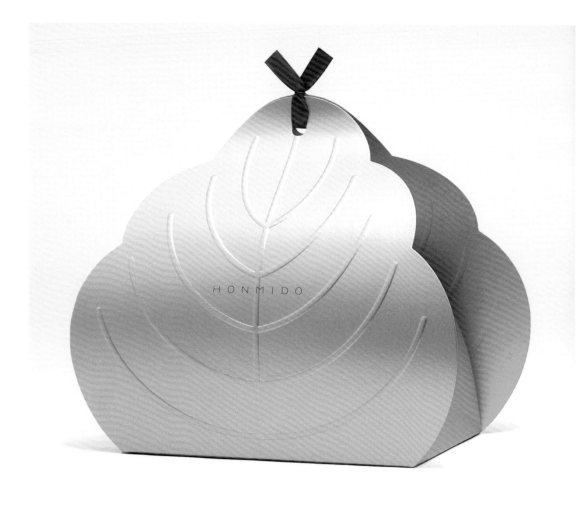

MALMÖ CHOKLADFABRIK
Ö-SERIEN

Client: Malmö Chokladfabrik, Jens Fylkner,
Jakob Fylkner
Senior Design: Peeter Ots
Design: Mika Nilsson
Client Direction: Johanna Augustin
Production Management: Johanna Larsson
Final Art: Anki Mac Pherson
Company: Pond Design
Country: Sweden
Category: Confectionery and sweet snacks
BRONZE PENTAWARD 2019

BEE SAMURAI THROAT LOZENGES

Design: Honggang Zhu
Company: Shenzhen Oracle Creative Design
Country: China
Category: Confectionery and sweet snacks
BRONZE PENTAWARD 2019

FORTNUM & MASON

Creative Direction: Chloe Templeman
Senior Design: Alice Douglas-Dean, Morgan Swain
Business Development: Alice Goss
Word Direction: Caroline Slade
Senior Production Project Management: Talitha Watson
Illustration: Paul Desmond
Company: Design Bridge London
Country: UK
Category: Confectionery and sweet snacks
SILVER PENTAWARD 2019

MACHIYENGA TREE TO BAR

Photography: Sumiko Miura
Company: Alejandro Gavancho
Country: Peru
Category: Confectionery and sweet snacks

BRONZE PENTAWARD 2020

POCKY THE GIFT

Creative Direction and Art Direction: Yoshihiro Yagi
Planning and Copywriting: Haruko Tsutsui
Design: Taiji Kimura (PEN), Haruko Nakatani and
(Creative Power Unit), Satomi Okubo (Dentsu)
Hirono Matsunaga (Creative Power Unit)
Planning: Takuya Fujita and Ryoya Sugano (Dentsu),
Mai Umegae and Kotaro Fujiwara (Dentsu Live)
Construction Management:
Masamitsu Usui (Dentsu Live)
Company: Dentsu
Country: Japan
Category: Confectionery and sweet snacks

SILVER PENTAWARD 2020

CADESIO

Design: Ester Bianchi
Photography: Claudia Bellotti
Company: Cadesio
Country: Switzerland
Category: Confectionery and sweet snacks

SILVER PENTAWARD 2020

RAW HALO

Creative Direction: Shaun Bowen
Design: Jennie Potts
Account Direction: Kate Thomas
Strategy Direction: Lisa Desforges
Company: B&B studio
Country: UK
Category: Confectionery and sweet snacks

BRONZE PENTAWARD 2020

On the packaging for **Xiangke Sunflower Seeds** three animals that like to eat these seeds are featured: a monkey, a hamster and a parrot. The mouths of the animals are the same shape as the sunflower seeds, and their surprised and satisfied expressions suggest that the seeds are big and delicious. In order to make the brand's packaging all-embracing, the images of a man, a woman and an old man were also created, whose wide-open mouths reveal their appetite for the tasty seeds.

Auf der Verpackung von **Xiangke Sunflower Seeds** sind drei Tiere zu sehen, die sehr gerne Sonnenblumenkerne essen: ein Affe, ein Hamster und ein Papagei. Die Münder der drei Tiere haben dieselbe Form wie die Saat und ihre überraschten und zufriedenen Gesichtsausdrücke lassen vermuten, dass die Kerne groß und köstlich sind. Um die Verpackung der Marke allumfassend zu gestalten, wurden außerdem die Bilder zweier Männer und einer Frau entworfen, deren weitgeöffnete Münder zeigen, dass sie großen Appetit auf die schmackhaften Snack haben.

Sur le packaging des graines de tournesol de la marque **Xiangke**, trois animaux amateurs de ces graines, que sont le singe, le hamster et le perroquet, sont illustrés avec la bouche en forme de graine de tournesol. Leurs expressions de surprise et de satisfaction font comprendre que les graines sont aussi grandes que délicieuses. Et pour renvoyer une image plus complète, les visages d'un homme jeune, d'un autre âgé et d'une femme, tous avec la bouche grande ouverte, prouvent leur goût pour ces savoureuses graines.

XIANGKE SUNFLOWER SEEDS

Creative Direction: Zhou Jingkuan
Design Direction: Sun Linlin
Illustration: Yang Xue, Li Ziqiong
Company: Shenzhen Left and Right Packaging Design
Country: China
Category: Savoury snacks

GOLD PENTAWARD·2019

HERO'S

Brand Strategy Direction: Stepan Avanesyan
Assistant Brand Strategy: Lusie Grigoryan
Creative Direction: Stepan Azaryan
Art Direction: Mariam Stepanyan
Project Management: Marianna Atshemyan
Graphic Design: Mane Budaghyan
Copywriting: Grace Jerejian
Company: Backbone Branding
Country: Armenia
Category: Savoury snacks

GOLD PENTAWARD 2020

FROM THE FOREST OF RUSK

Graphic Design and Illustration: Shoichiro Take
Copywriting and Production: Eriko Kunikata
Photography: Studio Work, Ryo Kawagoe
Company: Katal Seven
Country: Japan
Category: Savoury snacks

BRONZE PENTAWARD 2019

SEA MAN SEAWEED CHIPS

Strategic Creative Direction: Jesper von Wieding
Creative Direction: Thomas Kjær
Managing Direction: David Ramskov Hansen
Design: Louise Hvenegaard
Illustration: Frans Theis Jensen
Company: Pearlfisher
Country: UK
Category: Savoury snacks

BRONZE PENTAWARD 2019

RITZ

Creative Direction: Mark Link
Client Partner: Rebecca Barron
Senior Client Management: Phoebe Ridley-Fink
Company: Bulletproof
Country: UK
Category: Savoury snacks

SILVER PENTAWARD 2020

SQUEAKY POPS

Design and Illustration: Jason Reale
3D Modelling: Lyon Visuals
Client: Squeaky Treats, LLC
Company: & Reale
Country: USA
Category: Savoury snacks

SILVER PENTAWARD 2019

HILO LIFE

Design: PepsiCo Design & Innovation team
Company: PepsiCo Design & Innovation
Country: USA
Category: Savoury snacks

SILVER PENTAWARD 2020

JACOB'S

Founding Partner and CCO: Jonathan Ford
Founding Creative Partner and CCO: Karen Welman
Creative Direction: Jon Vallance
Design Direction: Stuart Madden
Chief Strategy Officer: Yael Alaton
Client Development Direction: Nic Robson
Head of Realisation: Jen Nathan
Company: Pearlfisher
Country: UK
Category: Savoury snacks

SILVER PENTAWARD 2019

SUPERMERCADOS CONSUM

Strategy and Creative Direction: Ana Niño
Art Direction: Jordi Escrivà
Account Management: Marta Álvarez
Account Excutive: Laura Benet and Beatriz Córcoles
Photography: Natxo Martínez
Company: Agencia Maslow
Country: Spain
Category: Savoury snacks

BRONZE PENTAWARD 2020

BAMA TEA TIME SNACK FOODS

Product Design: Weijie Chang, Tao Wang,
Jing Zhou, Luping Zhou
Company: Shenzhen Oneli Creative Design
Country: China
Category: Savoury snacks

BRONZE PENTAWARD 2020

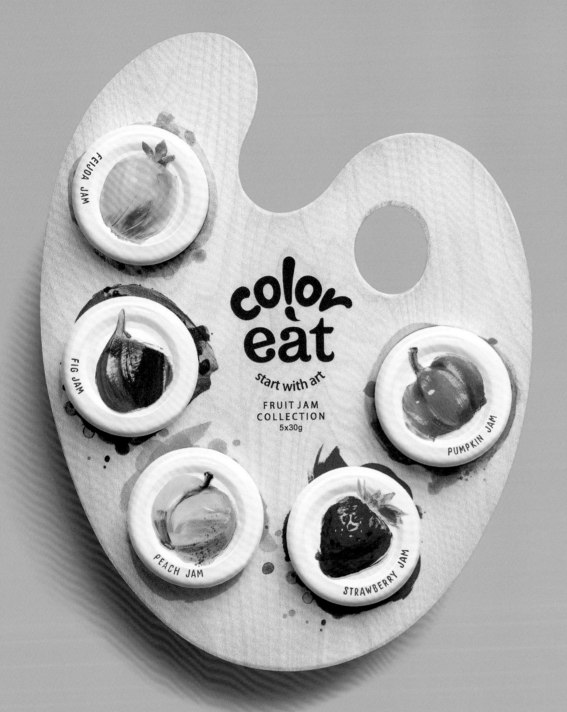

COLOREAT

Brand Strategy Direction: Stepan Avanesyan
Assistant Brand Strategy: Lusie Grigoryan
Creative Direction: Stepan Azaryan
Project Management: Meri Sargsyan
Design: Stepan Azaryan, Gevorg Balyan
Illustration: Mariam Stepanyan
Company: Backbone Branding
Country: Armenia
Category: Desserts, sweet foods and confection dishes
GOLD PENTAWARD 2019

Coloreat is a fruit jam collection with five different flavours: fig, strawberry, pumpkin, peach and feijoa. The packaging is a replica of an artist's palette aimed at making the ordinary breakfast routine more exciting and interactive for kids. With small jam jars as the paints, the toast becomes a canvas that children and parents can freely draw on, using the spoon as the paintbrush. Not only is it aesthetically pleasing, one jar comprises the daily recommended portion of jam for a child, which will help keep sugar consumption in balance.

Coloreat ist eine Marmeladenkollektion mit fünf verschiedenen Sorten: Feige, Erdbeere, Kürbis, Pfirsich und Feijoa. Die Verpackung ist einer Malerpalette nachempfunden und soll die gewöhnliche Frühstücksroutine für Kinder aufregender und interaktiver machen. Mit kleinen Gläsern als Farben wird der Toast zur Leinwand, auf dem Kinder und Eltern mit dem Löffel als Pinsel frei malen können. Das ist nicht nur ästhetisch ansprechend, ein Glas enthält auch die empfohlene Marmeladenmenge, die ein Kind täglich zu sich nehmen kann, was dabei hilft, den Zuckerkonsum im Auge zu behalten.

Coloreat est une gamme de confitures dans cinq parfums : figues, fraises, potiron, pêche et feijoa. Le packaging imite une palette de peintre afin que la routine du petit-déjeuner devienne plus amusante et interactive pour les enfants. En guise de peinture, les petits pots de confiture font de la tartine une toile sur laquelle petits et grands peuvent dessiner à leur gré à l'aide de la cuillère pour pinceau. L'esthétique de l'ensemble est attrayante, et un pot apporte la quantité journalière recommandée de confiture chez l'enfant, ce qui permet de contrôler la consommation de sucre.

Supha Bee Farm is one of the two main honey producers in Thailand which has its own bee farms with bee rearing and breeding facilities. The outstanding product is 100 % real pure honey with packaging that is specially designed and inspired by the structure of the beehive frame. The paper honeycomb is used together with the wooden box to emphasise the feeling that the honey bottle inside is directly from the beehive. The SB logo is designed simply to make it look similar to a bee.

Die Supha Bee Farm ist einer der beiden wichtigsten Honigproduzenten in Thailand, der eigene Bienenfarmen mit Bienenaufzucht und Brutanlagen besitzt. Das herausragende Produkt ist zu 100 % reiner Honig mit einer Verpackung, die speziell entworfen und von der Struktur des Bienenstockrahmens inspiriert wurde. Die Honigwabe aus Papier wird gemeinsam mit einer Box aus Holz verkauft, um das Gefühl zu unterstreichen, dass die darin enthaltene Honigflasche direkt aus dem Bienenstock kommt. Das SB-Logo ist so gestaltet, dass es einer Biene ähnlich sieht.

Supha Bee Farm est l'un des deux principaux producteurs de miel de Thaïlande possédant ses propres exploitations apicoles et installations d'élevage et de reproduction d'abeilles. Ce produit exceptionnel est un miel pur à 100 %, logé dans un emballage spécialement conçu et inspiré de la structure d'une ruche. Combiné à une boîte en bois, le papier alvéolé accentue l'impression que la bouteille de miel sort directement de la ruche. Le logo SB a été conçu pour ressembler à une abeille.

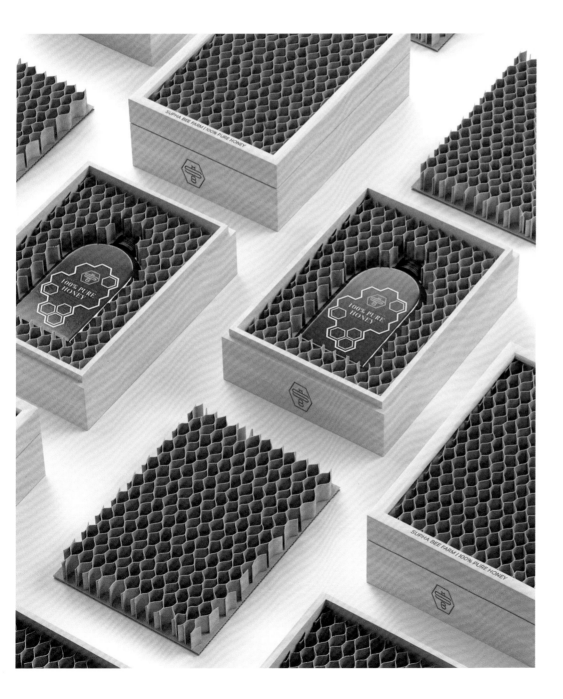

SUPHA BEE FARM HONEY

Executive Creative Direction: Somchana Kangwarnjit
Design: Rutthawitch Akkachairin, SKJ, Napapach Sunlee
Retouching: Pantipa Pummuang, Thiyada Akarasinakul, Somporn Thimkhao
Company: Prompt Design
Country: Thailand
Category: Desserts, sweet foods and confection dishes

GOLD PENTAWARD 2020

00:00

Design Lead: Yujie Chen
Design: Fengming Chen, Chinglang Chen, Jiarong Zeng, Yichao Fan, Qingwei Li, Haiyong Wang, Qing Yu
Company: inDare Design Strategy Limited
Country: China
Category: Desserts, sweet foods and confection dishes

SILVER PENTAWARD 2020

WAINWRIGHT'S

Executive Creative Direction: David Hodgson
CEO and Strategy Lead: Andrew Eyles
Senior Account Management: Charlie Spiers
Senior Visualisation: Simon Thomas
Artwork and Realisation: Steve Gordon
Company: Bluemarlin
Country: UK
Category: Desserts, sweet foods and confection dishes

BRONZE PENTAWARD 2019

MRGASTAN

Creative Direction: Stepan Azaryan
Brand Strategy: Lusie Grigoryan
Art Direction and Illustration: Mariam Stepanyan
Project Management: Marianna Atshemyan
Graphic Design: Mane Budaghyan
Copywriting: Grace Jerejian
Animation: Sahak Zarbabyan
Augmented Reality Partner: Arloopa
Music: Komitas Quartet, Yerevan State Chamber Choir
Company: Backbone Branding
Country: Armenia
Category: Desserts, sweet foods and confection dishes

BRONZE PENTAWARD 2020

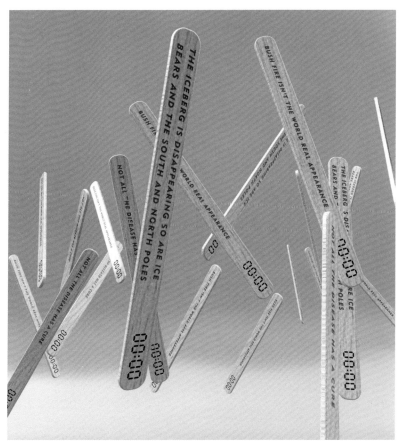

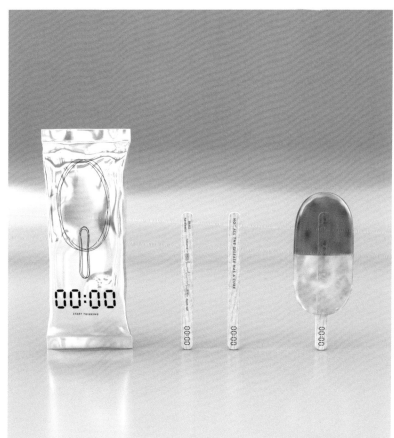

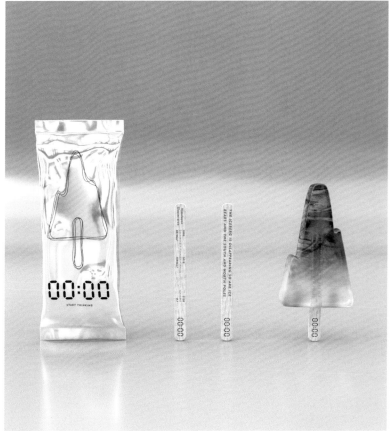

JEJU PREMIUM TART

Art Direction: Seoyoon Yang
Design: Seongmin Jeon, Hyeyoung Choi
Company: SPC Samlip
Country: Republic of Korea
Category: Desserts, sweet foods and confection dishes

SILVER PENTAWARD 2019

HONEY OF VARIOUS FLOWERS IN SHENGNONGJIA

Design: Xiang Shasha
Creative Direction: Zhang Yanhui
Customer Service Direction: Zhou Xiaoli
Illustration: Tong Meng
Company: Wuhan Pufan Advertising
Country: China
Category: Desserts, sweet foods and confection dishes

SILVER PENTAWARD 2020

YAGUMITAN

Design: Jiabo Lu, Kun Luo
Styling and Rendering: Jiabo Lu
Company: Shenzhen Qianhai Phecda Design
Country: China
Category: Desserts, sweet foods and confection dishes
BRONZE PENTAWARD 2020

STEP DESIGN

Design: Xinyuan Chen
Company: Step Design
Country: China
Category: Desserts, sweet foods and confection dishes
BRONZE PENTAWARD 2019

MANUKA EMPORIUM

Design: Onfire Design
Creative Direction: Matt Grantham
Design: Georgina Brothers, Sam Allan, Ewa Oliver
Company: Onfire Design
Country: New Zealand
Category: Desserts, sweet foods and
confection dishes
SILVER PENTAWARD 2019

JUST WHOLE FOODS

vegan
Delicious plant-based burgers made with wholemeal breadcrumbs.

organic
burger mix

High protein
High fibre
No palm oil

serving suggestion

JUST WHOLE FOODS

vegan
Tasty plant-based sausages lightly seasoned with herbs and spices.

organic
sausage mix

High protein
High fibre
No palm oil

serving suggestion

JUST WHOLE FOODS

vegan
The ultimate Middle Eastern street food delicately spiced with cumin and coriander.

organic
falafel mix

High protein
Gluten free

serving suggestion

JUST WHOLE FOODS

vegan
A moreish Mediterranean dip with toasted sesame seeds and garlic.

organic
houmous mix

High protein
High fibre
Gluten free

serving suggestion

JUST WHOLEFOODS

Design and Illustration: Rob Hall
Company: Studio h
Country: UK
Category: Food trends

GOLD PENTAWARD 2020

DELICIOUSLY ELLA

Creative Direction: Kate Marlow
Senior Design: Rachael Blowers
Design: Pui-Yee Cheung
Project Management: Dale Williams
Artwork: Nate Lally
Company: Here Design
Country: UK
Category: Food trends

GOLD PENTAWARD 2019

WECO

Client: Weco Agricultural
Client Representation: Yao Lin, Haifeng Xie
Creative Direction: Minghua Zheng
Design and Photography: Minghua Zheng,
Zhaonian Zhou
Copywriting: Mingming Zheng, Yong Zhu
Company: Monsoon Culture and Art
Country: China
Category: Food trends

SILVER PENTAWARD 2020

SANOVITA

Art Direction: Costin Oane
Design and Illustration: Horia Oane
Company: BroHouse
Country: Romania
Category: Food trends
BRONZE PENTAWARD 2020

KOS

Client: KOS Naturals
Design and Illustration: Juan Jose Montes
Company: Juan Jose Montes
Country: Colombia
Category: Food trends
BRONZE PENTAWARD 2019

LOGOTHETIS ORGANIC FARM

Creative Direction: Antonia Skaraki
Design: Andreas Deskas, Valia Alousi, Evri Makridis
Copywriting: Sotiria Theodorou
Company: A.S. Advertising
Country: Greece
Category: Food trends

SILVER PENTAWARD 2020

方家铺子

润胜莲生水，
颜如玉浅尝，
馨香暗起，
如春风唊嚼
丝丝柔韧，
窝香四溢\

方家铺子
干・燕窝
The bird's nest

净含量：50克

GIFTS FORM NATURE

MR. FANG'S STORE

Design: Sozo Design, Mr. Fang's Store
Company: Hangzhou SOZO Industrial Design
Country: China
Category: Food trends

SILVER PENTAWARD 2019

GO GOOD

Creative Direction: Donna McCort
Design: Leonie Whyte
Finished Artwork: Ben Dean, Mike Turnbull
Company: Dow Goodfolk
Country: New Zealand
Category: Food trends

BRONZE PENTAWARD 2019

OXFAM FAIR TRADE

Creative Direction: Joseph Robinson
Design: Sara Gunnarsson
Company: Quatre Mains
Country: Belgium
Category: Food trends

BRONZE PENTAWARD 2020

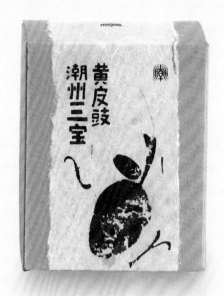
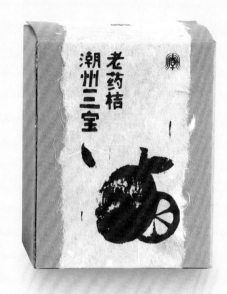

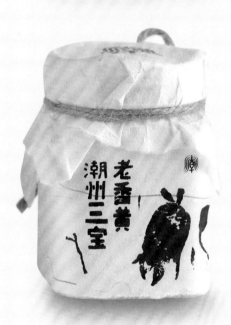

THREE TREASURES OF CHAOZHOU

Design Guidance: Yang Zhen
Design: Xu Yi Fei, Yang Jia Lu, Hu Yu Bin, Lin Qing Yi
Company: Firewolf Design
Country: China
Category: Food trends

SILVER PENTAWARD 2019

MONDELEZ CADBURY

Creative Direction: Asa Cook
Design: Kirsty Struthers
Associate Creative Direction and Art Direction:
Rob Ellis (VCCP)
Associate Creative Direction and Copywriting:
Peter Reid (VCCP)
Company: Design Bridge London
in collaboration with VCCP London
Country: UK
Category: Limited editions, limited series,
event creations

GOLD PENTAWARD 2020

To help Age UK fight the loneliness epidemic, **Cadbury** were asked to donate their words and create the "wordless bar". Keeping things simple, the milk pour motif was left exactly where it normally appears on the standard bar, and a stripped back graphic style was used for maximum "quietness". The bar occupies an almost empty space on the shelf, which boldly stood out precisely because the design is so minimal. It's not until someone picks up the bar that they see the message in a milk splash speech bubble on the back of the pack, telling them that 30p per bar sold is donated to Age UK. The Cadbury purple and the milk pour are so distinctive that the bar is immediately recognisable.

Um der Organisation Age UK zu helfen, die Epidemie der Einsamkeit zu bekämpfen, wurde **Cadbury** gebeten, ihre Worte zu spenden und die „wortlose Tafel" zu kreieren. Das Motiv der Milchgläser ist genau dort platziert, wo es auch sonst auf den Schokoladentafeln zu finden ist, für maximale „Ruhe" wurde ein zurückgenommener grafischer Stil verwendet. Die Tafel belegt damit eine fast leere Stelle im Regal, die vor allem deswegen heraussticht, weil das Design so reduziert ist. Erst wenn jemand die Tafel in die Hand nimmt, sieht er die Botschaft auf der Rückseite der Packung mit dem Hinweis, dass 30 Pence pro verkaufter Tafel an Age UK gespendet werden. Das Cadbury-Lila und die fließende Milch sind so markant, dass die Tafel sofort wiedererkannt wird.

Pour combattre le fléau de la solitude, Age UK a demandé à **Cadbury** de proposer une « tablette sans mots ». Pour faire simple, l'image du lait versé a été conservée à sa place habituelle, et un style graphique dépouillé a été choisi pour une « tranquillité » absolue. La tablette occupe un espace quasiment vide en rayon et se fait clairement remarquer grâce à ce design si minimal. C'est seulement quand on prend la tablette que l'on peut voir au dos le message dans une bulle de texte en forme d'éclaboussure de lait, expliquant que pour chaque tablette vendue, 30 pence sont reversés à Age UK. Le violet Cadbury et le lait versé sont tellement caractéristiques que la tablette est immédiatement identifiable.

CARNERO

Creative Direction and Graphic Design:
Emanuele Basso
Creative Direction: Elena Carella
Graphic Design and Illustration: Federico Epis
Company: The 6th
Country: Italy
Category: Limited editions, limited series,
event creations

GOLD PENTAWARD 2019

Carnero is the first biltong, a type of dried meat, produced in Italy. Inspired by the style of the Golden Age of Italian graphic design, the front of the packaging shows illustrations of Mr Carnero playing with his cows: the classic cow and the spicy cow. To help make the product stand out, the backs of the packets show 25 different visuals of the Carnero family and storyline, turning the pouches into a mural when displayed all together.

Carnero ist das erste Biltong, eine Art Trocken-fleisch, das in Italien hergestellt wird. Inspiriert vom Stil des Goldenen Zeitalters des italienischen Grafikdesigns, zeigt die Vorderseite der Verpackung Illustrationen von Mr. Carnero, die mit dem Bild der Kuh spielen: die klassische Kuh und die scharfe Kuh. Damit das Produkt herausssticht, sind die Verpackungen mit 25 Bildern der Carnero-Familie und ihrer Geschichte gestaltet und

Carnero est le premier biltong, un type de viande séchée, produit en Italie. S'inspirant du style de l'âge d'or du design graphique italien, l'avant du packaging affiche des illustrations de M. Carnero jouant avec ses vaches, la classique et l'épicée. Pour singulariser le produit, l'arrière du paquet compte 25 illustrations de la famille Carnero et son histoire. Mis côte à côte, les emballages forment alors une véritable fresque.

Figlia (meaning daughter in Italian) is a limited-edition batch of hand-crafted olive oil from Agricola Dargenio. The edition was inspired by the concept "Feminine by Nature", which relates to both the product and how it's made, whilst showing support for Agricola's first female CEO. Three hundred handmade ceramic bottles from the same region were created, and aside from a subtle stamp in the base, the bottles are purposefully left unlabelled so they may be repurposed. A series of illustrations were developed to form the foundations of their visual language, inspired by the bottle design and use of soft organic shapes to form delicate and minimal depictions of female faces. Like the bottles, the illustrations aim to celebrate the uniqueness of all things natural and come in a multitude of variations set around the same style and colour palette.

Figlia (bedeutet Tochter auf Italienisch) ist eine in limitierter Charge handgemachten Olivenöls von Agricola Dargenio. Die Edition wurde von dem Konzept „von Natur aus weiblich" inspiriert, das sich sowohl auf das Produkt als auch auf die Herstellungsweise bezieht und gleichzeitig Unterstützung für Agricolas erste weibliche CEO zeigt. Es wurden dreihundert Keramikflaschen regional gefertigt und abgesehen von einem einfachen Stempel auf dem Boden, haben die Flaschen selbst absichtlich keine aufgeklebten Labels, damit sie wiederverwendet werden können. Für die Etiketten auf der Verpackung und die losen Schildchen an der Flasche wurde eine Reihe von Illustrationen angefertigt, die subtile Abbildungen von weiblichen Gesichtern zeigen. Wie die Flaschen zielen auch sie darauf ab, Natürlichkeit und Einzigartigkeit zu zelebrieren und wurden als Unikate angelegt, die sich in Form und Farbe voneinander unterscheiden .

Figlia (fille, en italien) est une collection en édition limitée d'huile d'olive artisanale d'Agricola Dargenio. Le concept derrière cette gamme est celui de « féminine par nature » associé au produit et à sa fabrication, et preuve du soutien à la première femme PDG d'Agricola. Trois-cents bouteilles en céramique ont été fabriquées à la main dans cette région et à part un discret tampon à leur base, elles sont délibérément dépourvues d'étiquette pour en faciliter le recyclage. Les illustrations réalisées posent les bases du langage visuel, qui s'aligne sur le design des bouteilles et joue avec des formes organiques pour représenter des visages féminins de façon délicate et minimale. Comme les bouteilles, ces illustrations visent à célébrer la singularité de toutes les choses naturelles et se déclinent en une foule de variantes autour du même style et de la même palette de couleurs.

FIGLIA

Creative Direction: Andy Reynolds
Design Direction: Gianluca Crudele
Design: Louisa Luk
Ceramic Artwork: Salvatore Caraglia
Client Management: Euginia Chui
Photography: Scott Kimble
Company: Superunion
Country: UK
Category: Limited editions, limited series, event creations

SILVER PENTAWARD 2020

LADY M MOONCAKE GIFT SET PACKAGE

Design: BXL Creative Design, Lady M Confections
Client: Lady M Confections
Company: Shenzhen Baixinglong Creative Packaging
Country: China
Category: Limited editions, limited series,
event creations

SILVER PENTAWARD 2020

STACY'S

Design: PepsiCo Design & Innovation
Featured Artwork: Nomoco, Amrita Marino,
Alexander Bowman, Jane Beaird,
Jade Purple Brown, Eleni Kalokati
Company: PepsiCo Design & Innovation
Country: USA
Category: Limited editions, limited series,
event creations

SILVER PENTAWARD 2019

SHANGRI-LA INTERNATIONAL HOTEL MANAGEMENT LTD

Creative Direction: Tim Siro
Senior Design: Christie Widjaja
Visualisation: Dea Jovita
3D Design Direction: Aaron Lim
Design: Elysa Tan, Pamela Ng
Illustration: Jason Liw
Senior Visualisation: Ong Jian'An
Visualisation Direction: Charles Galland
3D Technical Design Direction: Toh Meng Lee
Print and Production Team Lead: Calvin Low
Production Management: Fenson Cheng
Artwork: Vivian Vindu Dinata
Senior Client Management: Andie Ngoh
Client Executive: Nur Farzana
Company: Design Bridge Singapore
Country: UK
Category: Limited editions, limited series, event creations

BRONZE PENTAWARD 2020

BAKERY FACTORY

Art Direction: Seoyoon Yang
Design and Illustration: Hyeyoung Choi
Company: SPC Samlip
Country: Republic of Korea
Category: Limited editions, limited series, event creations

BRONZE PENTAWARD 2020

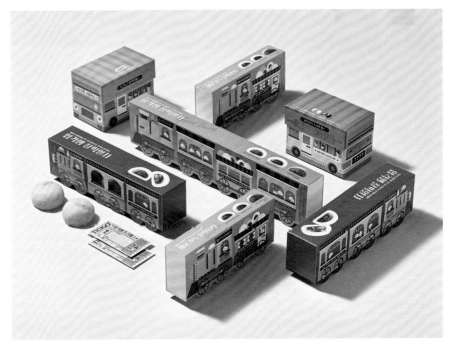

STARBUCKS

Senior Design: Carmen Lee
Design: WanFeng Wang
Senior Client Management: Ivy Wang
3D Technical Design Direction: Meng Lee Toh
Client Business Direction: Greenly Lu
Production Management: Fenson Cheng
Creative Direction: Tom Gilbert
Company: Design Bridge
Country: UK
Category: Limited editions, limited series,
event creations

SILVER PENTAWARD 2019

ARMATORE

Design: Lettera 7
Company: Armatore
Country: Italy
Category: Limited editions,
limited series, event creations

BRONZE PENTAWARD 2019

NOBLEZA DEL SUR

Creative Direction: Isabel Cabello
Design: Isabel Cabello
Design and Illustration: Ester Moreno
Company: Cabello x Mure
Country: Spain
Category: Limited editions, limited series,
event creations

BRONZE PENTAWARD 2019

XING SHI SHAN BRAND DESIGN

Client: Nanlian Agricultural
Design: One More Design
Creative Direction: Xia Jiangnan, Zhang Haiqiang,
Meng Shenhui, Huang Fupeng, Mao Jian, Qiu Yang
Company: One More Idea
Country: China
Category: Distributors'/retailers' own brands/
private labels

GOLD PENTAWARD 2020

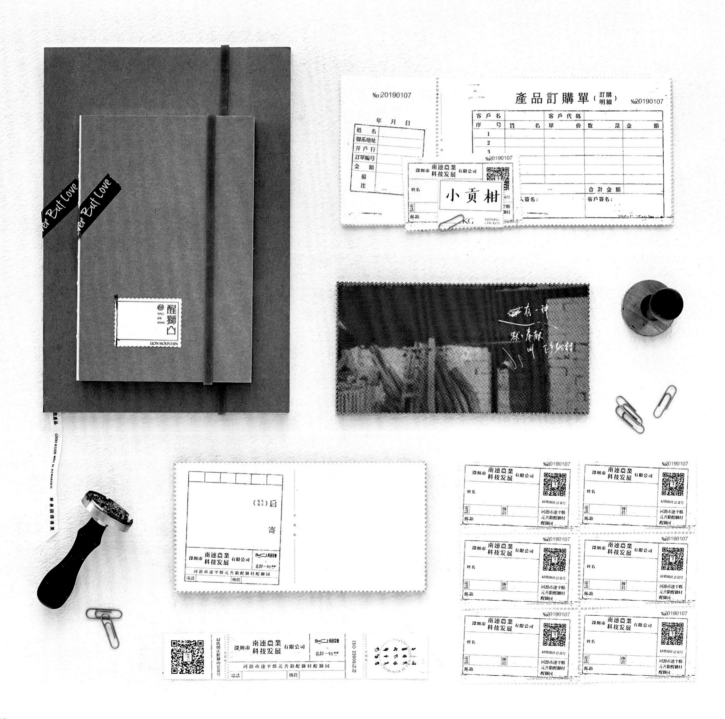

AH MORE THAN PASTA

Senior Design Direction: Ditte Glebbeek
Brand Direction: Evelyn Hille
Company: VBAT
Country: Netherlands
Category: Bread, cereals and pasta

SILVER PENTAWARD 2019

CONSUM SUPERMERCADOS

Strategic and Creative Direction: Ana Niño
Art Direction: Jordi Escrivà
Account Management: Marta Álvarez
Account Executive: Laura Benet, Beatriz Córcoles
Photography: Natxo Martínez
Company: Agencia Maslow
Country: Spain
Category: Distributors'/retailers' own brands/
private labels

SILVER PENTAWARD 2020

ALBERT HEIJN

Client: Albert Heijn
Creative Direction: Tahir Idouri
Design Direction: Jon Sonneveld
Design: Joost de la Housse
Account Direction: Sascha Goutier
Photography: Tobias Raymond
Illustration: Fred van Deelen
Company: Millford
Country: Netherlands
Category: Distributors'/
retailers' own brands/private labels
BRONZE PENTAWARD 2019

TESCO STORES PLC

Creative Direction: Sam Stone
Associate Creative Direction: Matt Goodchild
Design Direction: Jo Gold
Senior Design: Jennie Cooper,
Gareth Roberts, Antoine Bartmann
Design: Jia Ying Gnoh, Adam Chescoe,
Mimi VanHelfteren, Khrissie Farrands,
Ben Gale, Tom Wood, Kate Hirons
Client Partner: Julie Petard
Senior Account Direction: Clara Dipper
Account Direction: Lindsay Simpson
Account Management: Ruth Jenkins,
Imogen Walker, Annabel Baker
Planning Direction: John Clark
Senior Brand Planning: Natasha Samek,
Eftihia Spyropoulou, Elayne Read
Production Direction: Peter Cottington
Production Art: Joel Pearce
Artwork: Andy Donald
Company: Coley Porter Bell
Country: UK
Category: Distributors'/retailers' own brands/
private labels
SILVER PENTAWARD 2019

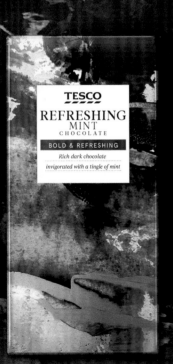

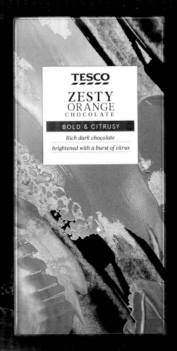

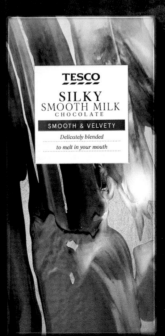

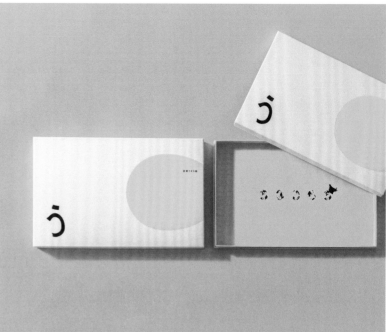

MURORAN UZURAEN

Art Direction: Nobuya Hayasaka
Creative Direction: Hitoshi Kobayashi
Design: Nobuya Hayasaka
Production: arica design
Client: Muroran Uzuraen
Company: arica design
Country: Japan
Category: Distributors'/retailers' own brands/
private labels

BRONZE PENTAWARD 2020

WAITROSE & PARTNERS

Creative Direction: Garrick Hamm
Client Services Direction: Wybe Magermans
Account Management: Bella Thompson
Design Direction: Mark Nichols
Design: Christopher Ribét, Becki Sewell,
Holly Mattacott-Cousins, Jane Harwood
Photography: Jonathan Gregson
Production Management: Mark Tosey
Artwork: Mark Tickner, Nursel Arslan
Retouching: Chris Fennel
Client and Head of Design
Waitrose & Partners: Ashley Vinall
Company: Williams Murray Hamm
Country: UK
Category: Distributors'/retailers' own brands/
private labels
BRONZE PENTAWARD 2019

GREEN LINE PRIVATE LABEL

Creative Direction: Nadie Parshina
Art Direction: Ann Burlakina
Junior Design: Nikita Gavrilov
Account Management: Kate Dorokhina
Company: Ohmybrand
Country: Russian Federation
Category: Distributors'/retailers' own brands/
private labels
BRONZE PENTAWARD 2020

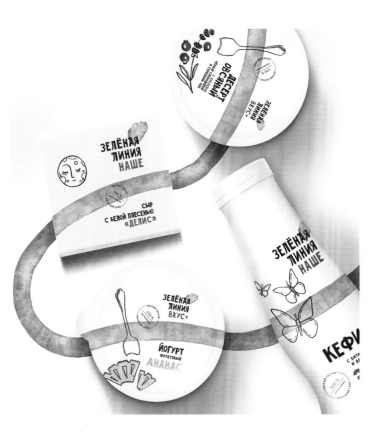

TUNA FISH CAN
LIKENED TO A FISHING BOAT

Design: Sayaka Kawagoe
Company: Toyo Seikan Group Holdings
Country: Japan
Category: Packaging concept (professional)

GOLD PENTAWARD 2019

This conceptual piece for a tuna fish can tells the story of how fresh tuna from the sea ends up on our plates. With delightful details decorating the fishing-boat-shaped can, the package created for **Toyo Seikan Group Holdings** was designed to bring happiness to the family dinner table and create instant brand recognition around a popular everyday food.

Dieses konzeptionelle Thunfischdose erzählt, wie frischer Thunfisch aus dem Meer auf unsere Teller gelangt. In Form eines Fischerboots, mit wundervollen Details verziert, wurde die Verpackung für **Toyo Seikan Group Holdings** entworfen, um Fröhlichkeit auf den Essenstisch zu bringen und um einen Wiedererkennungswert der Marke rund um ein beliebtes Alltagsessen zu schaffen.

Cette œuvre conceptuelle pour une boîte de conserve de thon explique comment le thon frais du grand large finit dans notre assiette. Parfaitement décorée, la boîte en forme de bateau de pêche a été conçue pour **Toyo Seikan Group Holdings** afin de donner une touche joyeuse aux repas en famille et d'assurer la reconnaissance immédiate d'un aliment populaire de tous les jours.

YINONG

Creative Direction: Jintao He
Design: Fanggui Chen
Illustration: Xiaofan Chen
Company: Shantou Datianchao Brand Planning
Country: China
Category: Packaging concept (professional)

GOLD PENTAWARD 2020

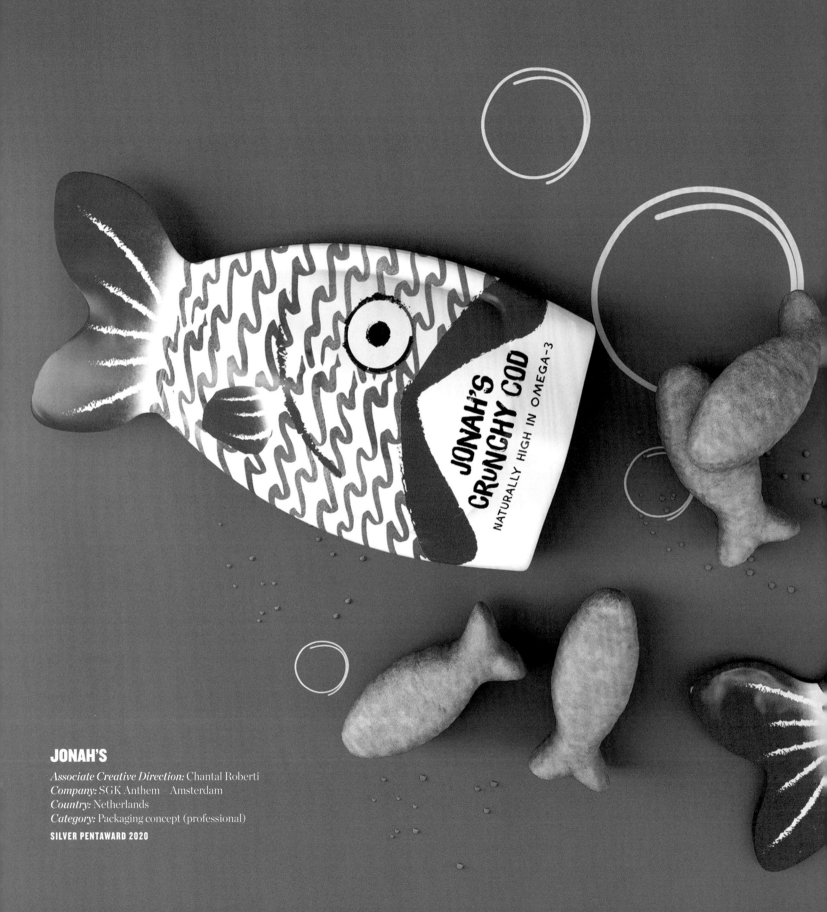

JONAH'S

Associate Creative Direction: Chantal Roberti
Company: SGK Anthem – Amsterdam
Country: Netherlands
Category: Packaging concept (professional)

SILVER PENTAWARD 2020

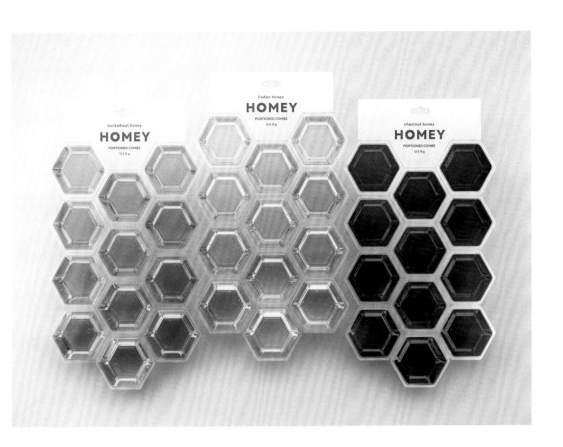

HOMEY

Art Direction: Katya Mushkina
CG Artwork: Bulgakov Nikita, Aleksey Shelukho
Copywriting: Aleksey Kalyan
Company: Katya Mushkina
Country: Russian Federation
Category: Packaging concept (professional)

BRONZE PENTAWARD 2019

GREEN REBELS UNITED

Senior Design: Fernando Ruiz Ibanez
Company: SGK Anthem – Amsterdam
Country: Netherlands
Category: Packaging concept (professional)

BRONZE PENTAWARD 2020

BEE-FEE

Design: Zuzanna Sadlik, Beata Faron
Company: Opus B Brand Design
Country: Poland
Category: Packaging concept (professional)

SILVER PENTAWARD 2019

GODIVA

Managing Direction: Malcolm Zhu
Group Creative Direction: Ryan Kam
Associate Creative Direction: Cao Jun, Vinc
Copywriting: Benjamin Woo
Creative Group Head: Forest Chen,
Emma Wu, Tom Guo
Senior Design: Boyce Liu, Charlie Wu,
Kim Zhou, Helen Ren, Awen Zhou
Account Direction: Hugh Shen
Company: Ivie
Country: China
Category: Packaging concept (professional)

SILVER PENTAWARD 2020

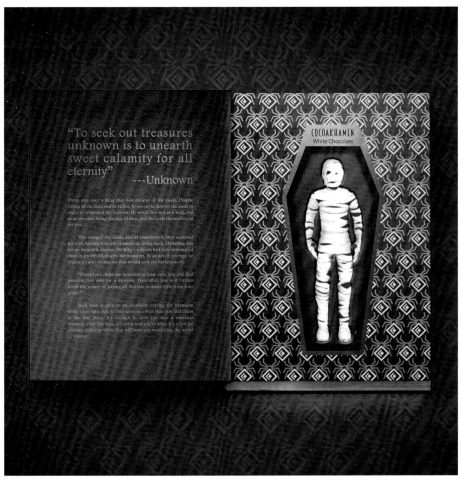

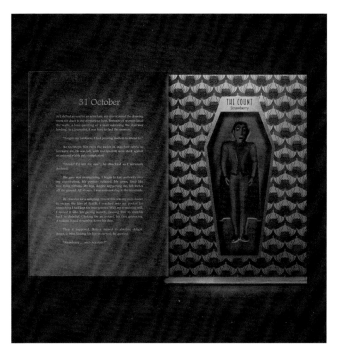

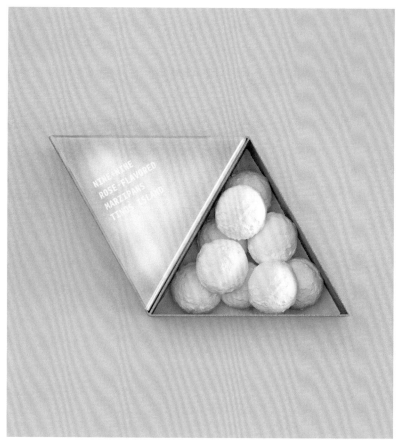

TINOS PROJECT

Lead Design and Creative Direction: Kostas Mentzos
Product Design: Cristina Seijas Fernández
Graphic Design: Anna-Maria Vlassopoulou,
Nour Hadwan, Yasmina Rasamny, Anastasia Efhetzi
Company: brand.new
Country: Greece
Category: Packaging concept (professional)

SILVER PENTAWARD 2019

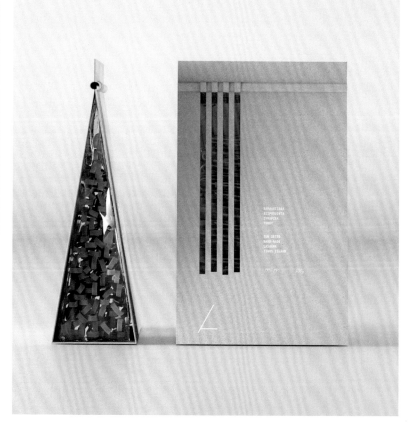

NAKED **STRAWBERRY**

BARE ALL BANANA

BARE YOGURT

Creative Direction: Paul Williams
Design: Rob Wilde
Company: Springetts
Country: UK
Category: Packaging concept (professional)

BRONZE PENTAWARD 2019

JIANGGUO WAWA

Creative Direction: Haozhen Luo
Company: Beijing Heziguai Creative Design
Country: China
Category: Packaging concept (professional)

BRONZE PENTAWARD 2020

HOT WAVE

Design, Creative Direction and Photography: Lin Wang
Supervision: Gu Chuan-Xi
School: Shanghai Institute of Visual Arts (SIVA)
Country: China
Category: Packaging concept (student)

GOLD PENTAWARD 2020

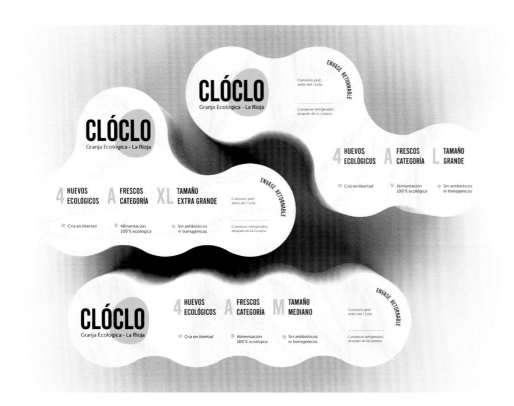

CLÓCLO

Creative Direction, Design and 3D Rendering
Design: África Álvarez Bueriberi
Instruction: Mónica Yoldi, Gracia de Prado,
Marcos Gallo
School: Escuela Superior de Diseño de La Rioja (Esdir)
Country: Spain
Category: Packaging concept (student)

GOLD PENTAWARD 2020

Clóclo is reusable organic egg packaging, intended to reduce the number of single-use containers. The set of different shapes and the graphic aesthetics emulate the appearance of the egg when it comes out of the shell, creating fluid forms that allow retailers to set up attractive combinations at the point of sale. Made of bent poplar wood, there are three styles which differentiate between M, L and XL eggs. Initially created with four egg slots, the structure can be easily scaled up to 6, 12 or more based on the consumer's needs.

Clóclo ist eine wiederverwendbare biologische Eierverpackung, die darauf abzielt, die Anzahl von Einmal-Verpackungen zu reduzieren. Das Set aus verschiedenen Formen und die grafische Ästhetik ahmen das Ei nach, wenn es aus der Schale kommt. Die fließenden Formen ermöglichen es dem Einzelhändler, attraktive Kombinationen im Laden zu bilden. Aus biegsamem Pappelholz hergestellt, gibt es drei verschiedene Stile für die Größen M, L und XL. Vorerst mit Platz für vier Eier hergestellt, kann die Struktur einfach auf sechs, zwölf oder noch mehr Eier, je nach den Bedürfnissen des Konsumenten, erweitert werden.

Clóclo est un emballage réutilisable pour œufs bio servant l'objectif de réduire le nombre de boîtes d'un seul usage. Les formes variées et l'esthétique graphique imitent l'aspect d'un œuf quand on en casse la coquille, ce qui donne des figures fluides idéales pour composer des combinaisons attrayantes dans les points de vente. Fabriquées en bois de peuplier courbé, les boîtes sont disponibles dans trois styles selon la taille M, L et XL des œufs. D'abord pensé pour quatre compartiments, cet emballage peut facilement passer à 6, 12 ou plus selon les besoins des consommateurs.

Boudin SF is a bakery and restaurant chain originally from San Franciscom known for its sourdough bread. It was established in 1849 by Isidore Boudin, the son of a family of master bakers from Burgundy, France, by blending the sourdough prevalent among miners in the Gold Rush with French techniques. Today, it is famous for its sourdough boule with clam chowder inside of it. This rebranding and packaging design recognises sustainability as longevity and delivers Boudin SF's same spirit but with a 21st-century vibe. This conceptual piece is part of a project from ArtCenter College of Design's first 100% plastic-free packaging course.

Boudin SF ist eine Bäckerei- und Restaurantkette, die ursprünglich aus San Francisco stammt und für sein Sauerteigbrot bekannt ist. Sie wurde 1849 von Isidore Boudin, dem Sohn einer Familie von Meisterbäckern aus Burgund, gegründet. Er kombinierte die Sauerteigkomponente, die bei den Minenarbeitern zur Zeit des Goldrauschs besonders beliebt war, mit französischen Backtechniken. Heute ist die Kette bekannt für Muschelsuppe im Sauerteigbrötchen. Das Design erkennt Nachhaltigkeit als Langlebigkeit an und verknüpft Boudin SFs Erbe mit dem Schwung des 21. Jahrhunderts. Dieses konzeptionelle Stück ist Teil eines Projekts des ersten 100%-plastikfreien Verpackungskurses des ArtCenter College of Design.

Boudin SF est une chaîne de boulangeries et de restaurants originaire de San Francisco qui est réputée pour son pain au levain. Fondée en 1849 par Isidore Boudin, fils d'une famille bourguignonne de maîtres boulangers, elle doit son succès au mariage du savoir-faire français de la boulangerie et du levain que les chercheurs d'or cultivaient à cette époque. Aujourd'hui, Boudin est célèbre pour sa chaudrée de palourdes servie dans une boule de pain au levain. Ce design de rebranding et de packaging fait rimer durabilité et longévité et transmet la même philosophie de Boudin SF, mais avec une approche du 21ᵉ siècle. Cette œuvre conceptuelle fait partie d'un projet pour le premier cours de création de packagings 100 % sans plastique à l'ArtCenter College of Design.

BOUDIN SAN FRANCISCO

Design and Art Direction: Yi Mao
Photography: Jack Strutz
Hand Modelling: Lemon Zhai
Instruction: Andrew Gibbs, Jessica Deseo
Advisor: Gerardo Herrera
School: ArtCenter College of Design
Country: USA
Category: Packaging concept (student)

GOLD PENTAWARD 2019

SWEET HOME

Design: Nazanin Behzadi Yeganeh
Company: NB nazaninbehzadi
Country: Iran
Category: Packaging concept (student)
SILVER PENTAWARD 2019

STANDARD

Design: Olga Prokhorova
Tutoring: Leonid Slavin, Alexander Nazarenko
School: British Higher School of Art and Design
Country: Russian Federation
Category: Packaging concept (student)

BRONZE PENTAWARD 2020

MILKY MOOD

Art Direction: Lilit Vartanyan
3D Modelling: Sergei Morozov
Copywriting: Svetlana Pozdnyakova
School: British Higher School of Art and Design
Country: Russian Federation
Category: Packaging concept (student)

BRONZE PENTAWARD 2020

ABC
THE REINVENTED CHOCOLATE

Creative Direction and Design: Carmen González,
Clara Hevia, Mar Sánchez-Morate
School: Elisava, Barcelona School of
Design and Engineering
Country: Spain
Category: Packaging concept (student)

SILVER PENTAWARD 2020

SEE'S CANDIES

Design: Donna Kang
Photography: James chou
School: ArtCenter College of Design
Country: USA
Category: Packaging concept (student)

SILVER PENTAWARD 2019

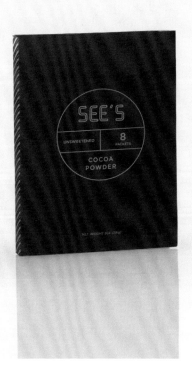

PESTOPESTO

Tutoring: Yevgeny Razumov
3D Modelling: Volodymyr Frantiichuk
School: British Higher School of Art and Design
Country: Russian Federation
Category: Packaging concept (student)

SILVER PENTAWARD 2019

RADUGA GORA

Design: Tatiana Fedrunova
3D Design: Pavel Gubin
School: British Higher School of Art and Design
Country: Russian Federation
Category: Packaging concept (student)

BRONZE PENTAWARD 2019

E&B

Design: Chen Xiaotong, Xiao Han
Design Direction: Michail Semoglou
School: Shanghai Institute of Visual Arts (SIVA)
Country: China
Category: Packaging concept (student)

BRONZE PENTAWARD 2019

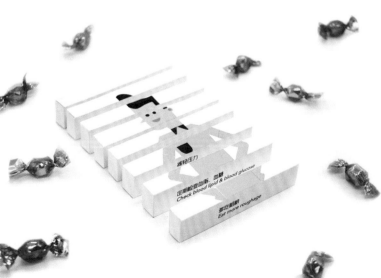

AKAN

Design: Keqiao Li
Supervision: Hu Ji-jun
School: Shanghai Institute of Visual Arts (SIVA)
Country: China
Category: Packaging concept (student)

SILVER PENTAWARD 2020

AKan
PRODUCT CATEGORY: canned sardines
SHELF LIFE: 24months
NET QUANTITY: 190
INGREDIENT LIST: sardine
STORAGE METHOD: Normal atmospheric
temperature, Avoid light, Moisture-proof

Constantly looking for the unknown surprise

Akio
アキオ
dusting powder
100 ml

Akio
アキオ
baby shower gel
500 ml

Akio
アキオ
baby oil
300 ml

Best of the category

Garments

Healthcare

body

Body care

Beauty

Distributors'/retailers' own brands/private labels

Packaging concept

Sponsored by

◩ GOLDEN ARROW

PINK ROSE COMPACT: A SUSTAINABILITY GAME CHANGER

Born to revolutionise the luxury packaging industry, **Golden Arrow** started with a mission in 1984 to use truly sustainable materials and production processes in order to protect our environment. Single-use plastics, often chosen by the packaging and printing industries, are massive contributors to global pollution and waste. We didn't want to be a part of that. From the very beginning we have worked to create **packaging that is eco-friendly, innovative and relentlessly luxurious**. Our latest concept is a testament to that mission: a high definition contour moulded fibre design that pairs sustainable materials with stunning form factors and vibrant colour options.

The Pink Rose Compact features a fibre-flow control system that combines vacuum pressure and tooling surface manipulation to create an ornate 3D design. And we didn't stop there. Included in our production is a process to fully integrate vivid colour directly into the material itself. Our Pink Rose design is also scented, and our collection of fragrances ensure that our packaging leaves a **multisensory impact** on your customers.

The result is a marvel of design and aesthetics – an elegant package complete with **tactile details and dazzling colours**, crafted entirely from environmentally responsible production processes and sustainable materials. Golden Arrow can now outfit brands with unique and brilliantly colourful 3D designs that fully express brand dedication to sustainability without compromising premium, luxurious quality.

Hinging on environmentally friendly ingenuity, Golden Arrow developed the **living hinge** – a moulded fibre joint rated for more than 2,000 openings. The living hinge opens up the imagined boundaries of what moulded fibre packaging can do by providing a lid or fold function for any package. The Golden Arrow Pink Rose Compact is a fluidly designed moulded fibre contour piece that offers brands **totally sustainable packaging with long-lasting durability**, premium quality and presentation.

PINK ROSE COMPAKT: EIN WENDEPUNKT FÜR DIE NACHHALTIGKEIT

Geboren, um die Luxusverpackungsindustrie zu revolutionieren, begann **Golden Arrow** 1984 mit der Mission, wirklich nachhaltige Materialien und Produktionsprozesse zu verwenden, um unsere Umwelt zu schützen. Einwegkunststoffe, die häufig von der Verpackungs- und Druckindustrie benutzt werden, tragen massiv zur globalen Umweltverschmutzung und zum Verschwendung bei. Wir wollten kein Teil davon sein. Von Anfang an haben wir daran gearbeitet, **Verpackungen zu entwerfen, die umweltfreundlich, innovativ und schonungslos luxuriös sind**. Unser neuestes Konzept ist ein Beleg für diese Mission: ein Design aus Faserguss mit hochauflösenden Konturen, das nachhaltige Materialien gemeinsam mit verblüffenden Formen und knalligen Farboptionen zusammenbringt.

Das Pink Rose Compact verfügt über ein Faserflusskontrollsystem, das Vakuumdruck und Vorrichtungen zu Oberflächenmanipulation kombiniert, um ein kunstvolles 3D-Design zu kreieren. Und damit haben wir nicht aufgehört. Zu unserer Produktion gehört ein Verfahren, um lebhafte Farben direkt in die Materialien selbst zu integrieren. Unser Pink Rose Design ist außerdem parfümiert, und unsere Duftkollektion sorgt dafür, dass unsere Verpackung einen **multisensorischen Eindruck** bei unseren Kunden hinterlässt.

Das Ergebnis ist ein Wunderwerk an Design und Ästhetik – eine elegante Verpackung, vollkommen mit **haptischen Details und schillernden Farben**, die vollständig aus umweltfreundlichen Produktionsprozessen und nachhaltigen Materialien hergestellt wird. Golden Arrow kann jetzt Marken mit einzigartigen und brillanten farbenfrohen 3D-Designs ausstatten, die das Engagement der Marke für Nachhaltigkeit vollständig zum Ausdruck bringen, ohne dabei Kompromisse bei der luxuriösen Premiumqualität einzugehen.

Angelehnt an umweltfreundlichen Einfallsreichtum entwickelte Golden Arrow den **Living Hinge** – eine geformte Faserformverbindung die auf mehr als 2.000 Öffnungen ausgelegt ist. Der Living Hinge öffnet die imaginären Grenzen dessen, was geformte Faserverpackung leisten kann, indem es jeder Verpackung eine Deckel oder eine Faltfunktion verleiht. Das Golden Arrow Pink Rose Compact ist eine fließend gestaltete Faserform mit Kontur, die den Marken eine **total nachhaltige Verpackung mit lang anhaltender Beständigkeit**, Premiumqualität und Präsentation bietet.

PINK ROSE COMPACT: UNE NOUVELLE DONNE EN DURABILITÉ

Fondé pour révolutionner l'industrie du packaging de luxe, **Golden Arrow** a débuté en 1984 avec pour mission d'employer des matériaux et des processus de production réellement écoresponsables et de protéger ainsi l'environnement. Souvent adoptés dans le domaine des emballages et de l'imprimerie, les plastiques à usage unique contribuent grandement à la pollution et aux déchets à l'échelle mondiale. Et nous ne voulions pas être complices. Nous avons donc dès le départ cherché à créer des **packagings écoresponsables, innovants et irrésistiblement luxueux**. Notre dernier concept en témoigne parfaitement, à savoir un design de forme haute définition par moulage de fibre qui combine matériaux durables, facteurs de forme sensationnels et options de couleurs vives.

Le boîtier Pink Rose Compact présente un mécanisme de contrôle du flux de fibre qui associe le pressage sous vide et le traitement de la surface d'outillage pour créer un design 3D raffiné. Mais ce n'est pas tout. Notre production inclut un processus d'intégration de couleurs vives directement dans la matière. Notre création Pink Rose est par ailleurs parfumée et grâce à notre collection de parfums, le packaging a un **impact multi-sensoriel** sur nos clients.

Le résultat est une merveille de design et d'esthétique, un emballage élégant assorti **de détails tactiles et de couleurs éclatantes**, entièrement conçu selon des processus de production écoresponsables et à base de matériaux durables. Golden Arrow apporte aux marques des designs 3D uniques et hauts en couleurs qui illustrent parfaitement son engagement envers le développement durable sans compromettre une qualité luxueuse.

S'appuyant sur une inventivité écologique, Golden Arrow a mis au point la **charnière vivante**, une articulation en fibre moulée conçue pour résister à plus de 2 000 ouvertures. Cette charnière vivante repousse les possibilités du packaging en fibre moulée en ajoutant à n'importe quel emballage un couvercle ou un rabat. Le boîtier Pink Rose Compact de Golden Arrow est une création en fibre moulée au design fluide qui offre aux marques un **packaging totalement écoresponsable et résistant**, de qualité supérieure et avec une présentation exceptionnelle.

GOLDEN ARROW

This basic make-up kit for **Chioture**, a vibrant and youthful make-up brand, focuses on the ritual surrounding the use of the product. Chioture stands for chic + capture and refers to the brand's idea of a "young fashion hunter" seeking "the simple life". With its adorable camera-like look, the innovative design of this loose powder case and brush effectively communicates the fun characteristics of the brand. The user unscrews the "lens" to access the powder and pulls out the brush, which is securely stored in the "grip". The "viewfinder" shows the logo and also doubles as a dock for the brush.

Dieses Make-up-Set von **Chioture**, eine lebhafte und jugendliche Make-up-Marke, fokussiert sich auf das Ritual, das die Verwendung des Produkts umgibt. Chioture steht für chic + capture (dt. „einfangen") und bezieht sich auf die Idee der Marke eines „jungen Modejägers", der das „arglose Leben" sucht. Das innovative Design dieser Puderdose und des Pinsels mit seinem bezaubernden kameraähnlichen Look vermittelt die humorvolle Charakteristik der Marke wirkungsvoll. Der Nutzer schraubt die „Linse" ab, um an das Puder zu gelangen, und zieht den Pinsel hervor, der sicher im „Griff" verstaut ist. Der „Sucher" zeigt das Logo der Marke und kann gleichzeitig als Halterung für den Pinsel genutzt werden.

Ce kit de maquillage pour la marque juvénile et colorée **Chioture** est adapté à l'environnement habituel dans lequel il est utilisé. Chioture est la contraction de chic + capture et renvoie à l'idée d'une « jeune chasseuse de mode » en quête d'une « vie simple ». Avec un adorable look d'appareil photo, le design innovant de ce boîtier de poudre libre et son pinceau transmet parfaitement les amusantes particularités de la marque. L'utilisateur dévisse la « lentille » pour ouvrir le poudrier et extrait le pinceau logé dans la « poignée ». Le logo se trouve sur le « viseur », qui sert également de support au pinceau.

CHIOTURE

Creative Direction: Guozheng Jiang, Dan Chen
Strategy Consulting Direction: Yang Shu
Product Design: Xinnan Zhang, Zilei Jiao
Account Executive: Jin Li
Company: Shanghai Nianxiang Brand Design & Consulting
Country: China
Category: Beauty
PLATINUM PENTAWARD 2020

STONEBRICK

Creative Direction: Sam O'Donahue
Client: Emart Inc
Photography: H. Factory, Junghoon Han
Company: Established
Country: USA
Category: Beauty

PLATINUM PENTAWARD 2019

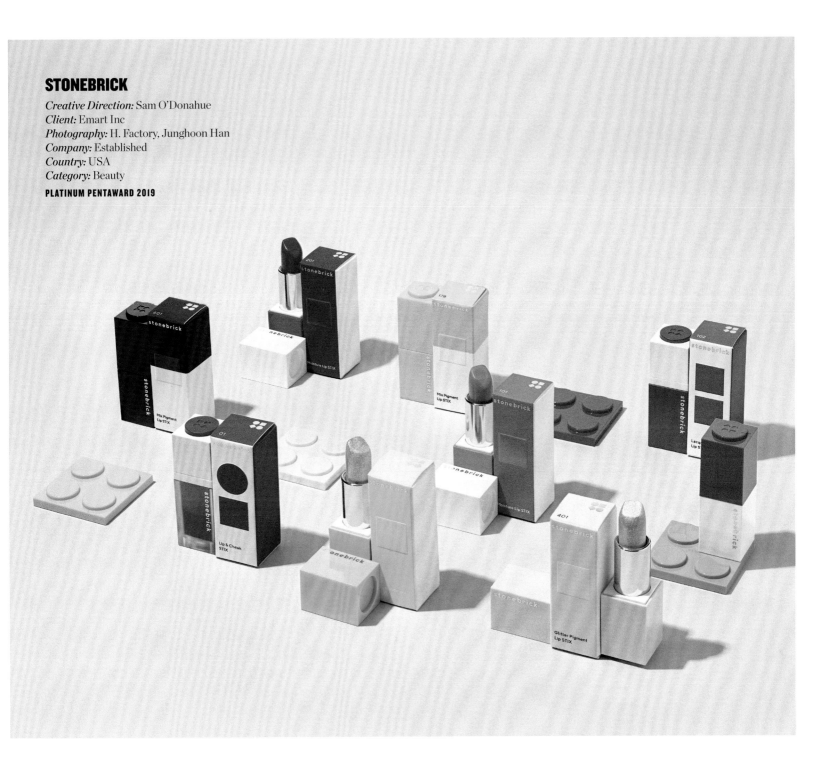

As a new line of makeup created for South Korea's largest retailer Emart, **Stonebrick** is the first fully customisable makeup range with individual magnetised components that snap together to create custom collections. The idea behind the line is to allow the customer to buy a tailor-made set of cosmetics in a playful, fun and joyful way. Lipsticks and face products also click together in different and exciting combinations for endless possibilities.

Als neue Make-up-Linie, die für Südkoreas größten Emart-Händler entworfen wurde, ist **Stonebrick** die erste komplett individualisierbare Make-up-Reihe mit einzelnen magnetischen Komponenten, die sich zu benutzerdefinierten Kollektionen zusammenfügen lassen. Die Idee ist es, dem Kunden die Möglichkeit zu geben, ein auf spielerische Art maßgeschneidertes Kosmetikset zu erwerben. Auch Lippenstifte und Gesichtspflege-produkte lassen sich in verschiedenen Kombinationen zusammenklicken.

Stonebrick est la nouvelle ligne de maquillage proposée par Emart, le plus grand détaillant de Corée du Sud. Il s'agit de la première gamme de produits de maquillage entièrement personnalisables, avec des éléments individuels aimantés qui s'assemblent pour former des collections uniques. L'idée est de permettre au consommateur d'acheter des produits cosmétiques personnalisés d'une manière amusante et originale. Les rouges à lèvres et les soins pour le visage se clipsent ensemble pour créer des combinaisons attrayantes infinies.

This re-invigorated packaging for **Petit Bateau's** baby, kid and adult clothing and underwear uses the brand's history as the focus for its redesign. In 1918, Étienne Valton, the son of the brand's founder, had the idea to cut off the legs of long underwear, inventing the world's first baby pants. Inspired by the brand's transformative heritage, the design utilises a "cut out" as the packaging signature, which highlights the brand's iconic clothes in a simple and fun way. The pack's new structure also enables the brand to communicate its story and legendary attributes on the back of the pack while better protecting what is inside.

Für diese neu belebte Verpackung für **Petit Bateaus** Baby-, Kinder- und Erwachsenenbekleidung und Unterwäsche wurde die Geschichte der Marke als Schwerpunkt für das neue Design genutzt. 1918 hatte Étienne Valton, der Sohn des Markengründers, die Idee, die Beine der langen Unterhosen abzuschneiden, und entwarf so die erste Babyunterhose der Welt. Inspiriert durch das transformative Erbe der Marke, verwendet das Design einen „Ausschnitt" als Verpackungscharakteristik, die die Erfindung auf einfache und lustige Art hervorhebt. Die neue Struktur der Packung ermöglicht es der Marke auch, ihre Geschichte und legendären Eigenschaften auf der Rückseite der Verpackung zu kommunizieren und gleichzeitig den Inhalt besser zu schützen.

Ce packaging redynamisé des vêtements et sous-vêtements pour bébés, enfants et adultes **Petit Bateau** base sa refonte sur l'histoire de la marque. Étienne Valton, fils du fondateur de la marque, eut l'idée en 1918 de couper les jambes des sous-vêtements longs, ce qui donna naissance aux premiers pantalons bébé au monde. S'inspirant de cet héritage transformateur, le design choisit comme signe distinctif une découpe qui dévoile les vêtements emblématiques d'une façon simple et amusante. Ce nouvel agencement de l'emballage permet aussi à la marque de communiquer au dos son histoire et ses attributs légendaires tout en protégeant davantage le produit qu'il renferme.

PETIT BATEAU

Managing Direction: Patrice Civanyan
Senior Design: Sarah Roberts
Design: Lysa Corporandy
Client: Petit Bateau
Company: Mutation
Country: France
Category: Garments
GOLD PENTAWARD 2020

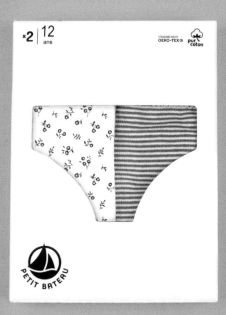

SOUTHBANK WATSON OUTFITTER UK

Creative Direction: Paul Roeters
Design: Jeroen Hoedjes
Company: Studio Kluif
Country: Netherlands
Category: Garments

GOLD PENTAWARD 2019

Southbank Watson Outfitter UK's **Button Eye Shirt** is part of a collection of limited-edition handmade shirts. What makes the packaging of their products unique is their clever button-eye concept in combination with the striking illustrations on the gift boxes. The shirt's black button with its red thread plays an unexpected yet important role in the packaging, resulting in an "eye-conic" and playful design.

Das **Button Eye Shirt** von Southbank Watson Outfitter UK ist Teil einer Kollektion handgefertigter Hemden in limitierter Auflage. Was die Verpackung ihres Produkts einzigartig macht, ist ihr geniales Knopfaugen-Konzept in Kombination mit ihren markanten Illustrationen auf den Geschenkboxen. Der schwarze Knopf des Hemds mit seinem roten Zwirn spielt eine unerwartete und doch wichtige Rolle in der Verpackung, die sich in einem „Augen-scheinlichen" und spielerischen Design niederschlägt.

Le modèle **Button Eye Shirt** de Southbank Watson Outfitter UK appartient à une collection de chemises faites main en édition limitée. Le packaging de leurs produits est unique grâce à l'astucieux concept d'œil-bouton et aux illustrations éclatantes sur les coffrets-cadeaux. Le bouton noir cousu avec du fil rouge crée la surprise et devient le protagoniste du packaging, donnant un design amusant au premier coup d'œil.

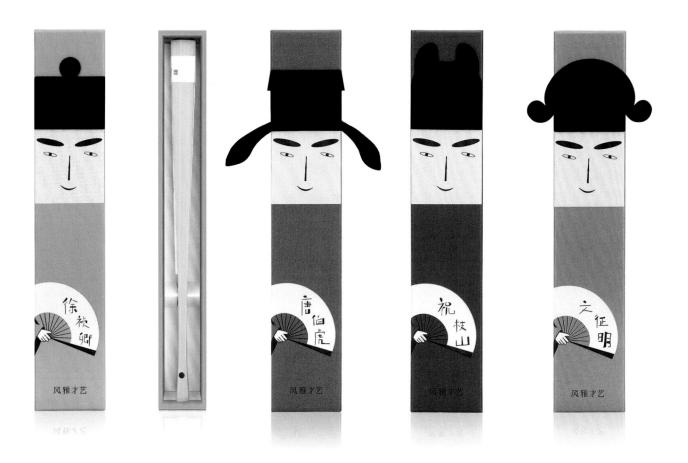

FOUR SCHOLARS IN JIANGNAN

Creative Direction: Jingfang Mei
Company: Hangzhou Dongyun Advertising Design
Country: China
Category: Garments
SILVER PENTAWARD 2019

GAMBOL

Creative Direction: Somchana Kanwarnjit
Creative Direction and Design: Chalayoot Komalanimi
Art Direction: Nonpakorn Thiapairat
3D Rendering: Pichit Klungwijit
Illustration: Thanakim Thanomton
Company: Strong Design
Country: Thailand
Category: Garments
BRONZE PENTAWARD 2020

ROLLOR PACKAGING

Head of Design and Implementation: Peter Hoogland
Packaging Design and Implementation Specialist:
Maarten Ornée
CEO and Founder: Teun van der Laan
CFO and Founder: Robert Hoes
Manufacturing: Smurfit Kappa MNL
Client: Loewe
Company: Rollor
Country: Netherlands
Category: Garments

BRONZE PENTAWARD 2019

ALICE'S ADVENTURES IN WONDERLAND

*Creative Direction, Art Direction
and Graphic Design:* Koji Matsumoto
Company: Grand Deluxe
Country: Japan
Category: Garments

SILVER PENTAWARD 2020

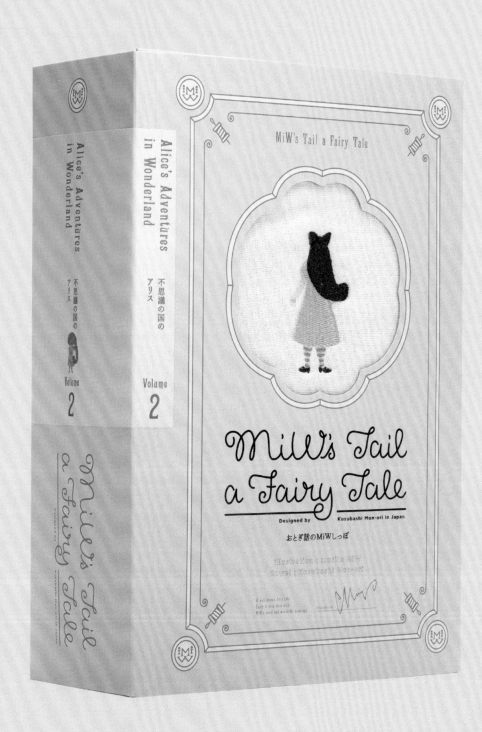

LOOKS SUNGLASSES PACKAGING

Design: Xiuling Zhou
Illustration: Shengri Cheng, Dongmei Huang
Project Management: Xiuhan Yang
Company: ZRP Printing Group
Country: China
Category: Garments

SILVER PENTAWARD 2020

NASTASIA ČERNOVSKI

Creative Direction: Dmitry Chigirin
Art Direction: Dmitry Krasnov
Senior Design: Irina Vasilyeva
Motion Design: Nikita Ryumshin
Retouching: Pavel Kostikov
Copywriting: Dmitry Chigirin
3D Design: Alexey Avduevsky
Account Direction: Sergey Kovalev
Account Management: Tatiana Borisova
Company: SOLL
Country: Russian Federation
Category: Garments
BRONZE PENTAWARD 2020

HIDARIUCHIWA

Art Direction and Design: Ryuta Ishikawa
Company: Frame inc.
Country: Japan
Category: Garments
BRONZE PENTAWARD 2019

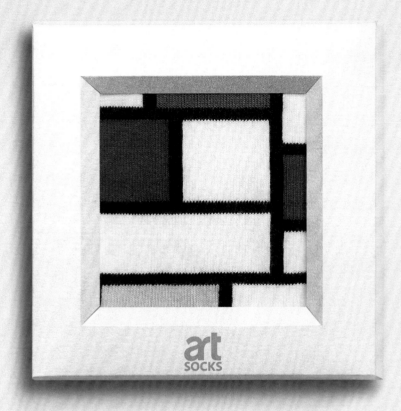

Composition with Large Red Plane, Yellow, Black, Gray and Blue
Piet Mondrian, 1921

ARTSOCKS

Creative Direction: Stepan Azaryan
Project Management: Meri Sargsyan
Design: Christina Khlushyan, Eliza Malkhasyan
Company: Backbone Branding
Country: Armenia
Category: Garments

SILVER PENTAWARD 2019

CANONPHARMA

Creative Direction: Valeria Repina
Art Direction: Anvar Kurbanov
Design: Alexey Zabrodin
Account Direction: Agata Suligovska
3D Design: Nikita Bulgakov
CG Artwork: Alexey Koler
Motion Design: Alexandr Filatov, Alexandr Yarysh
Company: Repina Branding
Country: Russian Federation
Category: Health care

GOLD PENTAWARD 2020

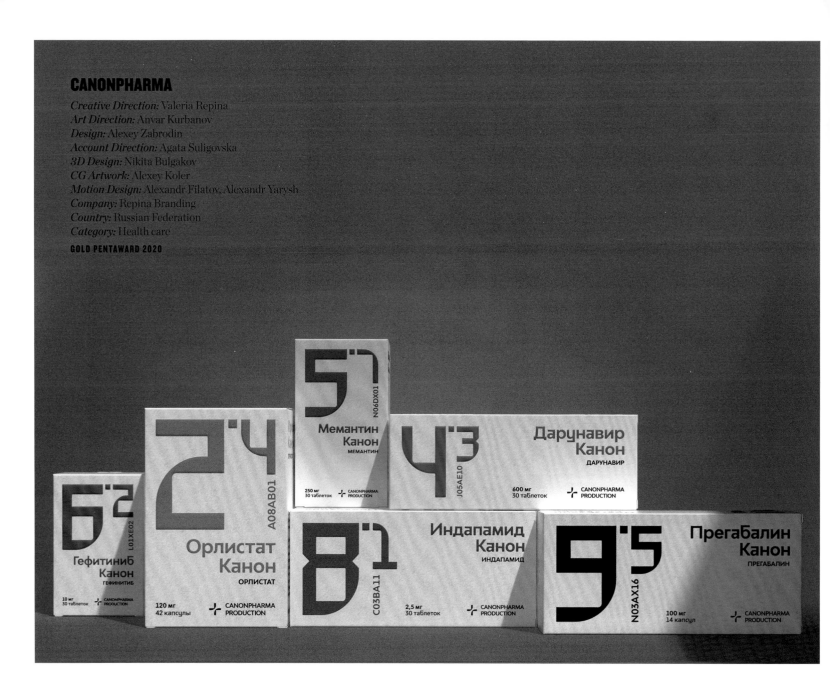

Canonpharma developed a revolutionary system based on colour-coding and numbering that enables easy navigation among a multitude of drugs and dosages. The first digit stands for the drug number within the pharmacological class while the second digit after the dot indicates the dosage, allowing the patient to simply name the group and number to the pharmacist. Great attention was given to the look of the digits so that these are clearly legible while bearing unique brand identification traits. Built on the contrast of hard and soft shapes, this design reflects the idea of advanced technologies united with customer care.

Canonpharma hat ein revolutionäres System entwickelt, das auf Farbcodierung und Nummerierung basiert und eine einfache Orientierung zwischen einer Vielzahl von Medikamenten und Dosierungen möglich macht. Die erste Ziffer steht für die Nummer des Medikaments innerhalb der pharmakologischen Klasse, während die zweite Zahl nach dem Punkt die Dosierung angibt, sodass der Patient dem Apotheker einfach die Gruppe und Nummer nennen kann. Großer Wert wurde auf das Aussehen der Ziffern gelegt, damit diese klar und deutlich lesbar sind und gleichzeitig eindeutige Merkmale zur Identifizierung der Marke tragen. Dieses Design, das auf dem Kontrast harter und weicher Formen aufbaut, spiegelt fortschrittliche Technologien wider und ist verbraucherfreundlich.

Canonpharma a mis au point un code révolutionnaire de couleur et de numérotation pour aider à s'y retrouver plus facilement parmi la foule de médicaments et de posologies. Le premier chiffre correspond au numéro du médicament dans la classe pharmacologique, alors que le second, après le point, indique la posologie ; le patient peut ainsi aisément donner au pharmacien le groupe et le nombre. Un soin tout particulier a été porté aux chiffres afin qu'ils soient clairement lisibles tout en dotant la marque d'une identification unique. Ce design, qui joue avec le contraste entre formes douces et angles, illustre l'application de technologies avancées à l'assistance aux clients.

In an attempt to defy gender bias, the condoms made by **SAIB** were designed to look like cosmetics, setting them apart from the more typical male-centred condom brands. The packaging uses text and visual expressions to resonate with women and the issues most relevant to them. As an extension of the company's mission to destigmatise negative perceptions around women's sexual agency in Korea, SAIB products are designed with bright colours and positive tones, so that women feel comfortable and proud to carry and use them, and let go of any shame or stigma.

In einem Versuch, mit Geschlechtervorurteilen aufzuräumen, wurden die Kondompackungen von **SAIB** so designt, dass sie wie Kosmetika aussehen und sich von den männlich-orientierten Kondommarken abheben. Die Sprache der Verpackung wendet sich an Frauen und soll für sie relevante Themen der Liebe und des Selbstwertgefühls hervorheben. Als Erweiterung der Mission des Unternehmens, negative Wahrnehmungen in Bezug auf die sexuelle Selbstbestimmung von Frauen in Korea zu entstigmatisieren, werden die SAIB-Produkte in hellen Farben und positiven Tönen gestaltet, sodass die Frauen sich wohlfühlen und stolz sind, sie mit sich zu tragen und zu benutzen, ganz ohne Scham und Diskriminierung.

Dans l'intention de défier les préjugés sexistes, les préservatifs de la marque **SAIB** ont été conçus pour paraître des produits cosmétiques, au lieu de s'aligner sur la concurrence plus axée sur le public masculin. Sur le packaging, le texte et les expressions visuelles trouvent un écho chez les femmes et parlent de sujets qui les concernent. En prolongement de la mission de la marque d'éliminer la stigmatisation liée au désir d'auto-détermination sexuelle des femmes en Corée, les produits SAIB sont conçus avec des couleurs vives et des tonalités positives, afin que les femmes se sentent à l'aise et fières de les utiliser et se libèrent de tout sentiment de honte ou de rejet.

SAIB INTIMATE COSMETIC

Executive Creative Direction: Jiwon Park
Design: Jungmin Choi, Eunchong Kim
Company: SAIB & Co.
Country: Republic of Korea
Category: Health care
GOLD PENTAWARD 2019

GOLDEN ERA NUTRITION

Design: Zhanqiang Yang
Illustration: Wenwei Dai
3D: Zhihong Liang
Company: Going Design
Country: China
Category: Health care

SILVER PENTAWARD 2020

CALLALY

Creative Direction: Chloe Templeman
Design: Faye Thomas
Sustainability Direction: Helen Hughes
Senior Production Management: Tal Watson
Senior Design: Cristina Tang
3D Branding Direction: Phil Bordet Stead
Design Direction: Natasha Dowdall,
Monique Bissell, Julian Waterson
Client Executive: Ellie Hammond-Hunt
Group Brand Experience Direction: Ed Mitchell
Company: Design Bridge London
Country: UK
Category: Health care
BRONZE PENTAWARD 2020

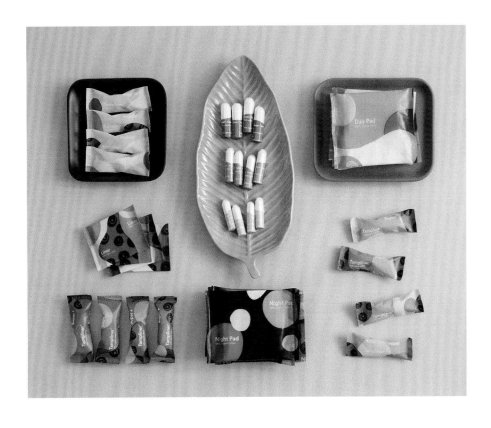

STARSHARING

Design: Wei Peng
Company: LionPeng Packaging Design Studio
Country: China
Category: Health care
BRONZE PENTAWARD 2019

RECKITT BENCKISER

Executive Creative Direction: Claire Robertshaw
Creative Direction: Tim Vary, Kate Galle
Design: Sam Ellis, Dan Norris, Charlotte Harrison,
Nathalie Bland, Leia Bygrave, Anthony Letterese
Image Creation: Damian Hughes, Natasha Dowdall
Print Consulting: David Benjamin
Strategy: David Helps, Hannah McDermid, Laura Ford
Client Services: Iona MacDonald, Seb Darke,
Sophie Hussein
Company: Design Bridge London
Country: UK
Category: Health care

BRONZE PENTAWARD 2020

PACK'D SUPPLEMENTS

Graphic Design and Art Direction: Davy Dooms
Client: Kristof Pirijns, David Box
Printing: BDMO, Devepack
Lab: Medix Laboratoires
Company: Davy Dooms Graphic & Brand Design
Country: Belgium
Category: Health care

BRONZE PENTAWARD 2019

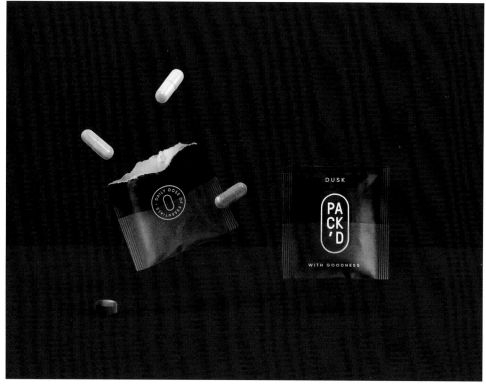

This packaging for **DUO** condoms and lubricants uses the logo as the focal point of the design. When looked at horizontally the letters of the word emerge as distinct shapes. In a vertical position they join together and form two human figures with arms reaching out for an embrace. Utilising the brand name and its reflection, this anthropomorphic design shape-shifts into a human couple. This design is also used on the products inside the package.

Diese Verpackung für **DUO** Kondome und Gleitmittel nutzt das Logo als Schwerpunkt des Designs. Wenn man horizontal darauf schaut, tauchen die Buchstaben des Wortes als unabhängige Formen auf. In vertikaler Position zeigen sie zwei Menschen, die sich umarmen. Unter Verwendung des Markennamens und seiner Spiegelung verwandelt sich das anthropomorphe Design in ein menschliches Paar. Das Design setzt sich auch auf den Produkten in der Verpackung fort.

Dans ce packaging pour les préservatifs et lubrifiants **DUO**, le logo est le point de mire du design. Horizontalement, les lettres prennent des formes différentes alors que verticalement, elles s'unissent pour former deux figures humaines sur le point de s'enlacer. En jouant avec le nom et un effet miroir, ce design anthropomorphique se convertit en un couple et se retrouve également sur les produits à l'intérieur.

DUO 2IN1

Design: Mousegraphics team
Company: Mousegraphics
Country: Greece
Category: Health care

SILVER PENTAWARD 2020

In India, myths and taboos around monthly periods often characterise menstruating women as unclean and impure. Even in urban areas, women still hesitate to ask for sanitary pads, and shopkeepers wrap menstrual products in newspapers and black plastic bags. As a way to help normalise the conversation around periods, **Don't Hide It. Period.** was launched. The limited-edition product uses this message as the main design concept. The phrase "don't hide it" was inspired by the sometimes embarrassing conversations around periods and seeks to remove the stigma around menstruation with its bold visuals and cheery wordplays.

In Indien charakterisieren Mythen und Tabus rund um die Monatsblutung menstruierende Frauen oft als unrein. Selbst in städtischen Gegenden trauen sich manche Frauen nicht, nach Damenbinden zu fragen, und Verkäufer verpacken Menstruationsprodukte in Zeitungen und schwarzen Plastiktüten. Um Gespräche über die Periode zu normalisieren, wurde **Don't Hide It. Period.** (dt. „Versteck es nicht") ins Leben gerufen. Das Produkt in limitierter Auflage nutzt seine Botschaft als Hauptdesignkonzept. Inspiriert von den manchmal peinlichen Dialogen über die Periode, brechen die starke Bildsprache und die selbstbewussten Sprüche das Stigma rund um die Menstruation auf. Die Doppeldeutigkeit des englischen Wortes "period" für „Periode" und „Punkt" am Satzende, macht die jeweilige Aussage zu einem echten Statement.

En Inde, les mythes et les tabous autour de la menstruation représentent souvent les femmes comme impures. Même dans les zones urbaines, les femmes hésitent encore à demander des serviettes hygiéniques, et les commerçants enveloppent les protections périodiques dans des feuilles de journaux et des sacs plastique noirs. **Don't Hide It. Period.** a été lancé pour essayer de normaliser la communication sur les règles. Le concept clé du design de ce produit en édition limitée est le propre message. La phrase « Don't hide it » (ne le cache pas) renvoient aux conversations parfois embarrassantes sur la menstruation et cherche à éliminer sa stigmatisation grâce à un visuel audacieux et des jeux de mots amusants, « period » ayant en anglais le double de sens de règles et de point.

DON'T HIDE IT. PERIOD.

Creative Direction: Neha Tulsian
Design: Sukriti Sahni
Photography: Raghav Kumar
Animation and Film-making: Nitin Shekhar
Social Media Management: Sukriti Sahni
Company: NH1 Design
Country: India
Category: Health care
SILVER PENTAWARD 2019

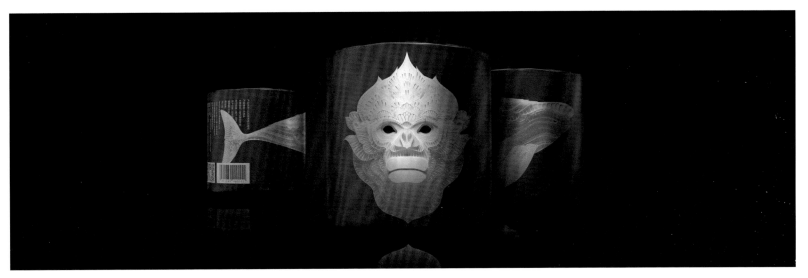

HILL SIDE

Creative Direction: Zhihua He
Design: Zhihua He
Client: Fengsheng Group
Company: Shanghai Version Design Group
Country: China
Category: Health care

SILVER PENTAWARD 2019

Hill Side is a new high-end brand of toilet paper which sees environmental protection and ecological balance as its core concepts. It uses special bamboo in the papermaking process, which is harvested by local farmers in Sichuan, supporting their incomes and respecting the ecological balance of the region. The black background gives a new look to traditional toilet roll packaging, featuring paper sculptures of endangered animals. The result is something that is both stylish and meaningful, aimed at young consumers who value the environment as well as the finer things in life.

Hill Side ist eine neue luxuriöse Toilettenpapiermarke, die den Schutz der Umwelt und die ökologische Balance als das Kernkonzept ihrer Marke sieht. Bei der Papierherstellung benutzen sie Bambus, der von Bauern in Sichuan geerntet wird, um somit deren Einkommen zu unterstützen und das ökologische Gleichgewicht der Region zu respektieren. Der schwarze Hintergrund gibt der Toilettenpapierrolle einen modernen Look und zeigt Papierskulpturen bedrohter Tierarten. Das Resultat ist etwas, das sowohl stil- als auch bedeutungsvoll ist und sich damit an junge Verbraucher richtet, die die Umwelt aber auch die schönen Dinge des Lebens schätzen.

Hill Side est une nouvelle marque haut de gamme de papier toilette dont les concepts clés sont la protection de l'environnement et l'équilibre écologique. La fabrication du papier se fait à partir d'un bambou spécial récolté par des producteurs locaux à Sichuan : la marque assure ainsi leur revenus et respecte l'équilibre écologique de la région. Le fond noir tranche avec l'emballage traditionnel des rouleaux de papier toilette, présentant des photos de sculptures en papier d'animaux menacés d'extinction. Le produit obtenu est aussi sophistiqué que plein de sens et s'adresse aux jeunes consommateurs attachés à la défense de l'environnement et aux choses raffinées du quotidien.

SK:LK-BODY CARE

Client: Beijing Youji Technology Development
Creative Direction: Tengxian Zou, Zhihua He
Design: Tengxian Zou, Haoting Zhang, Wenfang Ye
Render Division: Wenfang Ye
Company: Shanghai Version Design Group
Country: China
Category: Body care

GOLD PENTAWARD 2020

SK:LK-BODY CARE is a set of body care products, from hair care and shampoo to shower gel. To highlight the purity and gentleness of the products, the design for this range was completely stripped back. All it consists of is a simple ripple pattern, which outlines the numbers 0, 1 and 2, on a fine, soft matte material to communicate the sequence in which it should be used.

SK:LK-BODY CARE ist ein Set von Körperpflege-produkten, von Haarpflege und Shampoo bis hin zu Duschgel. Um die Reinheit und Sanftheit der Produkte zu unterstreichen, ist das Design für diese Reihe sehr minimalistisch. Es besteht aus nur einem Wellenmuster, das die Ziffern 0, 1 und 2 auf einem feinen, weichen und matten Material umreißt, und so die Reihenfolge vermittelt, in der die Produkte benutzt werden sollen.

SK:LK-BODY CARE est une gamme de produits de soin pour le corps incluant gel douche, shampooing et traitement capillaire. Pour transmettre la pureté et la douceur des produits, le design a été totalement épuré et se limite à un simple dessin ondulé qui trace les chiffres 0, 1 et 2 sur une surface matte et raffinée, indiquant ainsi l'ordre dans lequel utiliser les soins.

To ensure the best quality and aroma for its soaps, **24 SOLAR GARDEN** carefully chooses its plants and harvests them in the proper season. The company adds pure essential oils to their handmade soaps to help promote these sometimes overlooked ingredients, which are also highlighted with the 24 hand-painted plants that adorn the packaging. This further enhances their signature promise of only collecting the freshest and most seasonal plants for their essential oils.

Um die beste Qualität und einzigartiges Aroma für seine Seifen zu gewährleisten, wählt **24 SOLAR GARDEN** seine Pflanzen sorgfältig aus und erntet sie in der richtigen Saison. Das Unternehmen fügt ätherische Öle zu seinen handgefertigten Seifen hinzu, um die mitunter unterschätzten Zutaten hervorzuheben, die zusätzlich auf den 24 Zeichnungen von Pflanzen, aus denen die ätherischen Öle gewonnen werden, auf der Verpackung zu sehen sind. Das unterstreicht zudem ihr Markenversprechen, die frischesten Pflanzen der Saison für ihre ätherischen Öle auszusuchen.

Pour garantir une qualité optimale et préserver tout l'arôme de ses savons, **24 SOLAR GARDEN** choisit avec soin les plantes utilisées et les récolte à la bonne saison. L'entreprise ajoute des huiles essentielles pures à ses savons artisanaux pour promouvoir des ingrédients parfois oubliés : ces derniers sont aussi représentés dans les 24 plantes peintes à la main qui décorent le packaging. Cette approche ne fait que renforcer sa promesse de ne collecter que les plantes les plus fraîches et de saison pour élaborer ses huiles essentielles.

24 SOLAR GARDEN

Creative Direction: Lu Jun
Design: Lu Jun, Yang Yu Ping, Wang Xiao Qin
Illustration: Pan Feng, Zhang Li, Liu Jun Jie, He Jin Chao
Client: Shilin Xindian Agriculture Department
Company: Yunnan Minzu University
Country: China
Category: Body care
GOLD PENTAWARD 2019

BEAUTY CLASSIC

Executive Creative Direction: Somchana Kangwarnjit
Design: SKJ, Pongpipat Jetsadalak,
Thiyada Akarasinakul, Pantipa Pummuang
Company: Prompt Design
Country: Thailand
Category: Body care

SILVER PENTAWARD 2019

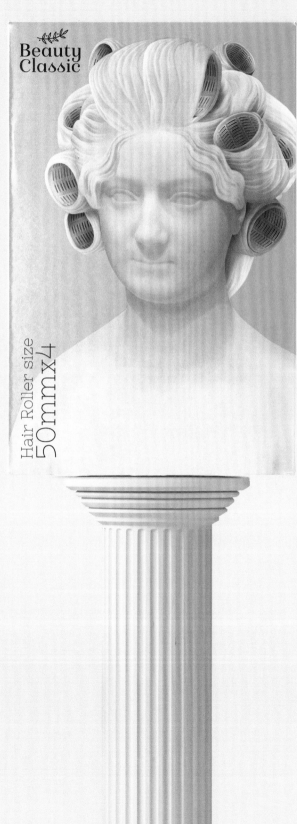

SOAPSMITH

Print Consulting: David Benjamin
Company: Bulletproof
Country: UK
Category: Body care
BRONZE PENTAWARD 2020

DERMICA

Client Services: Iona MacDonald,
Seb Darke, Sophie Hussein
Company: Goods
Country: Norway
Category: Body care
BRONZE PENTAWARD 2020

SHISEIDO PROFESSIONAL

Creative Direction: Aoshi Kudo
Colouring Direction: Keiko Hirano
Design: Midori Matsuishi, Ryosuke Kuga
Company: Communication Design Laboratory
Country: Japan
Category: Body care

SILVER PENTAWARD 2020

EQURE

Creative Direction: Valeria Repina
Art Direction: Alexandra Loginevskaya
Brand Strategy: Roman Pustovoit
Design: Polina Zagumenova
Company: Repina Branding
Country: Russian Federation
Category: Body care
BRONZE PENTAWARD 2019

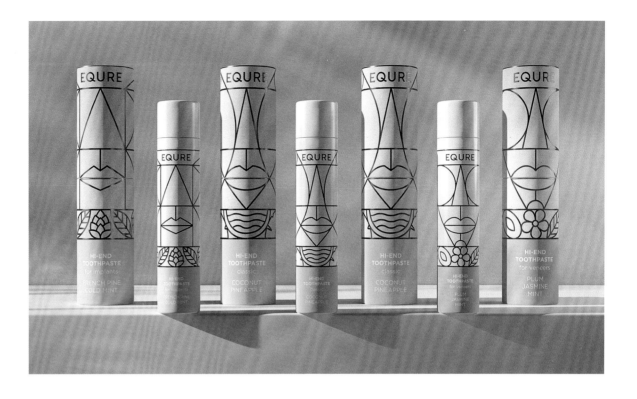

DENTISTE

Design: Karim Rashid
Company: Karim Rashid
Country: USA
Category: Body care
BRONZE PENTAWARD 2020

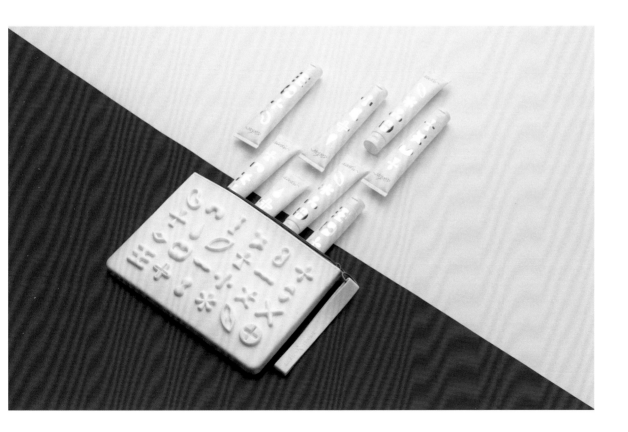

SKINHEAD

Art Direction: Alexander Frelikh
Company: DDC.Lab
Country: Russian Federation
Category: Body care

SILVER PENTAWARD 2019

UBIETY

Design and Design Direction: Phil Skinner
Creative Direction: Jamie Ellul
Illustration: Rebecca Sutherland
Photography: Red Forge Studios
Web Development: We are Duet
Company: Supple Studio
Country: UK
Category: Body care

BRONZE PENTAWARD 2019

COLOUR ZONE

Creative Direction: Guozheng Jiang, Dan Chen
Graphic Design: Sijie Pei, Ke Zheng
Industrial Design: Zilei Jiao, Xinnan Zhang, Lei Tang
Company: Shanghai Nianxiang
Brand Design & Consulting
Country: China
Category: Beauty

GOLD PENTAWARD 2019

The design for the make-up brand **Colour Zone** is built around the keywords contained in the brand's name. Using "zones of colour", the designer creates an exciting out-of-this-world look across the range of products. Shaped like a UFO, the products possess a futuristic colour gradient to highlight the wide range of unique colours available. Colour Zone reveals a parallel universe of make-up, offering endless possibilities for consumers to express themselves.

Das Design der Make-up-Marke **Colour Zone** basiert auf den im Markennamen enthaltenen Schlüsselwörtern. Mithilfe von „Farbzonen" hat der Designer eine aufregende Produktlinie geschaffen, die nicht von dieser Welt scheint. In Form von Ufos, zeigen die Produkte einen futuristischen Farbverlauf, um die einzigartige Vielfalt der erhältlichen Nuancen des Produkts hervorzuheben. Colour Zone offenbart damit ein Paralleluniversum des Make-ups, das den Konsumenten unendlichen Möglichkeiten bietet, sich selbst auszudrücken.

Le design pour la marque de cosmétique **Colour Zone** se base sur les mots clés formant son nom. À l'aide de « zones de couleur », le designer a créé un intéressant look hors du commun pour toute la gamme de produits. Rappelant un OVNI, le produit affiche un dégradé futuriste pour souligner le large éventail de couleurs uniques disponibles. Colour Zone dévoile ainsi un univers parallèle de maquillage aux possibilités infinies pour que les consommateurs y trouvent un mode d'expression.

BELEI

Executive Direction: Daniele Monti
Creative Direction: Jen Polaski, Carole Hurst
Design: Nicole Harter, Jenna Beck
Copywriting: Sarah Bergey
Brand Management: Lauren Kang
Production Lead: Kyle Fuson
Artwork Management: Michael Dwyer
Company: Amazon – Consumables Private Brands
Country: USA
Category: Beauty

GOLD PENTAWARD 2019

Pola Apex is a skincare brand which uses AI and big data to inform the latest skin analysis technology. It offers a personalised skin care solution for each individual, alongside its unparalleled design. Rather than a uniform package design, as is the norm, this skincare range offers packages featuring unique designs for each customer based on their skin type, created out of 8,620,000 pattern possibilities. The specialised printing technology creates label graphics that change with each printing, offering truly one-of-a-kind packaging.

Pola Apex ist eine Hautpflegemarke, die KI und Big Data nutzt, um die neuste Hautanalyse-Technologie zu präsentieren. Neben ihrem unvergleichbaren Design bietet sie eine personalisierte Hautpflegelösung. Statt des üblichen einheitlichen Verpackungsdesigns, liefert diese Pflegeserie eine einzigartige Gestaltung für jeden Kunden, basierend auf dessen Hauttyp, die aus 8 620 000 verschiedenen möglichen Mustern ausgewählt wurden. Die spezialisierte Drucktechnologie kreiert eine Etikettengrafik, die sich in jedem Druck verändert und so eine wirklich persönliche Verpackung schafft.

La marque de soins pour le visage **Pola Apex** a recours à l'IA et au big data pour offrir la technologie la plus avancée d'analyse de la peau. Elle propose un soin dermatologique personnalisé en plus d'un design hors pair. Plutôt que de parier sur les habituels emballages uniformes, cette gamme de soins présente pour chaque client un design unique en fonction de son type de peau parmi les 8 620 000 modèles possibles. Une technologie d'impression spéciale crée à chaque fois un graphisme différent, ce qui donne un packaging véritablement unique.

POLA APEX

Creative Direction: Chiharu Suzuki
Art Direction: Yushi Watanabe
Design: Kei Ikehata, Mai Karin Kamiyama
Company: POLA
Country: Japan
Category: Beauty
GOLD PENTAWARD 2020

SECRETOS DEL AGUA

Creative Direction: Eva Guadalupe
Design: Ana Mallent
Illustration: Fidel Cordón
Strategic Planning: Fede Reyna
Printing: Gráficas Royanes
Company: Meteorito Estudio
Country: Spain
Category: Beauty

BRONZE PENTAWARD 2019

INDARE

Team Lead: Chinglang Chen
Design: Fengming Chen, Yujie Chen, Jiarong Zeng,
Junlong Yang, Yanhui Yan, Linhan Peng,
Shuzhuan Huang
Company: inDare Design Strategy Limited
Country: China
Category: Beauty

SILVER PENTAWARD 2019

CHIOTURE

Creative Direction: Guozheng Jiang, Dan Chen
Strategy Consulting Direction: Yang Shu
Product Design: Xinnan Zhang, Zilei Jiao
Account Executive: Jin Li
Company: Shanghai Nianxiang Brand Design & Consulting
Country: China
Category: Beauty

SILVER PENTAWARD 2020

VYVYD STUDIO

Executive Creative Direction: Sam O'Donahue
Creative Direction: Lorena Seminario
3D Creative Direction: Peter Ash
3D Design: William Alusitz
Graphic Design: Andrea Kim, Cat Lee,
Hana Yoo, Hector Sos
Videography: Fabian Ohrn
Photography: Takahiro Igarashi
Company: Established
Country: USA
Category: Beauty

BRONZE PENTAWARD 2020

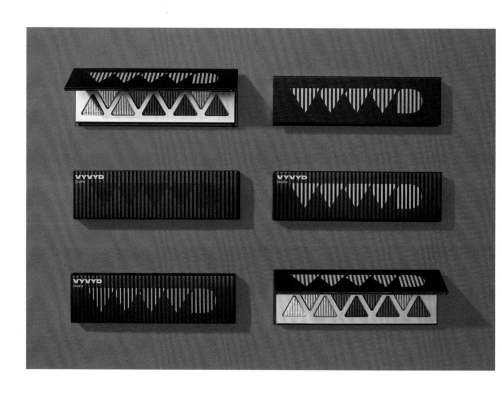

EN

Creative Direction: Yuji Tokuda
Design Direction: Mariko Yamasaki
Design: Makoto Takeda
Production: Takanori Amano
Photo Production (product): Shinya Omi,
Sumire Iwamoto
Product Photography: Takaya Sakano
Interior Photography: David Foessel
Retouching: Masahiko Furuta, Masaru Okuyama
Illustration: Haruko Hirano
Architecture: Archiee
Company: canaria inc.
Country: Japan
Category: Beauty

SILVER PENTAWARD 2019

ATHÉ

Executive Creative Direction: Sam O'Donahue
3D Creative Direction: Peter Ash
Graphic Design: Andrea Kim, Cat Lee, Hana Yoo
Company: Established
Country: USA
Category: Beauty
SILVER PENTAWARD 2020

SO YOUNG LIFE

Chief Design: Qi Yuan
Design: Leo Lee
Assistance: Song Xing Kai
3D Max: Tan Zeng Quan
Company: Leadshow (China) Brand Consulting
Country: China
Category: Beauty

BRONZE PENTAWARD 2020

SK:LK

Client: Beijing Youji Technology Development
Creative Direction: Tengxian Zou
Design: Tengxian Zou, Qi Tong, Yunfan Chen, Yi Song
Render Division: Wenfang Ye
Company: Shanghai Version Design Group
Country: China
Category: Beauty

BRONZE PENTAWARD 2019

REVLY

Executive Direction: Daniele Monti
Creative Direction: Toki Wolf, Carole Hurst
Design: Caitlin Field
Copywriting: Sarah Bergey, Dena Taylor
Brand Management: Lauren Kang
Production Lead: Kyle Fuson
Artwork Management: Jamie Hinderer
Company: Amazon – Consumables Private Brands
Country: USA
Category: Distributors'/retailers' own brands/
private labels

BRONZE PENTAWARD 2019

KICKS BEAUTY
SELF TAN

Creative Direction: Marie Wollbeck
Design Direction: Katrin Gullström
Design: Lovisa Ljungquist
Client Direction: Monika Varvne Uebel
Account Direction: Christine Schönborg
Company: BAS ID
Country: Sweden
Category: Distributors'/retailers' own brands/
private labels

SILVER PENTAWARD 2019

BLBM

Creative Direction: Zhihua He, Tengxian Zou
Design: Zhihua He, Vicky Tong, Suping Wu
3D Design: Wenfang Ye
Company: Shanghai Version Design Group
Country: China
Category: Distributors'/retailers' own brands/
private labels

BRONZE PENTAWARD 2020

LIFE

Design: Hagit Elias Adi, Amnon Rahav
Creative Direction: Ayelet Sadé
Company: Sadowsky Berlin
Country: Israel
Category: Distributors'/retailers' own brands/
private labels

BRONZE PENTAWARD 2020

THE TROUPE

Design: Lavernia & Cienfuegos team
Company: Lavernia & Cienfuegos
Country: Spain
Category: Packaging concept (professional)

GOLD PENTAWARD 2020

CODE OO-DESIGNED FOR POST-OOS

Client: Symrise
Design: Yang Ming Jie
Company: Yang Design
Country: China
Category: Packaging concept (professional)

GOLD PENTAWARD 2019

Code 00 believes that the post-2000 generation has a unique and more independent knowledge of skincare products. To attract this target group, their product design concept uses science fiction films as its inspiration. The solid metal of the packaging turns into the liquid metal droplets of the product, whilst the logo highlights the "00", like a pair of curious eyes or the infinity symbol. The ingenious container perfectly suits this dual-purpose moisturising lip and cheek ointment, which is an innovation in itself.

Code 00 glaubt, dass die Post-2000-Generation ein einzigartiges und unabhängigeres Wissen über Hautpflegeprodukte hat. Um diese Zielgruppe anzusprechen, nutzt ihr Verpackungsdesignkonzept Science-Fiction-Filme als Inspirationsquelle. Der Verpackung verwandelt sich in flüssige Metalltropfen, während das Logo die „00" wie ein Paar Augen oder als das Unendlichkeitssymbol in Szene setzt. Dieser Behälter passt perfekt zu der zweifach verwendbaren feuchtigkeitsspendenden Lippen- und Wangenpflege, die an sich schon eine Innovation darstellt.

Code 00 croit que la génération Z possède des connaissances plus personnelles et indépendantes des produits cosmétiques. Pour attirer cette cible, le design des produits s'inspire des films de science-fiction. Avec une surface métallisée, le packaging figure les gouttelettes de métal liquide du produit, alors que le logo, « 00 », s'affiche tel une paire d'yeux curieux ou le symbole de l'infini. L'ingénieux emballage va comme un gant à cette crème hydratante pour lèvres et pommettes, déjà toute une innovation en soi.

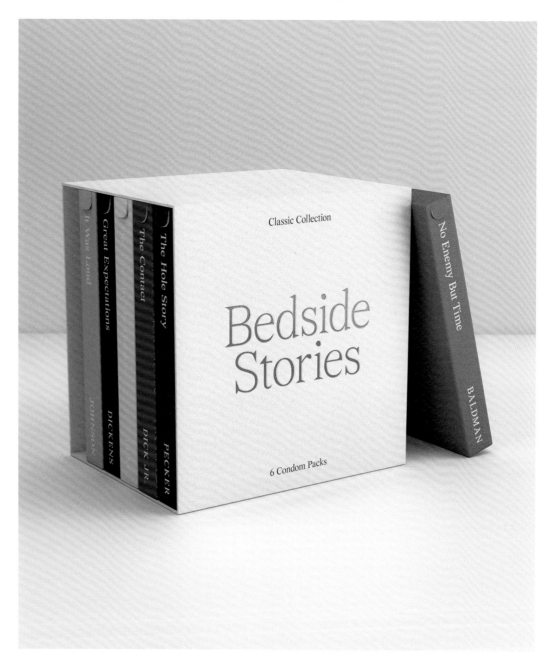

BEDSIDE STORIES

CG Artwork: Yuriy Smirnov
Senior Art Direction: Kirill Yermoshin
Art Direction: Margarita Indionkova
Copywriting: Vitalina Tonenkova
Illustration: Daria Kirei
Creative Direction: Paramon Parfenov
Company: DADA Agency
Country: Russian Federation
Category: Packaging concept (professional)

SILVER PENTAWARD 2019

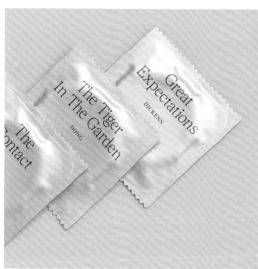

Bedside Stories aim to make choosing safe sex easier by removing the awkward necessity and creating an object which people can proudly keep on their nightstands. The packaging resembles a collection of books, with each condom wrapper taking its name from literary classics. No longer do you have to come up with a euphemism for condoms or shyly enquire at the counter, just ask for a volume of Dickens at the local chemist. And forget having to rummage in your drawer to search for condoms, they stand confidently next to the bed, as suitable for display as any book.

Bedside Stories haben es sich zur Aufgabe gemacht, die Entscheidung zu sicherem Sex einfacher zu machen, indem die peinliche Notwendigkeit verschwindet und ein Objekt kreiert wurde, dass die Leute stolz auf ihren Nachttisch stellen können. Die Verpackung ähnelt einer Buchkollektion, in der jede Kondomverpackung den Namen eines Klassikers trägt. Man muss sich nicht länger beschönigende Umschreibungen für Kondome ausdenken oder schüchtern an der Kasse danach fragen, jetzt kann man einfach um eine Dickens-Ausgabe in der örtlichen Apotheke bitten. Außerdem fällt das Durchwühlen der Schublade auf der Suche nach Kondomen weg. Sie können jetzt selbstbewusst neben dem Bett aufbewahrt werden, so wie jedes andere Buch.

L'objectif de **Bedside Stories** est de permettre une pratique sexuelle sûre en éliminant l'aspect embarrassant et en offrant un objet que l'on peut fièrement garder sur la table de nuit. Le packaging ressemble à une collection de livres, chaque emballage de préservatif tirant son nom d'un classique de la littérature. Plus besoin de recourir à un euphémisme pour parler de préservatifs ou de les mentionner avec gêne, il suffit de demander une œuvre de Dickens à la pharmacie. Et fini de fouiller dans vos tiroirs, vos préservatifs sont maintenant bien en vue à côté du lit, où ils ont autant leur place qu'un ouvrage.

GOODBABY®

Supervision: Cao Xue (Guangzhou Academy of Fine Arts),
Wang Liang (China Resources Sanjiu)
Art Direction: Duan Hongli (China Resources Sanjiu),
Chen Jiayi (JiaYi (Guangzhou) Design)
Project Management: Xu Mengzhen (China Resources Sanjiu)
Graphic Design: He Ge (JiaYi (Guangzhou) Design)
Consumer Analysis: Man Lan (China Resources Sanjiu)
Market Analysis: Lin Huangtao
(Guangzhou Academy of Fine Arts)
Company: China Resources Sanjiu Medical & Pharmaceutical
Country: China
Category: Packaging concept (professional)

BRONZE PENTAWARD 2020

SIMPLY COSMETIC

Design: Vishal Vora
3D Visualisation: Rmadhun
Company: Sol Benito
Country: India
Category: Packaging concept (professional)

BRONZE PENTAWARD 2019

OXO

Associate Creative Direction: Chantal Roberti
Company: SGK Anthem – Amsterdam
Country: Netherlands
Category: Packaging concept (professional)

BRONZE PENTAWARD 2020

999®

Supervision: Ding Xiong (Guangzhou Academy of Fine Arts),
Duan Hongli (China Resources Sanjiu)
Creative Direction: Liu Shan
(Guangzhou Academy of Fine Arts)
Project Management: Xu Mengzhen (China Resources Sanjiu)
Design: Ran Min (Guangzhou Academy of Fine Arts),
Zhou Wenjie (Guangzhou Academy of Fine Arts)
Company: China Resources Sanjiu Medical & Pharmaceutical
Country: China
Category: Packaging concept (professional)

BRONZE PENTAWARD 2020

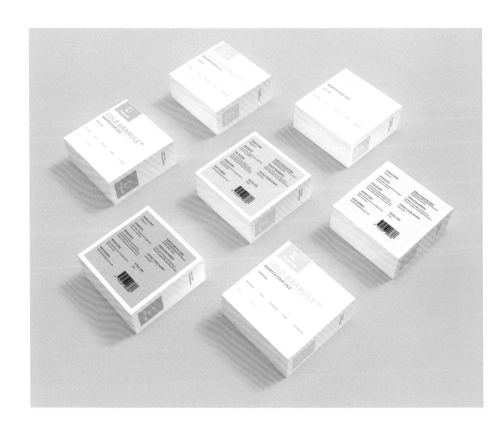

SO MUSH SUPPLEMENT

Executive Creative Direction: Somchana Kangwarnjit
Design: Rutthawitch Akkachairin, SKJ
Photography: Thiyada Akarasinakul,
Pantipa Pummuang, Somporn Thimkhao
Company: Prompt Design
Country: Thailand
Category: Packaging concept (professional)

SILVER PENTAWARD 2020

OOOPS! USE

Project Owner: Áron Kollmann
Team Lead: Szilveszter Buzási
Senior Account Management: Tímea Ungvári
Junior Account Management: Petra Budai
Copywriting: Anna Henzler
Graphic Design: Anita Fiertelmeister, Attila Orosz
3D Design: Tibor Varga
Company: 2Republic BTL Reklámügynökség Kft.
Country: Hungary
Category: Packaging concept (professional)
BRONZE PENTAWARD 2019

CUBESSENCE

Creative Direction: Haozhen Luo
Company: Beijing Heziguai Creative Design
Country: China
Category: Packaging concept (professional)

SILVER PENTAWARD 2019

AKIO

Design: Robert Dadashev
3D Visualisation: Pavel Gubin, Aleksey Koler
Copywriting: Alex Kalyan
Art Direction: Katya Mushkina, Robert Dadashev
Tutoring: Leonid Slavin, Yevgeny Razumov
School: British Higher School of Art and Design
Country: Russian Federation
Category: Packaging concept (student)
NXT-GEN PENTAWARDS 2020

More than anything, children love to play. **Akio** is a range of Japanese-style soap packaging that turns bathing into an amusing and interactive game. Thanks to the fun and graphic look of the containers, parents can distract a fussy child and keep them busy while they are getting clean. The removable kimono will surprise a toddler, grab their attention and help make bath time more fun and enjoyable.

Mehr als alles andere lieben Kinder das Spielen. **Akio** ist eine Reihe von Seifenverpackungen in Form von japanischen Figuren, die das Baden zu einem amüsanten und interaktiven Spiel machen. Dank des lustigen und grafischen Aussehens der Behälter können die Eltern ihr wählerisches Kind ablenken und beschäftigen, während sie es waschen. Der abnehmbare Kimono überrascht Kleinkinder, erregt ihre Aufmerksamkeit und hilft, die Badezeit lustiger und angenehmer zu gestalten.

Les enfants aiment jouer plus que tout autre chose. **Akio** est une marque de savons dont le packaging aux allures japonaises transforme la toilette en un divertissement interactif. Grâce à son look graphique amusant, les flacons permettent aux parents de distraire un enfant agité et de l'occuper pendant sa toilette. Le kimono amovible crée la surprise chez le bambin, retient son attention et fait de l'heure du bain un moment plus plaisant.

ART&FICT

Design: Evgeniia Zhuravleva
Tutoring: Leonid Slavin
Teaching: Yevgeny Razumov
3D Rendering: Dmitriy Saveliev
School: British Higher School of Art and Design
Country: Russian Federation
Category: Packaging concept (student)

GOLD PENTAWARD 2019

There are two approaches that form the basis for the **Art & Fict** cotton bud creative. Many people clean their ears with cotton buds but don't realise that you can very easily damage your eardrums. The first approach is to illustrate this, using the colourful cotton swabs to create an image of Van Gogh's self-portrait with a bandaged ear. The second idea revolves around cotton swabs being used to apply makeup. In this case, the coloured swabs combine to form the image of Marilyn Monroe in the style of pop art.

Zwei Ideen stecken hinter der Wattestäbchen-Kreation von **Art & Fict**. Die Erste basiert auf dem Fakt, dass viele Menschen ihre Ohren mit Wattestäbchen reinigen, aber nicht wissen, dass sie ihr Trommelfell dabei leicht beschädigen können. Van Goghs Selbstporträt mit verbundenem Ohr, zusammengestellt aus den gefärbten Spitzen der Stäbchen, steht dafür symbolisch ein. Die zweite Idee dreht sich um das Wattestäbchen, das zum Schminken zweckentfremdet wird. In diesem Fall bilden die Stäbchen ein Bild von Marilyn Monroe im Pop-Art-Stil.

Le design pour les cotons-tiges **Art & Fict** obéit à deux approches. Nombre de personnes se nettoient les oreilles à l'aide de bâtonnets ouatés sans être conscientes des risques pour leurs tympans. La première approche consiste à faire passer ce message en reproduisant à l'aide de cotons-tiges de couleur l'autoportrait de Van Gogh à l'oreille pansée. La seconde idée porte sur l'utilisation des bâtonnets pour le maquillage. Dans ce cas, la composition des cotons-tiges colorés forme l'image pop art de Marilyn Monroe.

WARM UP

Design: Alexander Shibaev
School: British Higher School of Art and Design
Country: Russian Federation
Category: Packaging concept (student)

SILVER PENTAWARD 2019

**BARNEYS NEW YORK
MEN'S SKINCARE**

Design: Hyek Im
Professor: Gerardo Herrera
School: ArtCenter College of Design
Country: USA
Category: Packaging concept (student)
BRONZE PENTAWARD 2019

HAHA DENTAL POSITIVE PASTE

3D Visualisation: Pavel Gubin
Tutoring: Leonid Slavin, Yevgeny Razumov
School: British Higher School of Art and Design
Country: Russian Federation
Category: Packaging concept (student)

BRONZE PENTAWARD 2019

NKDSKN SELF TANNING

Design, Art Direction and Hand Modelling:
Zach Ludlow
Photography: Zach Ludlow, James Chou
Instruction: Ania Borysiewicz
Advisor: Gerardo Herrera
School: ArtCenter College of Design
Country: USA
Category: Packaging concept (student)

SILVER PENTAWARD 2020

WHIRLPOOL HIGH-END NOURISHING MILK SET

Design: Tian-yi Zhang
Tutoring: Fang Jun
School: Shanghai Institute of Visual Arts (SIVA)
Country: China
Category: Packaging concept (student)

BRONZE PENTAWARD 2020

L'OREAL

Creative Direction and Design: Laura Homs,
Miquel Nadal, Venecia Palacios
School: Elisava, Barcelona School of
Design and Engineering
Country: Spain
Category: Packaging concept (student)

SILVER PENTAWARD 2020

COVËR

Design: Mayya Mikhaleva
3D Visualisation: Pavel Gubin
Copywriting: Vladimir Gumenyuk
Tutoring: Leonid Slavin, Yevgeny Razumov
School: British Higher School of Art and Design
Country: Russian Federation
Category: Packaging concept (student)

BRONZE PENTAWARD 2019

BAND-AID PACKAGING

Design: Lu Qin
Instruction: Professor Kong De Yang
School: Taihu University of Wuxi
Country: China
Category: Packaging concept (student)

BRONZE PENTAWARD 2020

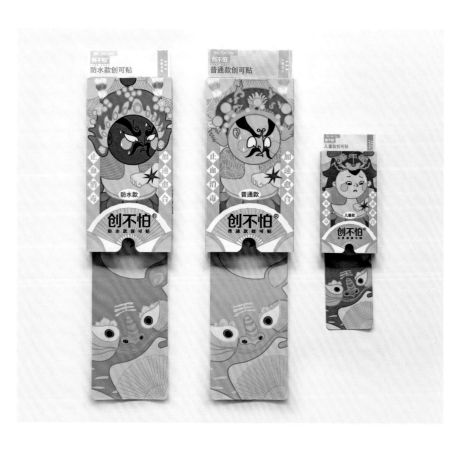

THE BLACK MARKET

Creative Direction and Design: Marina Orvañanos
School: Elisava, Barcelona School of
Design and Engineering
Country: Spain
Category: Packaging concept (student)

SILVER PENTAWARD 2019

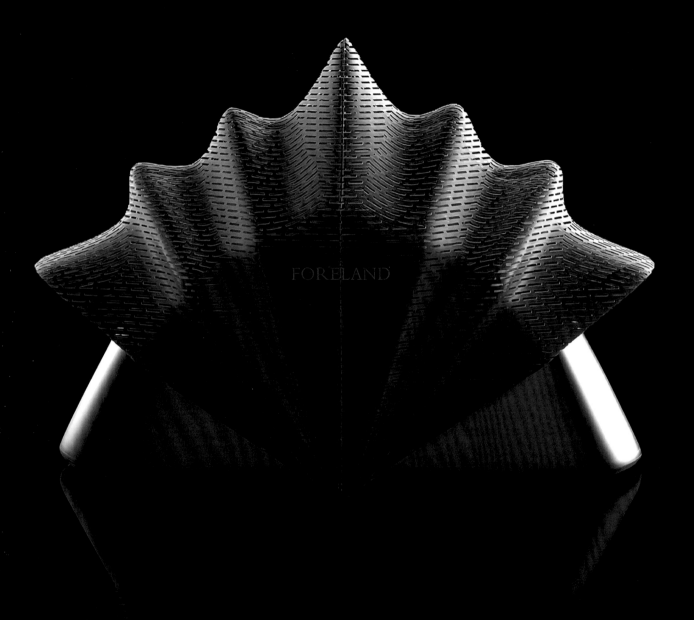

Best of the category

Perfumes

Make-up, body care, beauty products

Spirits

luxury

Fine wines, champagne

Casks & cases

Gourmet food

Limited editions, limited series, event creations

Distributors'/retailers' own brands/private labels

Packaging concept

ENDLESS POSSIBILITIES AND UNIQUE CHARM

Materials and craftsmanship are believed to be the cornerstones of packaging and packaging design for any product. Selecting both is where **creativity thrives** for a brand. **Baixinglong**, an expert in creative packaging design, does not stop at bringing your creativity to life; it makes your brand stick out from the rest as well.

Built on the **philosophy of harmony with nature**, Baixinglong opens up your brand to endless design possibilities and brings out the aesthetic qualities that ingeniously inject craftsmanship into materials.

When consumers shop for a product, they judge its look and quality both in a visual and tactile manner. It is the properties and visual language of materials that **produce varied visual effects and evoke different aesthetic emotions**. Baixinglong knows how to ignite amazing creativity around your products and brands, and how to flexibly deliver exquisite artisanry of great visual and tactile depth to magnetize consumers into action.

How consumers feel about a material is usually conditional upon a spectrum of elements of the material itself, including texture, grain, gloss and tactile feel. With its superb design and craftsmanship, Baixinglong excels at making the surface of the material even more highlighted and eye-catching by **amplifying the inherent properties of the material it chooses**, e.g., giving smooth surfaces a sleek feel, adding a primitive touch to a rough texture or leaving soft materials with a skin-like finish. This close association between the inherent properties and elevated ones of the material makes amazing packaging solutions. Baixinglong spoils you with a world of material and aesthetic choices to highlight your brands in a more diverse and flexible way.

UNENDLICHE MÖGLICHKEITEN UND EINZIGARTIGER CHARME

Materialien und Handwerkskunst gelten als die Pfeiler von Verpackung und Verpackungsdesign jedes Produkts. Bei der Auswahl von beidem gedeiht die **Kreativität** der Marke. **Baixinglong**, ein Experte für kreatives Verpackungsdesign, beschränkt sich nicht darauf, Ihre Kreativität zum Leben zu erwecken; Ihre Marke hebt sich dadurch auch vom Rest ab.

Aufgebaut auf der **Philosophie der Harmonie mit der Natur**, öffnet Baixinglong Ihre Marke für endlose Designmöglichkeiten und bringt die ästhetischen Qualitäten zum Vorschein, die auf raffinierte Art und Weise die Handwerkskunst in Materialien einbringt.

Wenn Konsumenten ein Produkt kaufen, beurteilen sie dessen Aussehen und seine Qualität sowohl visuell als auch haptisch. Es sind die Eigenschaften und die visuelle Sprache der Materialien, die **vielfältige visuelle Effekte erzeugen und unterschiedliche ästhetische Emotionen hervorrufen**. Baixinglong weiß, wie man unglaubliche Kreativität rund um Ihre Produkte und Marken herum entfacht und wie man flexibel exquisite Handwerkskunst von großer visueller und haptischer Tiefe flexibel einsetzt, um die Kunden in Aktion zu versetzen.

Wie Konsumenten über ein Material denken, hängt in der Regel mit einer Vielzahl an Elementen des Materials zusammen, wie Textur, Struktur, Glanz und Haptik. Mit seinem herausragenden Design und der Handwerkskunst tut sich Baixinglong damit hervor, die Oberfläche der Materialien noch mehr zu unterstreichen und zu einem Blickfang zu machen, indem es die **inhärenten Eigenschaften der Materialien verstärkt** und zum Beispiel die Entscheidung trifft, glatten Oberflächen ein geschmeidiges Gefühl zu verleihen, einer rauen Textur einen primitiven Zug zu verleihen oder weiche Materialien mit einer hautähnlichen Oberfläche zu versehen. Die enge Verbundenheit zwischen den inhärenten und den hervorgehobenen Eigenschaften des Materials sorgen für hervorragende Verpackungslösungen. Baixinglong verwöhnt Sie mit einer Welt der materiellen und ästhetischen Wahlmöglichkeiten, um Ihre Marken auf vielfältigere und flexiblere Art und Weise hervorzuheben.

DES POSSIBILITÉS INFINIES ET UN CHARME UNIQUE

On dit que matériaux et savoir-faire sont les pierres angulaires de l'emballage et du design de packaging d'un produit. Lorsqu'une marque opte pour les deux, **la créativité s'épanouit**. Experte en design de packaging créatif, l'agence **Baixinglong** ne se limite pas à donner vie à votre créativité : elle différencie votre marque de la concurrence.

S'appuyant sur la **philosophie de l'harmonie avec la nature**, Baixinglong ouvre pour votre marque un champ infini de possibilités et met en valeur les qualités esthétiques qui insufflent subtilement le savoir-faire dans les matériaux.

Quand les consommateurs achètent un produit, ils en jugent l'apparence et la qualité par la vue et le toucher. Les propriétés et le langage visuel des matériaux **provoquent divers effets visuels et suscitent différentes émotions esthétiques**. Baixinglong sait comment être des plus créatives au sujet des produits et des marques, et comment offrir un artisanat exquis d'une grande profondeur visuelle et tactile pour captiver les consommateurs.

Ce que ressentent les consommateurs relève d'une palette de caractéristiques de la matière elle-même, notamment sa texture, son grain, sa brillance et son toucher. Grâce à ses superbes conceptions et son savoir-faire, Baixinglong excelle à rendre une surface plus attrayante en **accentuant les propriétés intrinsèques du matériau** ; par exemple, en donnant aux surfaces lisses un aspect soyeux, en ajoutant une touche primitive à une texture rugueuse ou en dotant des matériaux souples d'une finition semblable à la peau. Cette relation étroite entre les caractéristiques inhérentes et celles rehaussées du matériau donne lieu à d'extraordinaires solutions de packaging. Baixinglong vous gâte avec un éventail de choix esthétiques et de matériaux pour mettre vos marques en valeur de manière fluide et variée.

BXL CREATIVE PACKAING

Perfeccionista is a single-estate limited-production wine, created using "thoughtful viticulture", a considerate and experienced method of winemaking. In order to connect emotionally with the consumer and position the product as a distinctive premium wine, packaging was developed that attaches value to the idea of imperfection, making each piece unique. For each of the 697 exclusive units produced, the wooden tags were broken by hand and individually ink-stamped.

Perfeccionista ist ein Wein aus einer limitierten Produktion, der durch „rücksichtsvollen Weinanbau" entstanden ist. Um eine emotionale Bindung mit dem Konsumenten einzugehen und um das Produkt als herausstechenden Premiumwein zu positionieren, wurde eine Verpackung entwickelt, die einen hohen Wert mit der Idee der Unvollkommenheit verbindet und so jedes Stück einzigartig macht. Für jede der 697 exklusiven Flaschen wurden die Holzschilder von Hand gebrochen und individuell mit Stempeln versehen.

Perfeccionista est un vin qu'un seul domaine viticole produit en quantité limitée par le biais d'une « viticulture consciencieuse », selon une méthode de vinification respectueuse et éprouvée. Afin de nouer un lien émotionnel avec le consommateur et de positionner le produit comme un vin haut de gamme, le packaging conçu donne de la valeur à l'idée d'imperfection, ce qui rend chaque pièce unique. Pour chacune des 697 unités exclusives produites, l'étiquette en bois a été cassée à la main et estampillée individuellement à l'encre.

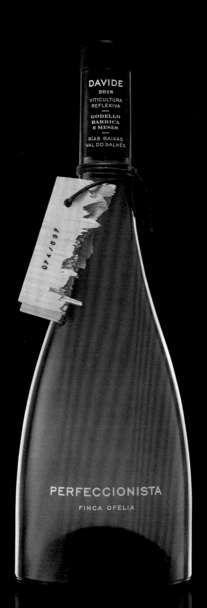

PERFECCIONISTA

Creative Direction: Roberto Núñez
Client: Bodega Davide
Printing: Avenadecor IPE
Copywriting: Roberto Núñez
Photography: Treviño
Assisting: Ángel Tello
Company: Roberto Núñez
Country: Spain
Category: Fine wines, champagne

PLATINUM PENTAWARD 2019

HENNESSY

Creative Direction: Julien Zylbermann, Marc Savary
Client: Hennessy V.S.
Artwork: Felipe Pantone
Company: Felipe Pantone – Appartement 103
Country: France
Category: Limited editions, limited series, event creations

PLATINUM PENTAWARD 2020

Released globally at a limited quantity of 70 pieces, this Collector's Edition from **Hennessy** was created in partnership with the world-renowned and pioneering street artist Felipe Pantone. The result of this collaboration is a super clean, shiny white PET box that once opened reveals the whole world of Felipe Pantone through a prism of graphical elements and textures. At the centre of the experience, the consumer is invited to build their own art sculpture around a customized Hennessy V.S bottle which is printed with the latest cutting-edge digital technologies in CMYK. The exclusive carafe stands on a pedestal in the centre of a grid of moiré-finished rods that consumers themselves can place, move and interchange to alter the bottle's optics.

Diese Collector's Edition von **Hennessy** wurde mit einer weltweit limitierten Stückzahl von 70 Flaschen in Partnerschaft mit dem Straßenkünstler Felipe Pantone entworfen. Das Ergebnis dieser Zusammenarbeit war eine glänzend weiße PET-Box, die nach dem Öffnen die Welt von Felipe Pantone durch ein Prisma von grafischen Elementen und Texturen offenbart. Im Zentrum des Erlebnisses steht der Verbraucher, der eingeladen ist, seine eigene Kunstskulptur um die Hennessy V.S-Flasche zu bauen, die mit den neuesten digitalen Technologien in CMYK gedruckt wurde. Die exklusive Karaffe steht auf einem Sockel in der Mitte eines Gitters aus Stäben mit Moiré-Muster, die der Kunde selbst positionieren, bewegen und verändern kann, um die Optik der Flasche zu verändern.

Avec un lancement mondial limité à 70 unités, cette édition Collector de **Hennessy** a été créée en collaboration avec Felipe Pantone, artiste de rue innovateur et de notoriété mondiale. Le fruit de ce travail est une boîte PET d'un blanc immaculé qui, une fois ouverte, révèle tout l'univers de Felipe Pantone à travers un prisme d'éléments graphiques et de textures. Au cours de l'expérience, le consommateur est invité à construire sa propre sculpture artistique autour d'une bouteille Hennessy V.S personnalisée et imprimée en quadrichromie à l'aide de technologies numériques de pointe. La carafe de luxe repose sur un piédestal au centre d'une grille de tiges moirées que le consommateur peut insérer, déplacer et permuter pour changer le visuel de la bouteille.

The bottles for **Yohji Yamamoto Parfums** are clear bullet-shaped containers wrapped with black rings that on closer inspection form his name, Yohji. On the backside of these letters, visible only by peering through the liquid, are phrases associated with each individual fragrance. Mode Zero, for example, reads "Be yourself. You're okay". When it came to packaging, Yamamoto is famous for his love of black, so the team went for a classic approach and opted for an all-black box, unadorned except for an embossed brand logo.

Die Flakons für **Yohji Yamamoto Parfums** sind durchsichtige Behälter in Form von Patronenhülsen mit Streifen aus schwarzem Klebeband, die bei genauem Hinsehen den Namen Yohji bilden. Auf der Rückseite dieser Buchstaben sind Sätze versteckt, die nur sichtbar sind, wenn man durch die Flüssigkeit hindurchsieht. Diese Sätze stehen in Verbindung mit jedem individuellen Duft. Mode Zero zum Beispiel enthält die Worte "Be yourself. You're okay". Wenn es um Verpackung geht, ist Yamamoto für seine Liebe zu Schwarz bekannt, weswegen sich das Team für einen klassischen Ansatz und eine schwarze Schachtel entschied, die bis auf das eingeprägte Marken-logo schmucklos ist.

Le bouteilles pour **Yohji Yamamoto Parfums** sont des flacons transparents de forme ogivale et entourés d'anneaux noirs qui, vus de près, composent le nom Yohji. Derrière les lettres, des phrases associées à chaque parfum ne sont lisibles qu'en regardant à travers le liquide. Par exemple, on peut lire sur la bouteille Mode Zero « Be yourself. You're okay ». Concernant le packaging, connaissant l'amour pour le noir de Yamamoto, l'équipe a suivi une approche classique et opté pour une boîte entièrement noire et sans décoration, à l'exception du logo en relief de la marque.

YOHJI YAMAMOTO PARFUMS

Packaging Concept and Design: Grisha Serov
Product Development: Anna Zhitareva
Glass Manufacturing: Groupe Pochet
Glass Bottle Finish Manufacturing: Dekorglass
Box Manufacturing: Zfoam
Company: Yohji Yamamoto Parfums
Country: Russian Federation
Category: Perfumes

GOLD PENTAWARD 2019

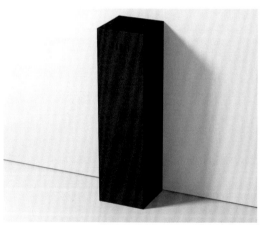

PERFUMED BRACELET

Creative Direction: Sébastien Servaire
Design: Candido Debarros
Technical Direction: Erwann Pivert
Company: Servaire & Co
Country: France
Category: Perfumes

GOLD PENTAWARD 2020

Through the development of its perfumed bracelet, **diptyque** continues its quest for innovation, offering customers consistently inventive and meaningful experiences. The bracelet takes into account the different perspectives of diptyque's three founders – an interior designer, a designer and a painter – with its new technique. The long rolled bracelet is perfumed via microencapsulation, which activates the fragrance by friction when the bracelet is unrolled. When snipped and tied around the wrist, it will provide three days of fragrance.

Durch die Entwicklung seines parfümierten Armbands setzt **diptyque** sein Streben nach Innovation fort und bietet den Kunden durchweg einfallsreiche und bedeutungsvolle Erfahrungen. Das Armband bezieht mit seiner neuen Technik die verschiedenen Perspektiven von diptyques drei Gründern mit ein; einem Innenarchitekt, einem Designer und einem Maler. Das lange aufgerollte Armband ist durch Mikroverkapselung parfümiert, die den Duft durch Reibung aktiviert. Zugeschnitten und um das Handgelenk gebunden, behält es seinen Duft für drei Tage.

En concevant son lien de parfum, **diptyque** poursuit sa quête d'innovation et offre aux clients des expériences invariablement créatives et éloquentes. D'un concept inédit, cet objet de la gamme prêts-à-parfumer intègre les différentes perspectives des trois fondateurs de diptyque, un architecte d'intérieur, un designer et un peintre. Le lien est imprégné de parfum par microencapsulation qu'il diffuse par friction quand il est déroulé. Une fois le lien coupé et attaché au poignet, ses qualités olfactives durent trois jours.

ZARA

Design: Victor Díez
Creative Direction: Nacho Lavernia,
Alberto Cienfuegos
Client: Zara
Company: Lavernia & Cienfuegos
Country: Spain
Category: Perfumes

SILVER PENTAWARD 2019

DKNY

Creative Direction: Sam O'Donahue
Company: Established
Country: USA
Category: Perfumes

BRONZE PENTAWARD 2019

THIS IS FOR U

Creative Direction: Nara, Garson
Design: Garson
Company: Boyish Studio
Country: China
Category: Perfumes

BRONZE PENTAWARD 2020

MARC JACOBS

Creative Direction: Sam O'Donahue
Company: Established
Country: USA
Category: Perfumes

BRONZE PENTAWARD 2019

NOKULT

Client Direction: Johanna Augustin
Production Management: Ellinor Kidd
Senior Design: Peeter Ots
Final Artwork: Anki MacPherson
Copywriting: Naama Forsrup
Company: Pond Design
Country: Sweden
Category: Perfumes

SILVER PENTAWARD 2020

PEPE JEANS

Design: Tailored Perfumes team
Company: Tailored Perfumes
Country: Spain
Category: Perfumes
SILVER PENTAWARD 2019

PEPE JEANS

Design: Tailored Perfumes team
Company: Tailored Perfumes
Country: Spain
Category: Perfumes
SILVER PENTAWARD 2019

SOAPSMITH

Design Lead: Alison Mehta
Design Direction: Beth Drummond,
Luke Chawner
Client Direction: Ella McKay
Photography: Carl Bartram
Senior Strategy: Tom Calvert
Illustration: Tom Abbiss-Smith
Company: Bulletproof
Country: UK
Category: Make-up, body care,
beauty products

GOLD PENTAWARD 2020

CHRISTIAN LOUBOUTIN

Folding carton production: Autajon Group team
Company: Autajon Group
Country: France
Category: Make-up, body care, beauty products

GOLD PENTAWARD 2019

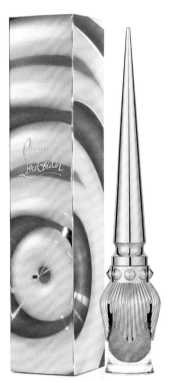

This make-up range for **Christian Louboutin** is a symbol of pure luxury. Reminiscent of Christmas ornaments or gilded icicles, the bottles revel in extravagance and perfectly suit the opulent products contained inside. The cartons are manufactured with a registered Fresnel lens laminated to white board, then printed with gold ink to give a truly eye-catching look. The elegant design is complete with white silk screen printed copy and an embossed logo.

Diese Make-up-Linie für **Christian Louboutin** ist ein Symbol des puren Luxus. An Weihnachtsschmuck oder vergoldete Eiszapfen erinnernd, schwelgen die Flaschen in Extravaganz und passen perfekt zu den opulenten Produkten im Inneren. Um einen richtigen Hingucker zu kreieren, zeigen die Schachteln eine Fresnellinse, die auf Weißkarton laminiert und anschließend mit Goldtinte bedruckt wird. Das elegante Design wird mit weißem Siebdruck und einem geprägten Logo vervollständigt.

Cette gamme de cosmétiques pour **Christian Louboutin** symbolise le luxe dans toute sa splendeur. Les flacons, qui ne sont pas sans faire penser à des décorations de Noël ou des stalactites de glace dorées, sont extravagants et vont comme un gant aux produits luxueux qu'ils renferment. Les boîtes sont recouvertes d'une lentille de Fresnel appliquée sur une surface blanche, puis imprimée à l'encre dorée pour donner un résultat des plus accrocheurs. Le design élégant est complété par une impression en sérigraphie de couleur blanche et un logo en relief.

WESTMAN ATELIER

Design: Angela Piner
Company: AVP Creative
Country: USA
Category: Make-up, body care, beauty products

SILVER PENTAWARD 2019

THANMELIN

Creative Direction: Guozheng Jiang, Dan Chen
Strategy Consulting Direction: Yanh Shu
Graphic Design: Fang Li, Qing Li
Product Design: Lexing Xu, Zilei Jiao
Senior Account Executive: Xiangbing Li
Company: Shanghai Nianxiang Brand Design & Consulting
Country: China
Category: Make-up, body care, beauty products

BRONZE PENTAWARD 2020

ASTALUXE SKINCARE SERIES

Creative Direction: Kazuhiro Niikura
Art Direction: Henri Harada
Design: Haruka Yamagata
Company: Kosé Corporation
Country: Japan
Category: Make-up, body care, beauty products

BRONZE PENTAWARD 2020

SERGE LUTENS

Creative Direction: Serge Lutens
Art Direction: Serge Lutens, Hiroshi Wakui
Design: Hiroshi Wakui
Company: Les Salons du Palais Royal Shiseido
Country: France
Category: Make-up, body care, beauty products

SILVER PENTAWARD 2020

JUNI COSMETICS

Founder and Direction: Madeleine White
Direction: Suzanne White
Direction and Senior Design: Nick Harvey,
Paul Robbins (Product Resolutions)
Logo Design: Carl Gamble
Company: Juni Cosmetics
Country: UK
Category: Make-up, body care, beauty products
SILVER PENTAWARD 2020

This luxury lipstick housed in a bespoke, plastic-free aluminium bullet is the debut product for **Juni Cosmetics** whose mission is to "leave a lasting impression, not a lasting problem". The bullet is octagonal, architectural and satisfyingly weighty, so it sits perfectly in your hand and feels substantial. Keen to enhance the raw beauty of aluminium rather than disguise it, they opted for a clear anodise and bead-blast finish that subtly catches the light. Additional design features, such as the bevelled lid and laser-etched "J" logo, add to the visual and tactile experience. The sleek, minimal packaging mirrors the high-tech lipstick formula, which is a make-up/skincare hybrid made of the finest organic and vegan-friendly ingredients.

Dieser luxuriöse Lippenstift, untergebracht in einem kunststofffreien Aluminiumprojektil, ist das Debüt-Produkt von **Juni Cosmetics**, deren Mission es ist, „einen bleibenden Eindruck und nicht ein bleibendes Problem zu hinterlassen". Die achteckige Form ist angenehm schwer und liegt perfekt in der Hand. Die klare Eloxierung und die Perlglanzoberfläche unterstützt die rohe Schönheit des Aluminiums und fängt das Licht ein. Zusätzliche Designmerkmale wie der angeschrägte Deckel und das gelaserte „J"-Logo tragen zum visuellen und haptischen Erleben bei. Die minimalistische Verpackung spiegelt die Hightech-Formel des Lippenstifts wider, der ein Make-up-/Hautpflege-Hybrid aus biologischen und veganen Inhaltsstoffen ist.

Ce rouge à lèvre de luxe logé dans un tube en aluminium sans plastique est le premier produit créé par **Juni Cosmetics**, dont la mission est de « laisser une impression durable, et non un problème durable ». Octogonal, architectural et agréablement lourd, ce tube tient bien dans la main et offre une sensation de solidité. Pour souligner la beauté brute de l'aluminium au lieu de le dissimuler, la marque a opté pour une finition anodisée incolore et microbillée qui capte subtilement la lumière. D'autres caractéristiques, comme le bouchon biseauté et le logo « J » gravé au laser, enrichissent l'expérience visuelle et tactile. Le packaging profilé et minimal est à l'image de la formule high-tech, un hybride entre maquillage et soin à base d'ingrédients bio et vegan.

CLÉ DE PEAU BEAUTÉ

Design: Shiseido
Art Direction and Design: Kaori Nagata
Illustration: Daria Petrilli
Creative Direction: Taisuke Kikuchi
Product Planning: Yuni Shimada
Make-up Direction: Lucia Pieroni
Production: Ai Tamura
Company: Shiseido
Country: Japan
Category: Make-up, body care, beauty products
BRONZE PENTAWARD 2019

PREANGE

Design: Hyang-mi Jang, Po-hee Lee
Product Design: Po-hee Lee
Direction: Hyang-mi Jang
Company: Coreana Cosmetic
Country: Republic of Korea
Category: Make-up, body care, beauty products
BRONZE PENTAWARD 2019

ONE BY KOSÉ

Creative and Art Direction: Naoko Yokokura
Design: Mami Futagami
Company: Kosé Corporation
Country: Japan
Category: Make-up, body care, beauty products

SILVER PENTAWARD 2019

VERY RARE SILENT DISTILLERY

Creative Direction: Mike Parsonson
Structural Design: Stewart Hobbs
Production Direction: Allen Luther
Business Direction: Bernard Gormley
Company: Nude Brand Creation
Country: UK
Category: Spirits

GOLD PENTAWARD 2020

YINXINGYUAN

Creative Direction and Design: XiongBo Deng
Client: Guangxi Yinxingyuan Liquor
Company: ShenZhen Lingyun Creative
Packaging Design
Country: China
Category: Spirits

GOLD PENTAWARD 2019

BUCHANAN'S RED SEAL

Strategy and Creative Direction: Pierre Delebois
Art Direction: Tim Devereaux
Product Design Direction: Harry Chong
Production Management: Steve Assandri
Company: forceMAJEURE Design
Country: USA
Category: Spirits

BRONZE PENTAWARD 2020

DYNASTY

Design, Creative Direction and
Account Direction: Qingfeng Meng
Company: Shenzhen Qizhi Brand Culture
Country: China
Category: Spirits

BRONZE PENTAWARD 2020

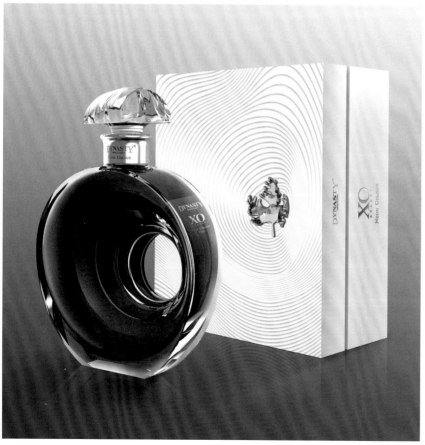

JSC SARAJISHVILI

CEO: Patrick Lerouge
Creative Direction: Julien
Clientele Direction: Florence
Art Direction: Elisabeth
CEO: Zurab Makharashvili (JSC Sarajishvili)
Marketing Direction: Tata Tavadze (JSC Sarajishvili)
Company: Mediane Creation
Country: France
Category: Spirits

SILVER PENTAWARD 2019

UMESHU THE AMBER

Art Direction: Amano Kazutoshi
Design: Ayana Shirai
Client: Liquor Innovation
Company: P.K.G.Tokyo
Country: Japan
Category: Spirits
SILVER PENTAWARD 2020

BAREKSTEN

Creative Direction: Tom Emil Olsen
Design Direction: Knut Harald Longva
Senior Design: Carl Bugge, Johannes Blomgren
Design: Agnieszka Gawlik
Junior Design: Emil Olsen
Photography: Christoffer Meyer
Brand Consultation: Thomas Danielsen
Key Account Management:
Beate Myren Romslo
Company: Kind
Country: Norway
Category: Spirits

SILVER PENTAWARD 2019

CHIVAS REGAL

Illustration: Greg Gossel
Design Finalisation and Range Extension: JDO
Company: Chivas Brothers
Country: UK
Category: Spirits

SILVER PENTAWARD 2020

TIGRE BLANC ALAMBIC EDITION

Glass Bottle and Decoration: Saverglass
Cap: TAPI
Labels: Nacara
Gift Box: Fabrik&Vous
Design and Photography: Tigre Blanc Paris
Company: Tigre Blanc Paris
Country: France
Category: Spirits

BRONZE PENTAWARD 2019

JAMESON WHISKEY, IRISH DISTILLERS JAMESON BOW STREET 18 YEARS OLD

Client: Jameson Whiskey Irish Distillers
Senior Design: Peeter Ots, Martin Ask
Client Direction: Fredrik Svalstedt
Copywriting: Naama Forsrup
Insight Direction: Naama Forsrup
Production Management: Niclas Hemlin
Final Art: Anna Johansson
Company: Pond Design
Country: Sweden
Category: Spirits

BRONZE PENTAWARD 2019

HARVEST MANOR

Design: Zhou Jingkuan
Company: Shenzhen Left and Right Packaging Design
Country: China
Category: Fine wines, champagne
GOLD PENTAWARD 2019

OSBORNE
VERY OLD RARE SHERRY

Design: Seriesnemo team
Company: Seriesnemo
Country: Spain
Category: Fine wines, champagne
SILVER PENTAWARD 2019

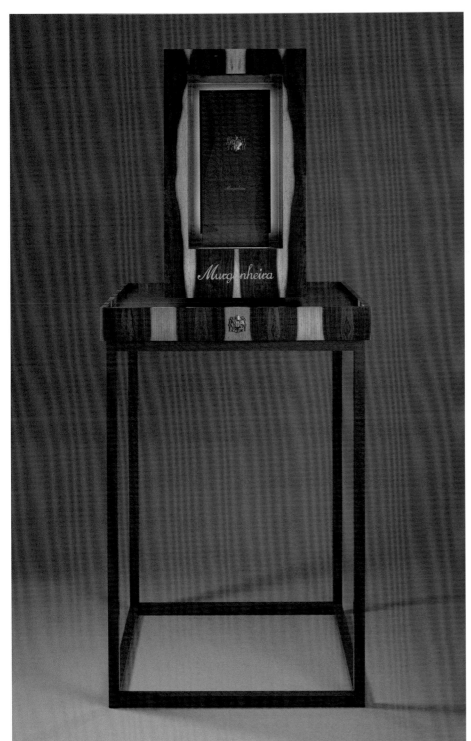

MURGANHEIRA

Design: Omdesign team
Company: Omdesign
Country: Portugal
Category: Fine wines, champagne

GOLD PENTAWARD 2020

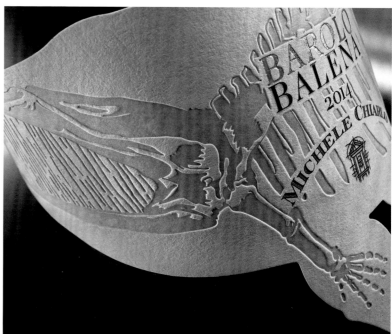

LUXORO

Design: Mario Di Paolo
Company: Spazio Di Paolo
Country: Italy
Category: Fine wines, champagne

SILVER PENTAWARD 2019

SABARIA

Design: Javi Garduño, Isra García
Company: Javier Garduño Estudio de Diseño
Country: Spain
Category: Fine wines, champagne
BRONZE PENTAWARD 2020

VELENOSI

Design: Mario Di Paolo
Company: Spazio Di Paolo
Country: Italy
Category: Fine wines, champagne
BRONZE PENTAWARD 2019

VALE D. MARIA PORT 1969

Design and Creative Direction: Pedro Roque
Company: RitaRivotti® Premium Packaging Design
Country: Portugal
Category: Fine wines, champagne

SILVER PENTAWARD 2020

MOD SÉLECTION CHAMPAGNE

Art Direction: Brent Hocking, Johan Liden
Design: Maya Peraza-Baker, Dan Snyder
Illustration: Maggie Enterrios
Photography: Mikon Von Gastel
Company: Aruliden
Country: USA
Category: Fine wines, champagne

BRONZE PENTAWARD 2019

M.G. HEUCQ

Art Direction, Graphic Design and Photography:
Alexandre Arzuman
Company: Alex Arzuman Studio
Country: France
Category: Fine wines, champagne

BRONZE PENTAWARD 2020

In celebration of their 180th anniversary, **The Dalmore** decided to mark the occasion with the release of an extremely old whisky (aged 60 years). To present this exceptional whisky made from two very old casks that were long stored at the Highland distillery, the designers created a unique bottle artwork and glorifier. The design intention was to embody the legacy of the distillery and symbolise the twin casks that came together to create this extremely limited-edition whisky. This resulted in a glorifier made of two casks covers joined together, and lead the concept and shape for the logo.

Anlässlich der Feier ihres 180. Jubiläums beschlossen **The Dalmore** einen extrem alten Whisky (60 Jahre gealtert) auf den Markt zu bringen. Um diesen außergewöhnlichen Whisky zu präsentieren, der aus zwei sehr alten Fässern stammt, die lange in der Highland-Distillery gelagert wurden, kreierten die Designer ein einzigartiges Flaschenkunstwerk und einen Hingucker. Das Design sollte das Vermächtnis der Brennerei verkörpern und die identischen Fässer symbolisieren, die bei der Herstellung dieses Whiskeys in limitierter Auflage zusammengebracht wurden. Das Ergebnis war eine Trophäe, die aus zwei verschiedenen Fassabdeckungen besteht, die zu einer zusammengefügt wurden und so das Konzept und die Form des Logos vorgeben.

Pour commémorer son 180ᵉ anniversaire, **The Dalmore** a décidé de marquer l'occasion en proposant un whisky très âgé de 60 ans. Pour présenter cette eau-de-vie d'exception vieillie dans d'anciens fûts longtemps conservés à la distillerie dans les Highlands, les designers ont conçu une bouteille unique glorifiant son contenu. L'intention était que cette œuvre d'art incarne l'héritage de la distillerie et symbolise les deux fûts ayant servi à l'élaboration de ce whisky en édition hautement limitée. Le résultat est un écrin composé de deux couvercles de fûts qui se chevauchent et définissent le concept et la forme du logo.

THE DALMORE

Photography: Studio 5•5
Creative Direction: Vincent Baranger
Design: Martin Lefèvre, Georges Diant, Clément Nambot, César Potel
Company: Studio 5•5
Country: France
Category: Casks & cases

GOLD PENTAWARD 2020

CÎROC VODKA

Creative Direction: Arron Egan, Jon Davies
Design: Martyn Wallwork
Supplier: Dapy Paris
Company: Butterfly Cannon
Country: UK
Category: Casks & cases

GOLD PENTAWARD 2019

Cîroc Vodka's Halo table server has been an icon of the brand's on-trade experience and popular in nightclubs for several years, but it needed a refresh. The solution was a deceptively simple structure inspired by contemporary luxury yacht design. With crisp, flowing curves it glows in an uninterrupted circle of light, a literal halo around Cîroc's distinctive bottle. The new design also incorporates two styles of illumination via one simple button, with a choice of either a constant light or multicoloured LEDs pulsing in sequence. The Halo itself is covered in Cîroc iridescent blue chrome, with a mirror finish that reflects light as well as the energy and vibrancy of night or daytime partygoers, whilst the Cîroc logo remains boldly visible, even when not illuminated.

Der **Halo** von **Cîroc Vodka** ist schon lange eine Ikone im Handel und in Nachtclubs beliebt, sein Design musste aber trotzdem aufgefrischt werden. Die Lösung war eine täuschend einfache Struktur, inspiriert von dem Look einer Luxusjacht. Ein leuchtender Kreis bildet buchstäblich ein Halo, einen Heiligenschein, um Cîrocs unverwechselbare Flasche. Das neue Design vereint zwei Beleuchtungsstile in einem Knopf, durch den man die Wahl zwischen konstantem Licht oder verschiedenfarbigen LEDs hat. Der Halo ist mit blauen Cîroc-Chrom überzogen, dessen Hochglanz-Finish sowohl das Licht als auch die Energie und die Lebendigkeit der Partygänger reflektiert, während das Cîroc-Logo auch im unbeleuchteten Zustand deutlich sichtbar bleibt.

Après des années de popularité dans les discothèques et à symboliser l'expérience commerciale de la marque **Cîroc Vodka**, le présentoir **Halo** avait besoin d'un coup de fraîcheur. La solution trouvée est une création d'apparence simple, inspirée du design contemporain des yachts de luxe. Ses courbes nettes et gracieuses font rayonner un cercle lumineux ininterrompu, tel un véritable halo autour de la bouteille originale de Cîroc. Un bouton permet de choisir entre deux styles d'éclairage : une lumière permanente ou des LED multicolores qui s'allument tour à tour. Le présentoir est recouvert de chrome bleu irisé Cîroc, avec un fini miroir réfléchissant la lumière ambiante et la vitalité des fêtards nocturnes ou en journée. Pour sa part, le logo Cîroc reste à tout moment très visible, même sans éclairage.

CHAMPAGNE TAITTINGER

Creative Direction: Vitalie Taittinger, Jérémy Malabre,
Justine Baillette, David Jankowski
Design: Jonathan Allègre, Mathieu Bourel,
Laura Kiritzé Topor
Product Development: Boris Pommeret
Company: Makao
Country: France
Category: Casks & cases

SILVER PENTAWARD 2019

WU

Design Guidance: Bosom
Photography: Hello Ogata
Company: 7654321 Studio
Country: China
Category: Casks & cases

SILVER PENTAWARD 2020

BLANDY'S

Design: Omdesign team
Company: Omdesign
Country: Portugal
Category: Casks & cases

BRONZE PENTAWARD 2020

EMPEREUS

Chairman, Asia Pacific: Monica Lee (Superunion)
Creative Direction: Ray Lan (Superunion)
Business Direction and Senior Design Direction:
Daniel Duh (Superunion)
Design: Jason Su, Penny Shi, Summer Dong,
Erica Chao (Superunion)
Project Management: Shift Feng (Superunion)
Account Management: Frank Feng (Superunion)
Credits: Xinmin Ke, Lihua Luo, Zengcai Gong, Bo Wu
(TRT); Ian Yen, Celine Derosier, Martin Mörck
Company: Beijing TRT Health Pharmaceutical
Country: China
Category: Casks & cases

BRONZE PENTAWARD 2019

THE SOUL OF MAOTAI-FLAVOUR

Creative Direction and Design: Li Zuo
Company: Guangzhou Wendao Advertising
Country: China
Category: Casks & cases

SILVER PENTAWARD 2020

CHAMPAGNE LOUIS ROEDERER

Co-Founder and Design Management: Gérald Galdini,
François Takounseun
Design Management: Emilie Etchelecou
Product Design: Florent Edmond
Company: Partisan Du Sens
Country: France
Category: Casks & cases

SILVER PENTAWARD 2019

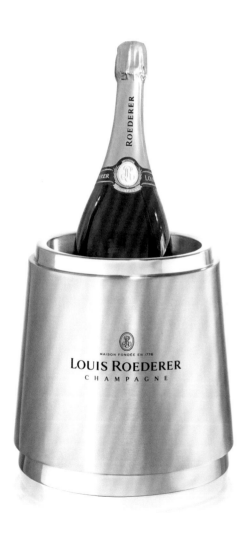

CHAMPAGNE TAITTINGER

Creative Direction: Vitalie Taittinger, Jérémy Malabre, Justine Baillette, David Jankowski
Design: Jonathan Allègre, Laura Kiritzé Topor, Laura Vandaële, Alice Moreau, Grégoire Chrétien
Product Development: Boris Pommeret
Company: Makao
Country: France
Category: Casks & cases

BRONZE PENTAWARD 2019

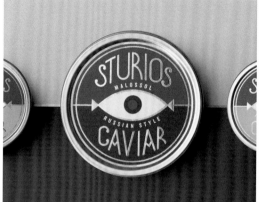

STURIOS

Creative Direction: Igor García
Strategy: Oliver Gutierrez
Company: lacía Branding & Packaging
Country: Spain
Category: Gourmet food

GOLD PENTAWARD 2020

Cinco Jotas acorn-fed Ibérico ham is Spain's national treasure, and such an authentic delicacy deserves extraordinary and unique packaging. Breaking with traditional packaging codes, this unconventional box has an unexpected shape that fits perfectly with the geometry of the product that it contains. The iconic hexagonal box holds one Cinco Jotas 100% Ibérico ham leg and a half piece of Cinco Jotas 100% Ibérico presa. Adorning the box are several birds of the Dehesa, the forest where the pigs live and feed from holm oak acorns. These birds have an important role in the life cycle of the acorn, which is essential to creating the flavour of the authentic 100% Ibérico Cinco Jotas Bellota ham.

Cinco Jotas iberischer Schinken vom Eichelschwein ist Spaniens Nationalschatz und eine so authentische Delikatesse verdient eine einzigartige Verpackung. Diese unkonventionelle Box bricht mit allen Verpackungscodes und hat eine unerwartete Form, die sich perfekt an die Geometrie des darin enthaltenen Produkts anpasst. Die sechseckige Box enthält eine Cinco Jotas 100 % Ibérico Schinkenkeule und ein halbes Stück des Cinco Jotas 100 % Ibérico presa. Die Box wird mit einigen Vögeln aus der Dehesa geschmückt, den Wäldern, in denen die Schweine leben und sich von den Eicheln der Steineiche ernähren. Diese Vögel spielen eine wichtige Rolle im Lebenszyklus der Eichel, die essenziell für den authentischen Geschmack des 100 % Ibérico Cinco Jotas Schinkens sind.

En Espagne, le jambon de porc ibérique nourri aux glands Cinco Jotas est un trésor national, un mets fin qui mérite un emballage unique et exceptionnel. Son packaging rompt avec les codes traditionnels et se présente dans une forme inédite qui épouse parfaitement la géométrie du produit qu'il renferme. La boîte hexagonale emblématique abrite un jambon Cinco Jotas 100 % ibérique et une demi-presa Cinco Jotas 100 % ibérique. Elle est décorée d'oiseaux de la dehesa, la forêt où les porcs vivent et s'alimentent des glands de chênes verts. Ces oiseaux jouent un rôle important dans le cycle de vie des glands, essentiels pour donner tout son goût au jambon de bellota Cinco Jotas 100 % ibérique.

CINCO JOTAS

Industrial Design: Marta Zabala
Art Direction: Clara De Sousa
Industrial Design Direction: Pep Trias
Craftsmanship Direction: Xavi Cuixart
Client Management: Mario González
Direction: Ignacio Muguiro
Company: Morillas Brand Design
Country: Spain
Category: Gourmet food

GOLD PENTAWARD 2019

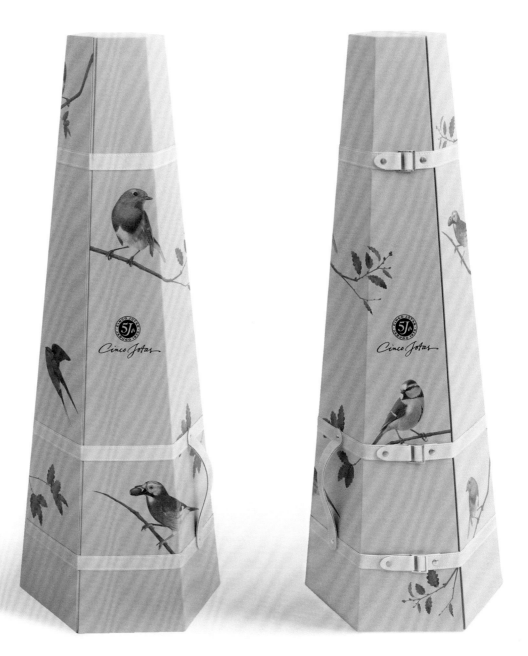

TORO ALBALÁ

Design: Seriesnemo industrial and graphic team
Company: Seriesnemo
Country: Spain
Category: Gourmet food

SILVER PENTAWARD 2020

Royal Duck is a premium brand of velvety smooth duck liver pâtés and rendered duck and goose fats. The product line consists of luxurious duck liver pâtés under the name DUX, and gourmet duck and goose fats under the name FATe. The jars are wrapped with eye-catching labels, each one telling its own unique yet analogous story with its main characters in the centre – leader Dux and Gastronomad Fate. Deservingly, the His and Her Royal Highness Dux and His and Her Majesty FATe portraits are embellished with a suitable frame lined with gold, gently complementing particular background colours that reflect the ingredients.

Royal Duck ist eine Premium-Marke für samtig weiche Entenleberpasteten und ausgelassene Enten- und Gänsefette. Die Produktlinie besteht aus luxuriösen Pasteten unter dem Namen DUX und dem Gourmet-Enten- und Gänsefett unter dem Namen FATe. Die Gläser sind mit ausdrucksstarken Etiketten umwickelt, von denen jedes eine eigene Geschichte erzählt, mit seinen Hauptcharakteren im Zentrum: Anführer DUX und Gastro-Nomade FATe. Standesgemäß wurden die Porträts von Seiner und Ihrer Königliche Hoheit DUX und Seiner und Ihrer Königlichen Hoheit FATe mit einem passenden, goldgesäumten Rahmen verziert, der die besonderen Hintergrundfarben ergänzt, die die Inhaltsstoffe widerspiegeln.

Royal Duck est une marque supérieure dont la gamme de produits compte d'onctueux foies gras de canard sous le nom de DUX, et de la graisse d'oie et de canard fondue raffinée sous le nom de FATe. Les bocaux sont enveloppés d'étiquettes attrayantes, chacune racontant une histoire unique bien qu'analogue aux autres, avec son protagoniste au centre de l'image, soit Leader Dux ou Gastronomad Fate. Les portraits de Son Altesse Royale Dux et de Sa Majesté FATe sont enjolivés d'un encadrement doré tout approprié qui agrémente noblement les couleurs de l'arrière-plan en accord avec les ingrédients.

ROYAL DUCK

Design: Marin Šubašić
Photography: Marin Šubašić
Copywriting: Marina Pavlić, Juraj Orehovec
Company: CAT01
Country: Croatia
Category: Gourmet food

SILVER PENTAWARD 2020

SAFE POWER

Design: Crystal So, Mavin Ma
Company: Safe Power Printing & Box MFG
Country: Hong Kong
Category: Gourmet food

SILVER PENTAWARD 2019

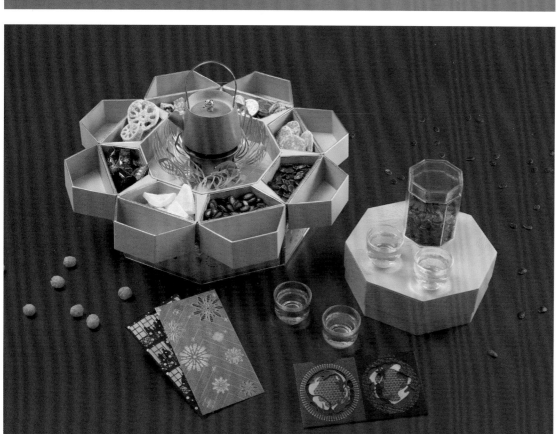

LA GLACERIE

Artistic Direction: Pierre Vanier
Company: PULP
Country: France
Category: Gourmet food

BRONZE PENTAWARD 2019

AUSTEVOLL SEAWEED

Creative Direction: Tom Emil Olsen
Design Direction: Knut Harald Longva
Senior Design: Carl Bugge
Design: Agnieszka Gawlik, Michał Leonczuk
Junior Design: Emil Olsen
Photography: Christoffer Meyer
Junior Photography: Simon Tonev
Brand Consultation: Thomas Danielsen
Key Account Management: Beate Myren Romslo
Company: Kind
Country: Norway
Category: Gourmet food

BRONZE PENTAWARD 2019

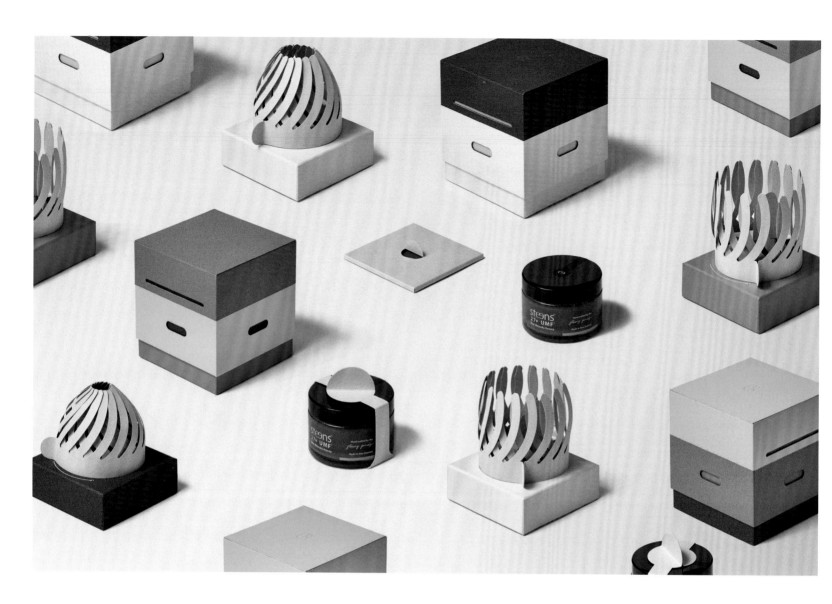

27+ UMF MANUKA HONEY

Client: P.A. & S.C. Steens
Design: David Trubridge
Cardboard Engineering: Think Packaging
Manufacturing: Wrapology International Ltd
Photography: Emirali Photography
Art Direction Photography and Editing: Ssaalltt
Company: Think Packaging
Country: New Zealand
Category: Gourmet food

SILVER PENTAWARD 2019

FORTNUM & MASON

Senior Design: Cameron Knott, Elle Holian
Creative Direction: Chloe Templeman
Business Development Direction: Alice Goss
Senior Creative Retouching: Nathan Jordan
Brand Experience and Technology Development:
Nick Holland
Senior Peoduction Project Management: Tal Watson
Direction of Storytelling: Holly Kielty
Company: Design Bridge London
Country: UK
Category: Gourmet food
BRONZE PENTAWARD 2020

MILTOS

Art Direction, Design and Photography: Yuta Takahashi
Company: Yuta Takahashi Design Studio
Country: Japan
Category: Gourmet food
BRONZE PENTAWARD 2020

The brief was to create new gift set packaging which would encourage the (re)discovery of **Hennessy XO**'s greatness and reach a new generation of luxury drinkers. With the knowledge that ice-cold water is a taste enhancer, the limited-edition box was made with a perfectly symmetrical diamond cut design carved out of a single injection-moulded block, giving the effect of a block of ice. When closed, the box seems to encase the fire of XO cognac, but when open, it becomes an elegant ice bucket to use on special occasions. Under the light, the facets make the block sparkle like real glass or diamonds, creating an enchanting and festive atmosphere for a new luxury ritual of cognac tasting.

Die Vorgabe war es, ein neues Geschenkset zu entwerfen, das die (Wieder-)Entdeckung von **Hennessy XO**s Profil fördern und eine neue Generation von Kunden erreichen sollte. Mit dem Wissen, das eiskaltes Wasser ein Geschmacksverstärker ist, wurde die in limitierter Auflage hergestellte Box mit einem perfekt symmetrischen Diamantenschnitt-Design aus einem einzelnen Spritzgussblock herausgearbeitet, der den Effekt eines Eisblocks nachstellt. Wenn sie geschlossen wird, scheint die Box das Feuer des XO Cognacs zu umschließen, wenn sie geöffnet ist, wird sie zu einem eleganten Eiskühler, den man zu besonderen Anlässen nutzen kann. Im Licht lassen die Facetten den Block glitzern wie echtes Glas oder Diamanten und schaffen damit eine bezaubernde, feierliche Atmosphäre für ein neues luxuriöses Ritual der Cognac-Verkostung.

Le brief créatif portait sur l'invention d'un coffret-cadeau afin de faire (re)découvrir toute la grandeur de **Hennessy XO** et atteindre une nouvelle génération d'amateurs de boissons de luxe. L'eau glacée étant un exhausteur de goût, le design de la boîte en édition limitée a été conçu comme un diamant taillé parfaitement symétrique à partir d'un bloc moulé en une seule injection ; l'effet obtenu est celui d'un bloc de glace. Quand la boîte est fermée, elle semble renfermer le feu du cognac XO ; ouverte, elle devient un élégant seau à glace à utiliser lors d'occasions spéciales. Sous une lumière, les facettes font étinceler le bloc tel du verre véritable ou des diamants, ce qui crée une atmosphère festive et féérique pour un luxueux rituel de dégustation de cognac.

HENNESSY XO

Global Creative Direction and CEO: Sébastien Servaire
Design Creative Direction: Candido de Barros
Design: Thomas Chouvaeff
Product Design Development Management: Erwann Pivert
Account Direction: Anne Pilliard
Film Artistic Direction: Sébastien Servaire, Marie Galanti
Photography: Claude Badée
Company: Servaire & Co
Country: France
Category: Limited editions, limited series, event creations

GOLD PENTAWARD 2019

ACQUA DI PARMA

CEO: Thierry Cazaux
Creative Strategy Direction: Marine Forlini-Crouzet
Art Direction: Damine Escaravage
Product Development and Innovation Direction:
Paola Paganini (Acqua di Parma)
Senior Product Management: Ginetta Rizzi
(Acqua di Parma)
Company: Chic
Country: France
Category: Limited editions, limited series,
event creations

GOLD PENTAWARD 2020

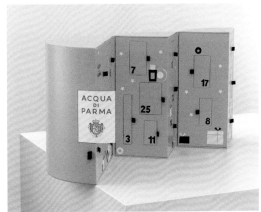

With advent calendars gaining popularity in the luxury market, **Acqua di Parma** took this as an opportunity to offer renewed value to the customer in an innovative way. Staying true to the brand DNA and building on its iconic cylinder, an ingenious folding structure was developed to hold 25 Acqua di Parma products of 11 different shapes and dimensions. The structure invites the consumer to take part in a smart, dynamic and delightful ritual. The luxury of the project is encapsulated in the elegance of the unfolding calendar, the delicacy of the magnetic opening and the high-quality of the product's manufacturing.

Da Adventskalender auf dem Luxusmarkt immer beliebter werden, sah **Acqua di Parma** dies als Möglichkeit, seinen Kunden auf innovative Weise neue Wertigkeit zu bieten. Um der Marken-DNA treu zu bleiben und auf dessen bekannte Zylinder aufzubauen, wurde eine geniale Faltstruktur entwickelt, die 25 Produkte von Acqua di Parma mit elf verschiedenen Formen und Dimensionen aufnehmen kann. Die Struktur lädt den Kunden dazu ein, an einem intelligenten, dynamischen und freudvollen Ritual teilzunehmen. Der Luxus dieses Projekts wird durch die Eleganz des aufklappbaren Kalenders, der Feinheit der magnetischen Öffnung und der hohen Qualität der Produktherstellung verkörpert.

Les calendriers de l'avent sont en vogue sur le marché des produits de luxe, et **Acqua di Parma** a saisi cette occasion pour se revaloriser auprès de ses clients de façon innovante. Fidèle à l'ADN de la marque et partant de son emblématique cylindre, une ingénieuse structure articulée a été conçue pour accueillir 25 produits Acqua di Parma de 11 formes et dimensions différentes et pour inviter le consommateur à suivre un rituel exquis. Le luxe de ce projet réside dans l'élégance du calendrier qui s'ouvre, dans la finesse de l'ouverture aimantée et dans la qualité supérieure des produits.

QUINTA DO CRASTO

Design: Omdesign team
Company: Omdesign
Country: Portugal
Category: Limited editions, limited series,
event creations

SILVER PENTAWARD 2019

VEUVE CLICQUOT

Off Trade Marketing Product Management:
Tahar Kassar (Veuve Clicquot/Moët Hennessy)
Creative Direction: Tanguy Kabouende
Company: Casanova
Country: France
Category: Limited editions, limited series,
event creations

SILVER PENTAWARD 2020

CLÉ DE PEAU BEAUTÉ

Creative Direction: Taisuke Kikuchi
Art Direction and Design: Kaori Nagata
Photography: Masato Kanazawa, Taihei Iino
Artwork: Ayana Otake
Kimono Making: Tachibana
Kimono Coordination: Katsumi Hayashi, SACRA
Company: Shiseido
Country: Japan
Category: Limited editions, limited series, event creations

SILVER PENTAWARD 2020

P&G SK-II

Creative Lead: Magdalena Gacek (P&G SK-II SK-II)
Executive Creative Direction: Jonathan Eshel
Managing Direction: Fabian Serrano
Direction of 3D and Brand Experience: Shohei Yagi
Art Direction: Hubert Wah, Anna Gregorio
Industrial Design: Evelyn Hayashi
Company: NiCE
Country: Singapore
Category: Limited editions, limited series,
event creations

BRONZE PENTAWARD 2020

KRUG X DEVIALET

Global Creative Direction and CEO: Sébastien Servaire
Graphic Design Development Management: Yaël Audrain
Account Direction: Anne Pilliard
Company: Servaire & Co
Country: France
Category: Limited editions, limited series,
event creations

BRONZE PENTAWARD 2019

MARIESTADS BRYGGERI

Creative Direction: Henrik Hallberg
Design: Lachlan Bullock, Victor Nilsson
Project Management: Maria Florell Janhammer,
Jeanette Zackrisson
Company: Neumeister Strategic Design
Country: Sweden
Category: Limited editions, limited series, event creations

BRONZE PENTAWARD 2019

JOHNNIE WALKER BLUE LABEL

Creative Lead: Jon Davies, Ben Cox
Account Lead: Maisie Flight
Illustration: Timorous Beasties
Company: Butterfly Cannon
Country: UK
Category: Limited editions,
limited series, event creations

BRONZE PENTAWARD 2020

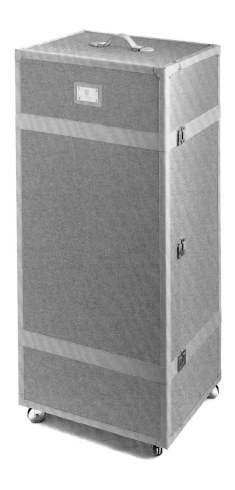

CINCO JOTAS

Industrial Design: Albert Pérez
Art Direction: Clara De Sousa
Industrial Design Direction: Pep Trias
Craftsmanship Direction: Xavi Cuixart
Client Management: Mario González
Direction: Ignacio Muguiro
Company: Morillas Brand Design
Country: Spain
Category: Limited editions, limited series, event creations

SILVER PENTAWARD 2019

HARVEY NICHOLS FOOD COLLECTION

Creative Direction and Design: Debrah Smith
Strategy Direction: Richard Village
Copywriting: Richard Village, Debrah Smith
Company: Smith&+Village
Country: UK
Category: Distributors'/retailers' own brands/
private labels

BRONZE PENTAWARD 2019

YAN TU

Creative Direction: Jonny Wang
Design: Jerry Liu
Company: East Orange
Country: China
Category: Distributors'/retailers' own brands/
private labels

SILVER PENTAWARD 2019

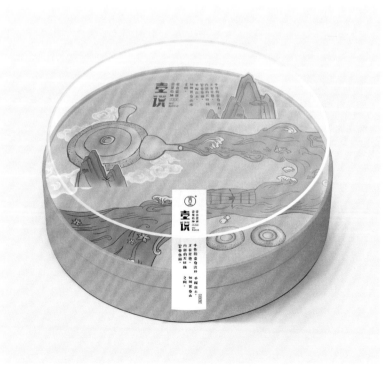

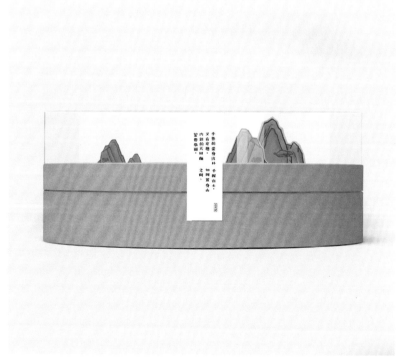

U-JEWELRY

Creative Direction: Tengxian Zou
Design: VDG
Company: Shanghai Version Design Group
Country: China
Category: Distributors'/retailers' own brands/
private labels

GOLD PENTAWARD 2019

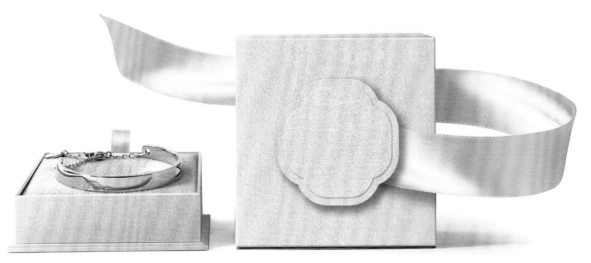

A Time Bottle is a perfume bottle made of reused ocean plastic which becomes unique over the years through everyday use. It's like beach glass, shaped slowly after being gently ground and shaped by the waves. In recent years plastic has been strongly associated with terms like mass production, but if it is turned into a material that can be used over a long time, not just mass produced then thrown away, it can also reduce the amount of plastic created. The idea behind A Time Bottle is to give plastic new value by becoming a long-term usable material, creating "antique plastic" which sees its value grow with the passage of time.

A Time Bottle ist ein Parfümflakon aus recyceltem Plastik aus dem Meer, das im Laufe der Zeit und durch den täglichen Gebrauch einzigartig wird – wie ein Stück Glas, das sanft von Meereswellen geschliffen und geformt wurde. In den vergangenen Jahren wurde Kunststoff stark mit Begriffen wie Massenproduktion in Verbindung gebracht, dabei kann man es über eine lange Zeit verwenden, anstatt es in rauen Mengen wegzuwerfen. So lässt sich die Herstellung von Plastik reduzieren. Die Idee hinter A Time Bottle ist, Plastik aufzuwerten, es als langfristig verwendbares Material zu nutzen und in „antikes Plastik" zu verwandeln, dessen Wert mit den Jahren steigt.

A Time Bottle est un flacon de parfum fabriqué à base de plastique récupéré des océans et dont l'aspect évolue avec le temps par son utilisation quotidienne. Il s'apparente aux morceaux de verre trouvés sur les plages, lentement taillés et polis par les vagues. Ces dernières années, le plastique est surtout associé à la production de masse, mais s'il devient un matériau avec une longue durée de vie au lieu d'être simplement produit puis jeté, il peut aussi réduire la quantité de plastique générée. L'idée derrière A Time Bottle est de revaloriser le plastique en le convertissant en un matériau utile à long terme, créant par là du « plastique antique » dont la valeur augmente avec le passage du temps.

A TIME BOTTLE

Art Direction and Design: Anna Sakaguchi,
Miki Kawamura
Company: Anna Sakaguchi / Miki Kawamura
Country: Germany
Category: Packaging concept (professional)
GOLD PENTAWARD 2019

NIGHT BEASTS ABSINTHE

3D: Jing Lin
Company: Leandro Crispim
Country: Singapore
Category: Packaging concept (professional)

SILVER PENTAWARD 2020

FAUST OLIVE OIL

Creative Direction: Pedro Vareta
Product Design, 3D Modelling and Rendering:
Ricardo Ribeiro
Graphic Design: Rui Magalhães
Project Management: Lourenço Neves
Company: VOLTA Brand Shaping Studio
Country: Portugal
Category: Packaging concept (professional)

SILVER PENTAWARD 2019

MONSIEUR LA HOUSSE

Concept, Creative Direction and Design:
Joost Identities
Perfume Design: Tanja Deurloo and Joost la Housse
Photography: Studio_M Amsterdam, Rob van Dam
Cartonnage: Vrijdag Premium Printing
Company: Joost Identities
Country: Netherlands
Category: Packaging concept (professional)
BRONZE PENTAWARD 2019

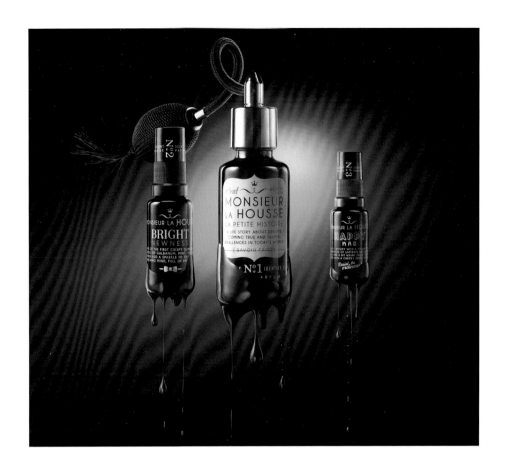

MYAIR

Creative Direction and Design: Anna Rufova
3D Visualisation: Nikita Bulgakov
Company: Anna Rufova
Country: Russian Federation
Category: Packaging concept (professional)
BRONZE PENTAWARD 2019

ROARING 40, FURIOUS 50

Art Direction: Ewa Nocuń
Creative Direction: Paweł Frej
Design: Arkadiusz Tkacz
Company: Hi Brands
Country: Poland
Category: Packaging concept (professional)

BRONZE PENTAWARD 2020

COLUMNA

Design: Sara Faulkner
Company: JDO
Country: UK
Category: Packaging concept (professional)

BRONZE PENTAWARD 2020

BRABANT WHISKY

Design and 3D Visualisation: Untactil team
Company: Untactil
Country: Spain
Category: Packaging concept (professional)

SILVER PENTAWARD 2019

SALUTE

Design: Yanlong Zhou
Supervision: Gu Chuan-Xi
School: Shanghai Institute of Visual Arts (SIVA)
Country: China
Category: Packaging concept (student)

GOLD PENTAWARD 2020

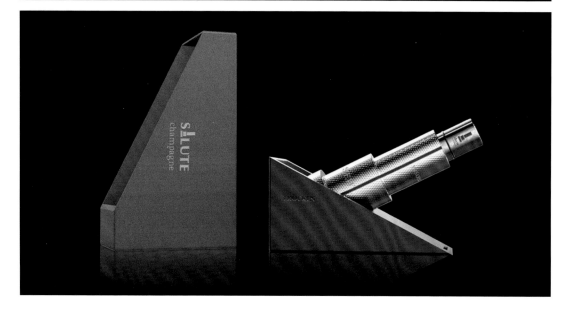

MING

Design: Kong Haoru
Visual Consultation: Liu Yuxin
School: North China University of Science
and Technology
Country: China
Category: Packaging concept (student)

GOLD PENTAWARD 2019

SCNT

Design: Elena Zaitseva
3D Design: Pavel Gubin
School: British Higher School of Art and Design
Country: Russian Federation
Category: Packaging concept (student)

SILVER PENTAWARD 2019

SEREMONI PERFUME PACKAGING

Fabrication Assisting: Xinda Wang
School: School of the Art Institute of Chicago
Country: USA
Category: Packaging concept (student)

SILVER PENTAWARD 2019

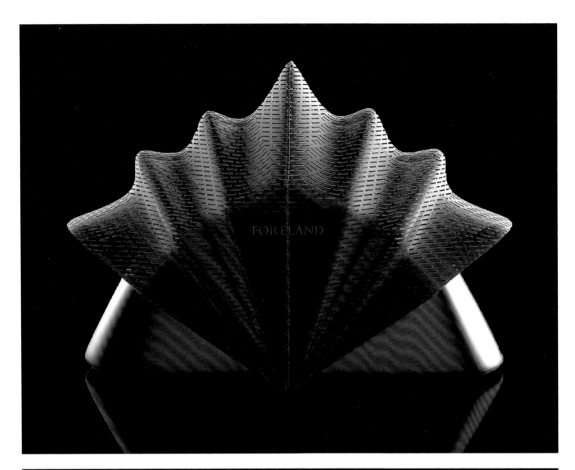

FORELAND

Design: Dai Dong
Supervision: Hu Jijun
School: Shanghai Institute of Visual Arts (SIVA)
Country: China
Category: Packaging concept (student)

SILVER PENTAWARD 2019

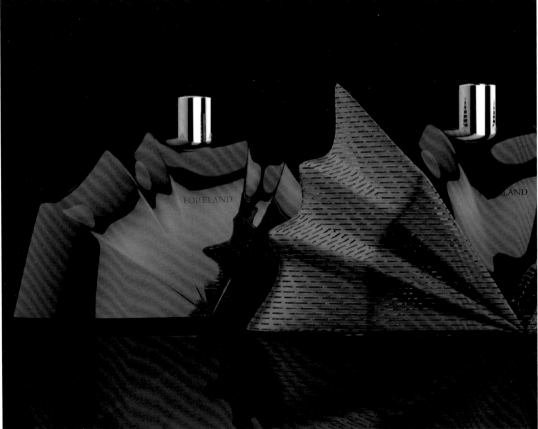

FERMENT IMMEDIATELY

Design: Qiong-Yin Wang, Wan-Ru Yang, Xin-Ru Wu,
Yi-Ru Chen, Chia-Yi Chao, Yi-Tung Chen
School: Ling Tung University
Country: Taiwan
Category: Packaging concept (student)

SILVER PENTAWARD 2020

JEEP VOYAGER

Design and Art Direction: Grace Susilo
Photography: Timothy Huang, Grace Susilo
Instruction: Dan Hoy
School: ArtCenter College of Design
Country: USA
Category: Packaging concept (student)

BRONZE PENTAWARD 2020

SHOW TAIL

Design: Liu Yuanzhuo
Supervision: Gu Chuanxi
School: Shanghai Institute of Visual Arts (SIVA)
Country: China
Category: Packaging concept (student)

BRONZE PENTAWARD 2019

RAY

Design: Pei Ziwen
Supervision: Hu Jijun
School: Shanghai Institute of Visual Arts (SIVA)
Country: China
Category: Packaging concept (student)

BRONZE PENTAWARD 2019

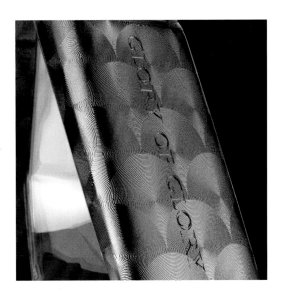

MOËT & CHANDON

Creative Direction and Design: Lorena Jiménez,
Miquel Nadal, Valentina Reyes
School: Elisava, Barcelona School of
Design and Engineering
Country: Spain
Category: Packaging concept (student)
BRONZE PENTAWARD 2020

OTAMATI

Creative Direction and Design: Jessica Sandoval
School: Elisava, Barcelona School of
Design and Engineering
Country: Spain
Category: Packaging concept (student)
SILVER PENTAWARD 2020

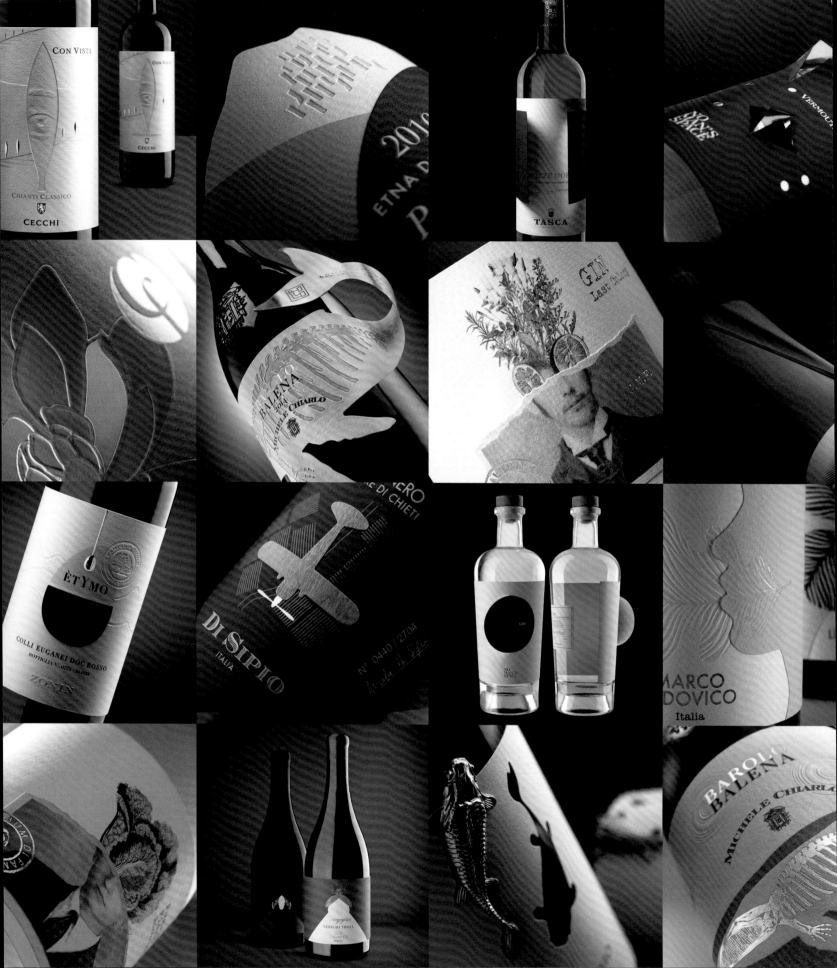

WE BOTTLE CREATIVITY

Spazio Di Paolo, established by Mario Di Paolo, is a creative hub for the wine and spirits sector specialising in marketing and packaging design. For over 50 years, our experience has made its way into the visual arts. We began as a professional photographic studio focused on contemporary art and advertising in the late 1960s. The studio evolved during the subsequent years into a marketing and packaging business with a **focus on the wine and spirits sector**.

Spazio di Paolo is an award-winning studio and among the most recognisable internationally. **Knowledge and passion drive our business**. With a completely innovative organisational structure and approach that goes beyond the traditional idea of a communication agency, Spazio Di Paolo is perceptive and creative, with a holistic ability to adapt to market trends.

A rounded knowledge of all printing techniques and the constant study of agricultural techniques, from the use of the land to the bottling stage, has allowed us to **create unique communication ideas and avenues**, which have developed into modern and refined "must-haves" when publicising the biodiversity of products to the consumer.

We have contributed to **creating a new and stronger relationship** between the territory and the local producer through original narratives by using the potential of the printing and labelling machines at their best. Each project is designed and engineered to be fully automated within the production process.

WIR FÜLLEN KREATIVITÄT AB

Spazio Di Paolo, gegründet von Mario Di Paolo, ist ein kreatives Zentrum für den Wein- und Spirituosensektor, das sich auf Marketing und Verpackungsdesign spezialisiert hat. Seit über 50 Jahren hat unsere Erfahrung ihren Weg in die bildenden Kunst gefunden. Wir haben als ein professionelles Fotostudio angefangen, das sich Ende der 1960er-Jahre auf zeitgenössische Kunst und Werbung spezialisierte. Das Studio entwickelte s ich in den darauffolgenden Jahren zu einem Marketing und Verpackungsunternehmen mit Schwerpunkt **auf dem Wein- und Spirituosensektor**.

Spazio Di Paolo ist ein Studio, das viele Preise gewonnen hat und ist eines mit dem international höchsten Wiedererkennungswert. **Wissen und Leidenschaft befeuern unser Geschäft**. Mit einer vollkommen innovativen Organisationsstruktur und Herangehensweise die weit über die traditionelle Idee einer Kommunikationsagentur hinausgeht, ist Spazio Di Paolo scharfsinnig und kreativ mit einer umfassenden Fähigkeit zur Anpassung an Markttrends.

Ein umfassendes Wissen aller Druckverfahren und das andauernde Lernen von landwirtschaftlichen Techniken, von der Landnutzung bis zu Abfüllprozessen, haben es uns ermöglicht, **einzigartige Kommunikationsideen und -wege zu schaffen**, die sich zu modernen und raffinierten Must-Haves entwickelt haben, wenn es darum geht, dem Konsumenten die Biodiversität der Produkte vorzustellen.

Wir haben durch originäre Narrative dazu beigetragen, eine **neue und stärkere Beziehung** zwischen dem Territorium und den lokalen Produzenten zu schaffen, indem wir das Potenzial der Druck- und Etikettenmaschinen optimal genutzt haben. Jedes Projekt ist so konzipiert und konstruiert, dass es innerhalb des Produktionsprozesses komplett automatisiert werden kann.

LA CRÉATIVITÉ MISE EN BOUTEILLE

Fondé par Mario Di Paolo, **Spazio Di Paolo** est un pôle de création pour le secteur du vin et des spiritueux, spécialisé dans le marketing et le design de packaging. Depuis plus de 50 ans, nous nous sommes forgé une expérience dans les arts visuels. Nous avons débuté à la fin des années 60 comme studio photo professionnel avec des projets principalement d'art contemporain et de publicité. Le studio a ensuite évolué pour se tourner vers le marketing et les emballages, avec une spécialisation sur **le secteur vitivinicole et des spiritueux**.

Spazio di Paolo est aujourd'hui un studio primé qui a sa place parmi les plus grands noms sur la scène internationale. **Le savoir-faire et la passion sont les moteurs de notre activité**. Grâce à une structure organisationnelle innovatrice et une approche qui va au-delà de l'idée traditionnelle d'une agence de communication, Spazio Di Paolo est sagace et créatif, doté d'une faculté holistique à s'adapter aux tendances du marché.

Nous **élaborons des idées et des voies de communication uniques** grâce à des compétences éprouvées dans tous les procédés d'impression et l'étude en continu des techniques agricoles, de l'exploitation des sols à la phase de mise en bouteille. Sophistiquées et contemporaines, nos conceptions s'avèrent incontournables pour promouvoir la biodiversité des produits auprès du consommateur.

Nous avons œuvré pour **établir une relation nouvelle et plus solide** entre le territoire et le producteur local par le biais de mises en récit originales, en exploitant au mieux le potentiel des machines d'impression et d'étiquetage. Chaque projet est conçu et développé de façon à être entièrement automatisé au sein du processus de production.

SPAZIO DIPAOLO
WINE&SPIRITS PACKAGING DESIGN / ARTS

www.spaziodipaolo.it

FARROW & BALL

F&B®

DORSET ENGLAND

COLOUR BY NATURE

NATURAL HISTORY MUSEUM

DUTCH ORANGE No. W76

MODERN EMULSION

Best of the category
Household maintenance
Home improvement
Electronic
Non-electronic
Packaging brand identity programs
Pet products
Entertainment

other markets

Tobacco and products for smokers
Self-promotion
Baby products
Sustainable design
Distributors'/retailers' own brand/private labels
Packaging concept

Sponsored by

MADE TO BE OPENED

Combining sustainability, innovation, beauty and exclusivity,
we develop small masterpieces of design for the premium beverage market.
Creations designed to preserve and customize excellence, making it memorable.
Exclusive closures that are "Made to be opened".

Tapi | UNIQUENESS INSIDE
BEAUTY ON TOP

COLLECTION | SIGNATURE | REVÒ

tapigroup.com

UNIQUENESS INSIDE, BEAUTY ON TOP

Founded in 2000, the team of professionals at **Tapì** is young, dynamic and enthusiastic. We think of ourselves as a **"global boutique"** designing closures for the premium and super-premium segments of the drinks market.

Our ability to innovate means we have become a multinational group that is recognised for its **originality, design and focus on aesthetics**. Being the first to drive market trends is our main aim. It's what fuels us every day to carry out our mission of introducing the value of beauty to the world, expressed through the products we design.

A focus on sustainability has always been in our DNA. To best describe how it is ingrained in all our company processes, best practices and Tapì product ranges, we have created LEI. **Standing for low environmental impact, LEI encapsulates Tapì's mission** in one simple concept: offering to our target markets products and services that have a minimal environmental impact, guaranteeing the protection of our planet.

INNERE EINZIGARTIGKEIT, SCHÖNHEIT AN DER SPITZE

Tapì wurde im Jahr 2000 gegründet und hat ein Team von Fachkräften, die jung, dynamisch und enthusiastisch sind. Wir sehen uns als eine „globale Boutique", die Verschlüsse für die Premium- und Superpremiumsegmente des Getränkemarkts entwirft.

Dank unsere Innovationsfähigkeit sind wir zu einer multinationalen Gruppe geworden, die für ihre **Originalität, ihr Design und ihren Fokus auf Ästhetik** bekannt ist. Unser Hauptziel ist es, die Ersten zu sein, die Markttrends beeinflussen. Das treibt uns jeden Tag an, unsere Mission zu erfüllen und den Wert der Schönheit in die Welt zu bringen, der durch die von uns entworfenen Produkte zum Ausdruck kommt.

Der Fokus auf Nachhaltigkeit war schon immer Teil unserer DNA. Um am besten zu beschreiben, wie das Thema in all unseren Unternehmensprozessen, unserem Erfolgsrezept und den Tapì-Produktreihen verinnerlicht ist, haben wir LEI entwickelt. LEI steht für für **Low Environmental Impact (dt. niedriger Umwelteinfluss) und fasst Tapìs Mission** in einem einfachen Konzept zusammen: Wir bieten unseren Zielmärkten Produkte und Dienstleistungen an, die einen minimalen Einfluss auf die Umwelt haben und garantieren so den Schutz unseres Planeten.

SINGULARITÉ À L'INTÉRIEUR, BEAUTÉ EN TÊTE

Fondée en 2000, l'équipe de professionnels de **Tapì** est jeune, dynamique et enthousiaste. Nous nous considérons comme une « **boutique globale** » qui conçoit des bouchons pour les marques premium et super premium du marché des boissons.

Grâce à notre capacité d'innover, nous sommes devenus un groupe multinational reconnu pour **son originalité, son design et l'accent qu'il met sur l'esthétique**. Notre objectif premier est d'être des prescripteurs de tendances : c'est notre moteur au quotidien pour mener notre mission de révéler au monde la beauté qui s'exprime à travers les produits que nous concevons.

La durabilité a toujours été une priorité ancrée dans notre ADN. Nous avons créé le concept « LEI » pour expliquer comment cette approche durable est instillée dans tous nos procédés, nos bonnes pratiques et la gamme de produits Tapì. **LEI – Low Environmental Impact – résume toute la mission de Tapì** en une idée simple : offrir à nos marchés cibles des produits et des services dont l'impact sur l'environnement est minime en vue de contribuer à protéger notre planète.

www.tapigroup.com

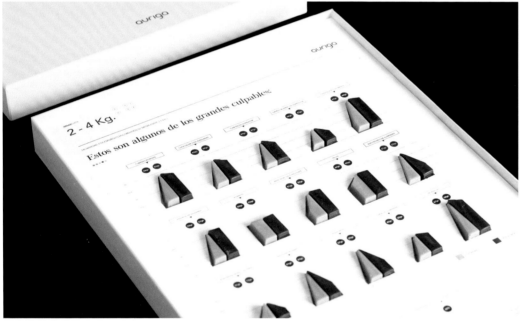

AURIGA

Creative Direction: Javier Bidezabal
Art Direction: Johana Dueñas, Eduardo España, Javier Bidezabal
Copywriting: Eduardo España
Design: Carmina Escudero, Carmen Cuadrado
Photography: Pedro Maìrnez, Agustín Escámez (Q&Cumber)
Production: Tamar Valdenebro
General Account Direction: Cristina Hernández, Raquel Guerrero
CEO: Balba González Camino
Client: Auriga
Company: Auriga
Country: Spain
Category: Self-promotion

PLATINUM PENTAWARD 2019

This self-promotional piece by **Auriga** features a set of four chocolate boxes with edible infographics. To create a standout seasonal gift for their clients, they turned Christmas data into a design which was simple to understand and interactive. Using premium materials, each box is designed to be an experience allowing users to take a tour through all the data and information whilst enjoying a delicious treat. Different shapes and flavours of chocolate represent different kinds of information, creating something pleasing both to the eyes and to the taste buds.

Dieses Selbstvermarktungsstück von **Auriga** beinhaltet ein Set aus vier Schokoladenschachteln mit essbaren Infografiken. Um ein herausstechendes Geschenk zu schaffen, wurden Weihnachtsdaten in ein Design verwandelt, das einfach zu verstehen, und interaktiv ist. Mit hochwertigen Materialien entworfen, erläutert jede Grafik Fakten, während die Käufer einen Leckerbissen genießen können. Die unterschiedlichen Formen und Sorten der Schokolade repräsentieren verschiedene Informationsarten und sind sowohl bekömmlich für die Augen als auch für den Magen.

Cette création d'autopromotion par **Auriga** se compose d'un lot de quatre boîtes de chocolats aux infographies comestibles. En vue d'offrir à ses clients un cadeau d'exception pour les fêtes, la marque a converti des données sur Noël en un design intuitif et interactif. Chaque boîte est fabriquée à l'aide de matériaux haut de gamme et pensée comme une expérience : les destinataires découvrent ainsi les informations tout en savourant une délicieuse gâterie. Les formes et les goûts des chocolats correspondent à divers types d'informations, ce qui donne une composition plaisante tant visuellement que pour les papilles.

This packaging for Dutch retailer **Hema** encloses a range of inflatables for summer fun. The design concept was to show a variety of summer products that look like they have been dropped into mini swimming pools, and there's even a typical ladder that leads into the pool visible on the box, bringing the image to life. All the toys have been designed exclusively by Hema and represent the retailer's most famous icons, like a smoked sausage, Takkie the dog, a tompouce pastry and an ice cream cone. Hema's overall ambition is to stop putting plastic products into plastic packaging, so cardboard boxes were chosen to package and protect the products inside.

Die Verpackung für den niederländischen Einzelhändler **Hema** betrifft eine Reihe von aufblasbaren Spielzeugen für den Sommerspaß. Das Designkonzept zeigt eine Vielfalt an Produkten, die aussehen, als ob sie in Minischwimmbecken fallen gelassen wurden. Es gibt sogar eine Leiter, die in das auf der Schachtel sichtbare Schwimmbecken führt und die das Bild zum Leben erweckt. Alle Spielzeuge wurden exklusiv von Hema entworfen und repräsentieren die bekanntesten Symbole des Einzelhändlers, wie die gebratene Wurst, Takkie den Hund, einen niederländischen Tompouce-Kuchen und eine Eistüte. Hema hat es sich zum Ziel gesetzt, Plastikprodukte nicht mehr in Plastik zu hüllen, daher wurden Kartonagen gewählt, um die Produkte darin zu verpacken und zu schützen.

Ce packaging pour la chaîne de magasins néerlandaise **Hema** renferme une collection d'objets gonflables pour les activités estivales. L'idée du design était de montrer un éventail de produits semblant avoir été jetés dans des mini-piscines : on y voit même la typique échelle à emprunter pour entrer dans l'eau pour une image plus réaliste. Tous les jouets ont été exclusivement conçus par Hema et représentent les icônes de la chaîne, comme une saucisse fumée, le chien Takkie, un mini-gâteau et un cône de glace. L'objectif d'Hema est d'arrêter de vendre des produits en plastique dans des emballages en plastique, d'où le choix de boîtes en carton pour emballer et protéger ses produits.

HEMA

Concept and Design: Richard Mooij (Magnet Design), Hema design team
Packaging Management: Kirsten Wiarda (Hema)
Project Management: Laura Vermeer (Hema)
Company: Magnet Design
Country: Netherlands
Category: Entertainment

PLATINUM PENTAWARD 2020

STIIK

Art Direction: Kazutoshi Amano
Design: P.K.G.Tokyo / kad ltd.
Product Design: Eiji Sumi
Concept: Kenji Wada
Client: Ko Design Concept
Company: P.K.G.Tokyo
Country: Japan
Category: Household maintenance
GOLD PENTAWARD 2019

METHOD

Senior Direction of Industrial Design: Sean McGreevy
Senior Graphic Design: Michelle Byle
Company: Method Products
Country: USA
Category: Household maintenance

SILVER PENTAWARD 2020

COLORWRAP

Creative Direction and Art Direction: Koichi Sugiyama
Design and Illustration: Minako Endo
Production: Yasushi Funaki
Company: MARU
Country: Japan
Category: Household maintenance

BRONZE PENTAWARD 2019

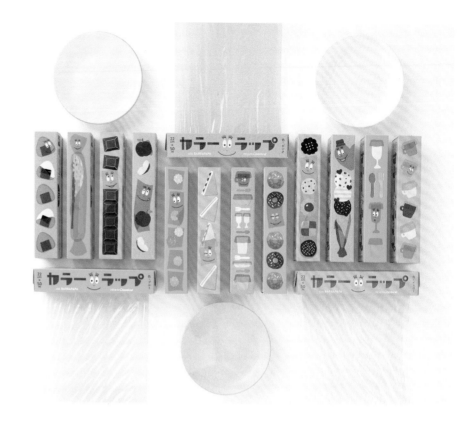

LIVING GREEN

Creative Direction and Design: Debbie Hyde
Design: Mahani Jones
Photography: Melanie Jenkins
Shrink Wrap Printing: Sato New Zealand Ltd
Box Printing: Forbes Packaging
Client: Living Green Group
Company: Brother Design
Country: New Zealand
Category: Household maintenance

SILVER PENTAWARD 2019

JUSTWASH

Creative Direction: Antje Hoffmann, Marc Schmidt
Design: Ann-Katrin Schumann, Verena Hirschberger
Client: Jan-Eric Syring (NU Business GmbH)
Company: alvonsbranding
Country: Germany
Category: Household maintenance

SILVER PENTAWARD 2019

CIF BEAUTIFUL BOTTLE

Creative Direction: Mike Webster
Design: Tim Ryan, Toni Papaloizou, Jon Shaw
CAD Design: Sach Chauhan
Company: 1HQ Brand Agency
Country: UK
Category: Household maintenance

BRONZE PENTAWARD 2020

BONSAI

Creative Direction: Andrey Amlinsky
Art Direction and Design: Olkas Voron
Photography: Anna Zemlyankina
Company: Amlinsky Creative Strategies and Olkas Voron
Country: Russian Federation
Category: Household maintenance

BRONZE PENTAWARD 2019

PRIMAL NATURAL SPONGE

Design: LEDNIK design & photography
Packaging Design, Illustration and Photography:
Alesia Kutsian, Aliaksei Hvozdzeu
Client: Tsyn East Trade
Company: Alesia Kutsian, Aliaksei Hvozdzeu
Country: Belarus
Category: Household maintenance

BRONZE PENTAWARD 2020

MEDICI THREAD

Design: Elena Zaitseva
Country: Russian Federation
Category: Household maintenance

SILVER PENTAWARD 2020

Every DIY store offers a tremendous range of wood finishes. As a rule the packaging design illustrates either their use and effect or the benefits of the brand, but it's not always obvious what type of product it is. **Brite** is an exclusive brand of coatings for wooden surfaces that offers a wide selection of innovative paints and varnishes with organic ingredients. The distinctive packaging design for Brite not only helps the consumer choose the right product but also highlights the brand's passion for wood. The name of each product type is carved from wood and given a main role in the packaging design, whilst the hyper-decorative style of typography illustrates the effect that different types of finishes can provide.

Jeder Baumarkt bietet eine riesige Auswahl an Holzversiegelung an. In der Regel zeigt das Verpackungsdesign entweder die Anwendung und Wirkung oder die Vorteile der Marke, aber es ist nicht immer offensichtlich, um welche Produktart es sich handelt. **Brite** ist eine exklusive Marke für Holzanstriche, die eine große Auswahl an innovativen, biologischen Farben und Lacken anbietet. Das unverwechselbare Verpackungsdesign für Brite hilft dem Kunden nicht nur, das richtige Produkt auszuwählen, sondern unterstreicht auch die Leidenschaft der Marke für Holz. Der Name jedes Produkttyps ist in Holz geschnitzt und spielt die Hauptrolle im Verpackungsdesign. Gleichzeitig veranschaulicht die dekorative Typografie die verschiedenen Arten der Oberflächenbehandlung.

Tous les magasins de bricolage proposent un choix considérable de finitions pour le bois. D'ordinaire, le design du packaging illustre soit leur utilisation et leur résultat, soit les bénéfices de la marque, mais le type de produit n'est pas toujours explicite. **Brite** est une marque exclusive de revêtements pour les surfaces en bois, avec une large gamme de peintures et de vernis innovants à base d'ingrédients biologiques. Le packaging original pour ses produits aide le consommateur à choisir ce qu'il cherche tout en prouvant la passion de la marque pour le bois. Le nom de chaque type de produit est sculpté dans du bois et a tout le protagonisme, alors qu'une typographie dans un style décoratif montre l'effet obtenu avec divers types de finitions.

BRITE

Creative Direction: Alexey Fadeev,
Anastasia Tretyakova
Art Direction and Design: Alexey Baiteev
Project Management: Natalia Bloshenkova
CEO: Alexey Andreev
Executive Direction: Ksenia Parkhomenko
Company: Depot Branding Agency
Country: Russian Federation
Category: Home improvement

GOLD PENTAWARD 2020

METHOD

Industrial Design: Sean McGreevy
Senior Brand Design: Tammy Dyer
Senior Digital Design: Cat Oshiro
Company: Method Products PBC
Country: UK
Category: Home improvement

GOLD PENTAWARD 2019

DULUX VALENTINE

Creative Direction: Robin Quiquempoix,
Léa Le Guyader, Romaric Travard
Account Direction: Diane Rochet
Founder: Isabelle Marchand
Client: Aurore Frontczak, Capucine Duchesne
Company: Elixir Design
Country: France
Category: Home improvement

SILVER PENTAWARD 2019

YIN SHANG YIN

Creative Direction: Yu Guang
Design: Wu Chang Fei
Company: Shenzhen Greensong Design
Country: China
Category: Home improvement

SILVER PENTAWARD 2019

FARROW & BALL

Creative Lead: Arron Egan
Account Lead: Phoebe Hillier
Company: Butterfly Cannon
Country: UK
Category: Home improvement

SILVER PENTAWARD 2020

FATBOY

Creative Direction: Paul Roeters
Design: Studio Fatboy, Jeroen Hoedjes
Company: Studio Kluif
Country: Netherlands
Category: Home improvement

BRONZE PENTAWARD 2019

BLACK AND WHITE TELEVISION AROMATHERAPY

Design: Polaris team
Company: Shenzhen Baixinglong Creative Packaging
Country: China
Category: Home improvement

BRONZE PENTAWARD 2020

PLAT-O TRAYBLE

HYGGE CANDLE

Art Direction: Kiyoshi Ishida
Design and Illustration: Harumi Sasaki
Design: Yurika Dohi
Client: MASH Beauty Lab
Supplier: DAIYO.Inc.
Company: Underline Graphic Inc.
Country: Japan
Category: Home improvement

BRONZE PENTAWARD 2019

Targeting 18- to 29-year-olds, the design for **Mi Sports Bluetooth Headset Mini** took its ideas directly from the young audience it aimed to impress. Nowadays this younger generation uses emojis to chat with each other, rather than typing out words. The strategy was to reflect this language, hence the emoji-like packaging, which makes clever use of the product in the design. The black earphones of the headset can be seen as the eyes of the emoji, whilst the controller becomes the mouth. There are multiple colour variations and graphics available, each showing a different emoji.

Das Design für das **Mi Sports Bluetooth Headset Mini** richtet sich an die Zielgruppe der 18- bis 29-Jährigen und bezieht seinen Look direkt von der jungen Kundschaft, die es beeindrucken will. Heutzutage verwendet die junge Generation Emojis, um zu chatten, statt Wörter auszuschreiben. Die Strategie bestand darin, diese Sprache widerzuspiegeln, daher die emojiähnliche Verpackung, die das Produkt geschickt in das Design integriert. Die schwarzen Kopfhörer des Headsets können als Augen des Emojis gesehen werden, während der Controller zu dessen Mund wird. Es gibt viele verschiedene Farbvarianten, die je ein anderes Emoji zeigen.

La population des 18-29 ans, public ciblé par **Mi Sports Bluetooth Headset Mini**, a été la source d'inspiration directe de son design. Cette génération emploie des emojis plutôt que du texte pour converser. La stratégie était donc de refléter ce langage, d'où un packaging aux allures d'emoji et qui fait un usage astucieux du produit : les écouteurs noirs du casque représentent les yeux, et le contrôleur fait office de bouche. L'emballage se décline en plusieurs couleurs et graphismes pour représenter différents emoji.

MI

Design Direction: Lu Chen
Design and Illustration: Weijie Jiang
Packaging Engineering: Zhizhuang Song
Company: Xiaomi
Country: China
Category: Electronic

GOLD PENTAWARD 2019

INSTAX

General Management: Kazuhisa Horikiri
Design: Akihiko Ikegami
Company: Fujifilm Corporation
Country: Japan
Category: Electronic

GOLD PENTAWARD 2020

MI

Creative Direction: Lu Chen
Graphic Design: Weijie Jiang
Packaging Structure Design: Zhizhuang Song
Company: Xiaomi
Country: China
Category: Electronic

SILVER PENTAWARD 2020

MI

Creative Direction: Lu Chen
Graphic Design: Jiangpeng Su
Packaging Structure Design: Zhizhuang Song
Company: Xiaomi
Country: China
Category: Electronic
SILVER PENTAWARD 2020

BASEUS

Design: YiCheng Luo, PeiJia Wang
Company: Shenzhen Times Innovation Technology
Country: China
Category: Electronic

SILVER PENTAWARD 2019

HEMA

Design: Richard Mooij (Magnet Design)
Client: Kirsten Wiarda (Hema)
Project Management: Brenda Berkholst (Hema)
Photography: Frans van Wijk
Company: Magnet Design
Country: Netherlands
Category: Electronic

BRONZE PENTAWARD 2019

MI

Creative Direction: Lu Chen
Graphic Design: Jiangpeng Su
Illustration: Yan Ni
Packaging Structure Design: Zhizhuang Song
Company: Xiaomi
Country: China
Category: Electronic

BRONZE PENTAWARD 2020

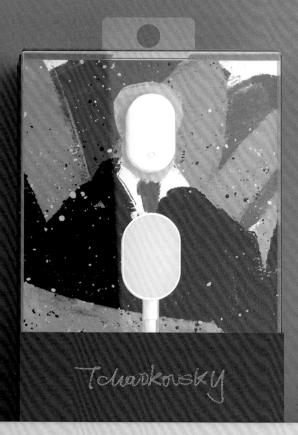

MI

Design Direction: Lu Chen
Design and Illustration: Yan Ni
Packaging Engineering: Zhizhuang Song
Company: Xiaomi
Country: China
Category: Electronic

BRONZE PENTAWARD 2019

MI

Creative Direction: Lu Chen
Graphic Design: Weijie Jiang
Illustration: Yan Ni
Packaging Structure Design: Zhizhuang Song
Company: Xiaomi
Country: China
Category: Electronic

BRONZE PENTAWARD 2020

SAKURA SHIMIZU

Art Direction: Nobuya Hayasaka
Creative Direction: Hitoshi Kobayashi
Design: Nobuya Hayasak
Production: arica design
Client: Sakura Shimizu
Company: arica design
Country: Japan
Category: Non-electronic

GOLD PENTAWARD 2020

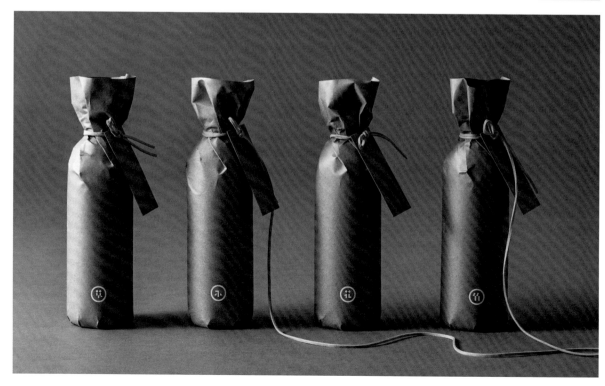

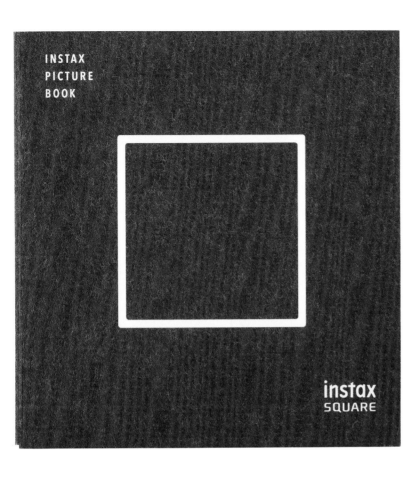

INSTAX SQUARE PICTURE BOOK

Design: Daisuke Sato, Akane Wakabayashi
Company: Fujifilm Corporation
Country: Japan
Category: Non-electronic

GOLD PENTAWARD 2019

OKAERI

Client: Yamachiku Co., Ltd.
Creative Direction: Katsuaki Sato
Art Direction and Design: Takenori Sugimura
Package Design: Yoichi Yoshinaga
Company: Katsuaki
Country: Japan
Category: Non-electronic

SILVER PENTAWARD 2020

ARPHIC

Client: ARPHIC Technology
Art Direction and Design: Hong Da Design Studio
Printing: JIL Print
Photography: Wagn Tzu Hao
Marketing Management: Chiou Ethan
Marketing: Lin Rina
Company: Hong Da Design Studio
Country: Taiwan
Category: Non-electronic

SILVER PENTAWARD 2020

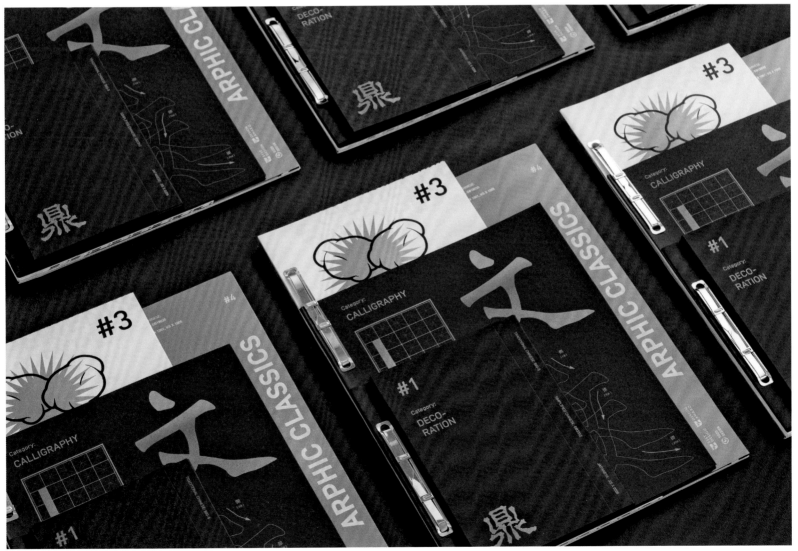

BRUYNZEEL HOLLAND

Founding Partners and Creative Direction:
Vincent Limburg, Heidi Boersma
Company: Guts&Glorious,
Brand and Packaging Designers
Country: Netherlands
Category: Non-electronic

SILVER PENTAWARD 2019

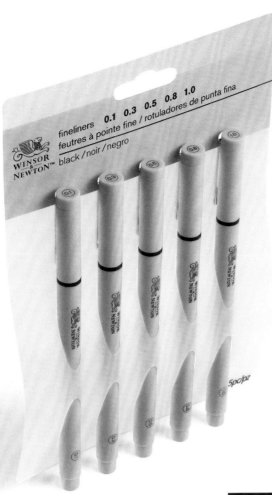

WINSOR & NEWTON

Design Direction and Graphic Design: Emily Fox
Structural Design: Emily Fox, Damian Fournival
Client: Colart
Global Brand Direction: Isabelle Ottiger (Colart)
Senior Brand Management: Marine Fau-Huet (Colart)
Company: Lewis Moberly
Country: UK
Category: Non-electronic
BRONZE PENTAWARD 2019

BETAS

Design: Zhong Hui, Chen Zengli
Company: Huzhou South Taihu Lake Shanghai Normal
University Innovation Design Center
Country: China
Category: Non-electronic
BRONZE PENTAWARD 2020

Aimed at a younger audience, **Song He** whiskey is a blended grain whiskey contained in four fun, stylish and easy-to-carry bottles. The design uses four animal characters, one for each bottle, to represent four different energies for gift-giving: the squirrel representing Kindness, the monkey Justice, the rabbit Wisdom and the bear Power.

Auf eine jüngere Kundschaft zugeschnitten, ist der **Song He** Whiskey, der aus verschiedenen Getreidesorten besteht und in vier stylishen, leicht zu tragenden Flaschen erhältlich ist. Das Design nutzt Tierfiguren, eine für jede Flasche, um die vier verschiedenen Dynamiken des Verschenkens zu repräsentieren: das Eichhörnchen für Freundlichkeit, den Affen für Gerechtigkeit, den Hasen für Weisheit und den Bären für Stärke.

S'adressant à un public jeune, le whisky de grain blended **Song He** est proposé dans quatre bouteilles élégantes et faciles à transporter. Sur chacune d'elles se trouve un personnage animal représentant l'une des quatre motivations pour faire un cadeau : l'écureuil symbolise la bonté, le singe la justice, le lapin la sagesse et l'ours le pouvoir.

SONG HE

Art Direction: Zhang Xiaoming
Company: Unidea Bank
Country: China
Category: Packaging brand identity programmes
GOLD PENTAWARD 2020

CARLSBERG

Founder and Creative Partner: Spencer Buck
Associate Creative Direction: Jonathan Turner-Rogers
Senior Creative Strategy: Rob Wynn-Jones
Account Direction: Laura Lancaster,
Hannah Bartholomew
Design Direction: Jonathan Ferriday
Senior Account Management: Lottie Pettinger
Senior Design: Ali Bartlett, Dave Badock
Design: Jasmine Rees
Junior Design: Liv Beresford-Evans
Client: Carlsberg
Chief Commercial Officer: Jessica Spence (Carlsberg)
Global Design Direction: Jessica Felby (Carlsberg)
Head of Marketing: Richard Whitty (Carlsberg)
Global Brand Direction: Julian Marsili (Carlsberg)
VP Marketing: Russell Jones (Carlsberg)
Design-to-print Management: Rob Martin (Carlsberg)
Design Management: Benjamin Hoffman (Carlsberg)
Company: Taxi Studio
Country: UK
Category: Packaging brand identity programmes
GOLD PENTAWARD 2019

PATISSERIE
BY GASTROPOLIS

GASTROPOLIS FOOD MARKET

Client: Collective LLC
Creative Direction: Armenak Grigoryan
Art Direction and Design: Karen Gevorgyan
Copywriting: Ani Gevorgyan
Company: formascope design
Country: Armenia
Category: Packaging brand identity programmes

SILVER PENTAWARD 2019

ASIAN

Kamar Business Centre, Vazgen Sargsyan 2 / foodmarket@gastropolis.am

ASIAN
BY GASTROPOLIS

+374 (11) 511 511
foodmarket@gastropolis.am
Kamar Business Centre, Vazgen Sargsyan 2

ASIAN
BY GASTROPOLIS

+374 (11) 511 511
foodmarket@gastropolis.am
Kamar Business Centre, Vazgen Sargsyan 2

AIDEN & COCO

Design: Hsuan-Yun Huang
Photography: Gaby Chang
Company: HsuanYun Huang
Country: USA
Category: Packaging brand identity programmes

BRONZE PENTAWARD 2020

SHEVET BREWING & DISTILLING CO

Creative Lead: Jon Davies, Ben Cox
Account Lead: Kate Weakley, Mafalda Volz
Company: Butterfly Cannon
Country: UK
Category: Packaging brand identity programmes

BRONZE PENTAWARD 2020

CUT RUM

Creative Direction: Ben Cox
Company: Butterfly Cannon
Country: UK
Category: Packaging brand identity programmes

BRONZE PENTAWARD 2019

LA DISTILLERIE GÉNÉRALE

Client: Spirits Partners, La Distillerie Générale, Pernod Ricard
Project Direction: Paul-Charles Ricard
Design and Artistic Direction: Paul-Bertrand Mathieu (PBM Design Studio)
Design: Gary Soreil, Mara Bourguignon, Eszter Hegedűs
Photography: Eva Iova
Company: PBM Design Studio
Country: France
Category: Packaging brand identity programmes
SILVER PENTAWARD 2020

BEAK PICK

Brand Strategy Direction: Stepan Avanesyan
Creative Direction: Stepan Azaryan
Project Management: Meri Sargsyan
Design: Eliza Malkhasyan, Stepan Azaryan
Illustration: Elina Barseghyan
Company: Backbone Branding
Country: Armenia
Category: Packaging brand identity programmes

BRONZE PENTAWARD 2019

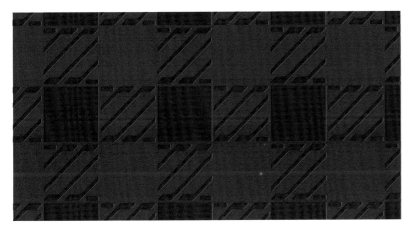

TIM HORTONS

Creative Direction: Miles Marshall
Design: Amy Cobain, Niall Burr, Jamie Nash,
Nick Cross, Jessie Froggett, Sam Jepson
Artwork: James Chilvers, James Norris
Retouching: Mick Connor
Account Management: Isabelle Erixon
Account Direction: Nicola Eager
Company: Turner Duckworth
Country: UK
Category: Packaging brand
identity programmes

SILVER PENTAWARD 2019

FAUNA PET FOOD

Design: Kristina Nyjordet, Thomas Larsen
Illustration: Kristina Nyjordet, Petter Tangen
Design Implementation: Kim Monsen
Logo Design: Robin Mientjes
Client Management: Christian Braaten
Project Management: Hilde Bjerkan
Photography: Johan Wildhagen
Case Photography: Dag Dalvang
Client: Unil
Client Contact: Ingela Falk
Company: Scandinavian Design Group
Country: Norway
Category: Pet products

GOLD PENTAWARD 2019

CAT PERSON

Creative Direction and Design: Brian Steele
Structural Design: Chris Granneberg
Food Packaging: Mythology
Illustration: Paul Davis
Company: Slate
Country: USA
Category: Pet products
GOLD PENTAWARD 2020

Transform this box into a Paw Puzzler that provides hours of feline fascination.

Cat Person

Transform this box into a Cat Chalet. It's the perfect kitty crash-pad.

Cat Person

Eat, play, purr

This isn't just a box…

Cat Person

Cat Person

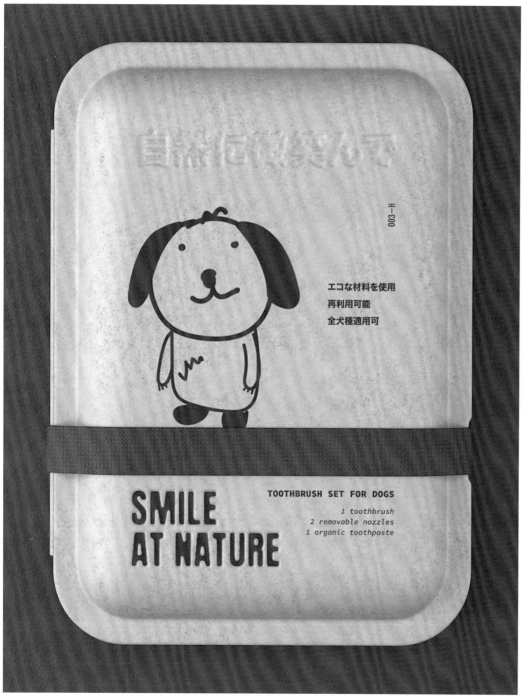

自然に微笑んで

H-003

エコな材料を使用
再利用可能
全犬種適用可

SMILE
AT NATURE

TOOTHBRUSH SET FOR DOGS
1 toothbrush
2 removable nozzles
1 organic toothpaste

TOOTHBRUSH SET FOR DOGS

Design, Structural Design and Art Direction:
Anastasia Igolnikova
3D Rendering: Yaroslav Sotov
Company: Anastasia Igolnikova
Country: Russian Federation
Category: Pet products

SILVER PENTAWARD 2020

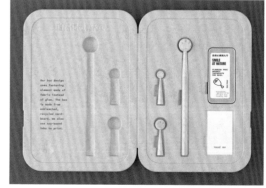

INTRATUIN

Art Direction: Paul Roeters
Design: Rob Corman
Company: Studio Kluif
Country: Netherlands
Category: Pet products
BRONZE PENTAWARD 2020

BOMBELLY

Creative Direction and Graphic Design:
Ján Paukovic
Company: The Twentytwo
Country: Slovakia
Category: Pet products
BRONZE PENTAWARD 2020

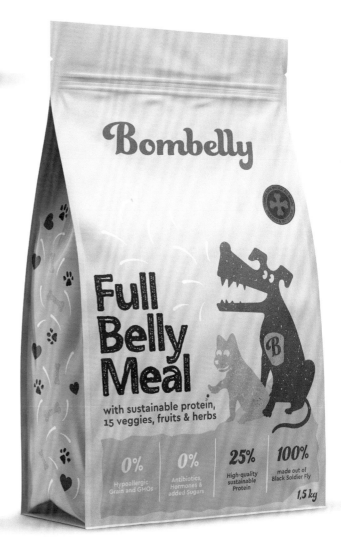

DANO

Design and Illustration: Bart Nagel
Technical Artwork: Joost Verbruggen
Copywriting: Martijn de Vreeze, Copycommando
Company: Now Even Better
Country: Netherlands
Category: Pet products

SILVER PENTAWARD 2019

REAL KATZENNAHRUNG

Creative Direction: Michelle Romeo-Wiegman
Design: Lissanne Snoek
Art Direction (Communication): Gerard Teuben
Illustration: Willemijn de Lint
Manufacturing: Real, SB-Warenhaus GmbH
Supplier: Partner In Pet Food
Company: Yellow Dress Retail
Country: Netherlands
Category: Pet products

BRONZE PENTAWARD 2019

BRISTLY BRUSHING STICK

Brand Strategy Direction: Stepan Avanesyan
Assistant Brand Strategy: Lusie Grigoryan
Creative Direction and Design: Stepan Azaryan
Project Management: Meri Sargsyan
Design: Gevorg Balyan
Client: Bristly Brushing Stick
Company: Backbone Branding
Country: Armenia
Category: Pet products
BRONZE PENTAWARD 2019

ALFASAN NATURALLY

Owner and Creative Direction: Kevin Davis,
Kyanne Bückmann
Company: Bowler & Kimchi
Country: Netherlands
Category: Pet products
SILVER PENTAWARD 2019

Out of nostalgia for **Seagull Camera**, a famous camera brand founded in 1958, Shanghai Seagull Digital Camera Co., Ltd. decided to restart the product line and remanufacture this iconic product. It is not only a digital camera but also a time machine that can capture every special moment, place and event. The use of copper and brown leather in the packaging are characteristic of Chinese industry of the 1950s, whilst the exquisite bronzing and lock add to the collectability of the product.

Aus Nostalgie für die **Seagull Camera**, entschied die Kameramarke Shanghai Seagull Digital Camera Co., Ltd., die 1958 gegründet wurde, sein beliebtes Produkt neu aufzulegen. Dabei handelt es sich nicht nur um eine Digitalkamera, sondern auch um eine Zeitmaschine, die besondere Momente, Orte und jedes Ereignis aufzeichnen kann. Die Verwendung von Kupfer und braunem Leder für die Verpackung sind charakteristisch für die chinesische Industrie der 1950er-Jahre, während die exquisite Bronzefarbe und der Verschluss jedes Sammlerherz höher schlagen lässt.

C'est par nostalgie pour **Seagull Camera**, la célèbre marque d'appareils photo fondée en 1958, que Shanghai Seagull Digital Camera Co., Ltd. a décidé de relancer la gamme et de refabriquer ce produit emblématique. Plus qu'un appareil numérique, cette machine à remonter le temps capture les moments, les lieux et les événements spéciaux. Pour le packaging, le recours au cuivre et au cuir brun est typique de l'industrie chinoise dans les années 1950, alors que le superbe brunissement et le mode de fermeture font du produit un objet de collection.

SEAGULL CAMERA

Design: Zhihao Zhang
Company: KHT Brand
Country: China
Category: Entertainment
GOLD PENTAWARD 2019

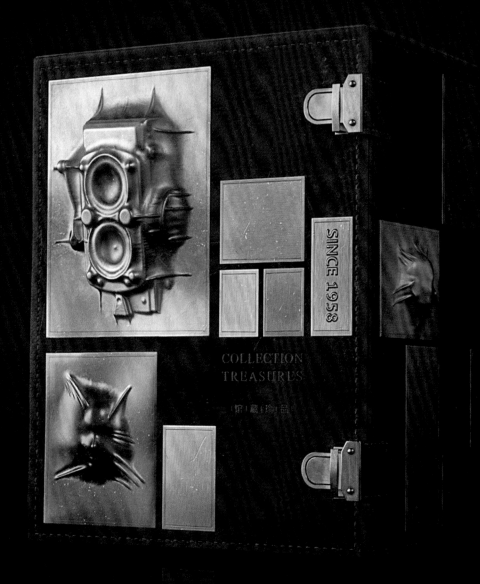

BRAND LOYALTY

Art Direction: Paul Roeters, Jeroen Hoedjes
Design: Jeroen Hoedjes
Company: Studio Kluif
Country: Netherlands
Category: Entertainment

GOLD PENTAWARD 2020

In preparation for the 2020 UEFA European Football Championship, **Brand Loyalty** designed football mascots for young football fans to represent each country: a lion for the Netherlands, a rooster for France, an eagle for Poland, etc. The packaging has a round die-cut on both the front and back, allowing the football to be visible, whilst the mascot illustration on the football is carried over onto the packaging.

Als Vorbereitung auf die europäische Fußball-meisterschaft 2020 entwarf **Brand Loyalty** Fußball-maskottchen für junge Fans, die die Mitgliedsländer repräsentieren sollten: einen Löwen für die Niederlande, einen Hahn für Frankreich, einen Adler für Polen usw. Die Verpackung hat sowohl auf der Vorder- als auch auf der Rückseite eine runde Stanzung, durch der der Ball sichtbar ist. Das Zusammenspiel der Illustrationen auf Ball und Verpackung erweckt das Fußballtier zum Leben.

En prévision de la Ligue des champions de l'UEFA 2020, **Brand Loyalty** a conçu pour les jeunes amateurs de football des mascottes correspondant à chaque pays : un lion pour les Pays-Bas, un coq pour la France, un aigle pour la Pologne, etc. Grâce à une ouverture circulaire à l'avant et à l'arrière, le packaging laisse apprécier le ballon illustré d'une mascotte dont l'image se prolonge sur l'emballage.

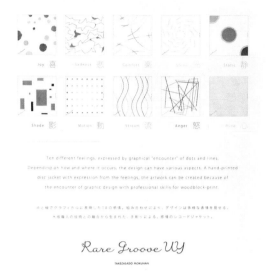

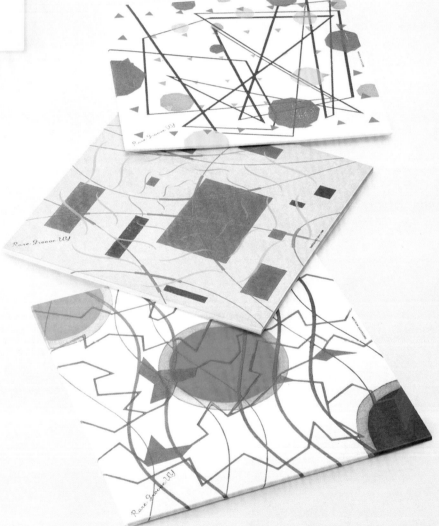

RARE GROOVE UY

Creative Direction: Kenji Takenaka
Art Direction: Yoshiki Uchida
Design: Yoshiki Uchida, Satori Nami,
Takuya Wada
Print Direction: Kenji Takenaka
Creative Team: Kazuki Nojima,
Daiki Nagai, Hiroka Yabushita
Company: cosmos
Country: Japan
Category: Entertainment

SILVER PENTAWARD 2019

YOUWHO
SALIVA COLLECTION KIT

Creative Direction and Art Direction: Yena Choi
Concept Execution: Jinha Seo
Main Graphic Design: Soomin Jo
Illustration and Motion Graphics: Soomin Jo,
Jinha Seo
Company: B for Brand
Country: Republic of Korea
Category: Entertainment

BRONZE PENTAWARD 2020

PUFFIN KIDS

Design Direction: Liao Jie
Product Design: Song Tianman
Graphic Design: Liao Jie, Zheng Yihan
Illustration: Natasha Durley
Company: PuffinKids, Liao Jie
Country: China
Category: Entertainment

BRONZE PENTAWARD 2020

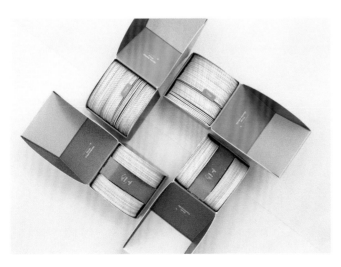

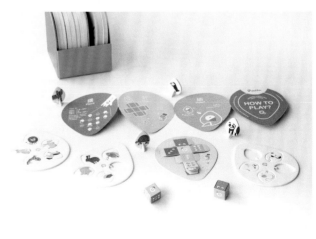

NEUDIES

Client: Nuedies
Product Design, Graphic Design, Illustration,
Photography and Art Direction: Enrique Diaz Rato
Company: Enrique Diaz Rato
Country: USA
Category: Entertainment
BRONZE PENTAWARD 2019

BLOKKER

Creative Direction: Paul Roeters
Design: Rob Corman
Company: Studio Kluif
Country: Netherlands
Category: Entertainment
SILVER PENTAWARD 2019

AGRRR MONSTERS

Art Direction: Alex Bychkov
Design: Nady Sapozhnikova, Irina Travnikova
Company: Addict Design Studio
Country: Russian Federation
Category: Entertainment

SILVER PENTAWARD 2020

MAKO CREATIONS

Design: David Rayer
Account Management: Delphine Oberto
Company: Ovis Nigra
Country: France
Category: Entertainment

BRONZE PENTAWARD 2019

HUANG SHAN

Art Direction: Chen Yingsong
Graphic Design: Cheng Wenbin, Tang Zhong
Company: Shenzhen Yuto Packaging Technology
Country: China
Category: Tobacco and products for smokers

GOLD PENTAWARD 2019

LIBERTINE
WHOLE FLOWER CBD VAPE STICKS

Chief Creative Officer: Damon Gorrie
Creative Direction: Adam Walko
Chief Strategy Officer: Georgia Levison
Design Direction and Design: Rebecca Ingersoll
VP of Client Services: Kate Dell'Aquila
Illustration: Jessica Benhar
Company: Safari Sundays
Country: USA
Category: Products for smokers

GOLD PENTAWARD 2020

OMURA

Creative Direction: Adam Walko
Design Direction: Matthew Smiroldo
VP of Client Services: Kate Dell'Aquila
Chief Strategy Officer: Georgia Levison
Company: Safari Sundays
Country: USA
Category: Tobacco and products for smokers

SILVER PENTAWARD 2019

SEPTWOLVES

Design: Yuanbu Yin
Company: Shenzhen Oracle Creative Design
Country: China
Category: Tobacco and products for smokers

BRONZE PENTAWARD 2019

VUSE

Strategy: Francesco Marziale
Creative Direction: Tristan Macherel,
Christine Raftopoulos
Account Direction: Marcia Clapson
Company: Landor
Country: UK
Category: Products for smokers

BRONZE PENTAWARD 2020

ROACH

Group Account Direction: Kiki Saxon
Creative Direction: Leigh Chandler
Strategy Direction: Emily Cristoforis
Strategy: Katie Hughes
Associate Design Direction: Tom Feilla
Senior Design: Lucie Mouchet
Company: Vault49
Country: USA
Category: Products for smokers

SILVER PENTAWARD 2020

CAMEL

Group Account Direction: Kiki Saxon
Senior Account Management: Hayley Hogan
Creative Direction: Sam Wilkes
Senior Design: Chris Wise
Company: Vault49
Country: USA
Category: Products for smokers

BRONZE PENTAWARD 2020

THEORY WELLNESS

Structural Design and Manufacturing: Duallok
Brand Agency: HIPPO Premium Packaging
Client: Theory Wellness
Creative Direction: Dane Whitehurst
Managing Direction: Rosie Reardon
Design: Dane Whitehurst, Ben Moody, Alex Parker
Photography: Lucy Parker
Copywriting: Alethea Price
Company: Burgopak
Country: UK
Category: Tobacco and products for smokers

BRONZE PENTAWARD 2019

HUANGSHAN

Design: Li Jianghui, Liu Qingsong, Xiao Jie
Client: China Tobacco Anhui Industrial
Manufacturing: Shenzhen Jinjia Group
Company: Shenzhen Qianhai Blueprint
Culture Communication
Country: China
Category: Tobacco and products for smokers

SILVER PENTAWARD 2019

TIANGAOYUNDAN

尽早戒烟有益健康
戒烟可减少对健康的危害

天高雲淡

本公司提示
吸烟有害健康
请勿在禁烟场所吸烟

KUNGFU

Design: Li Xie, Liang Liu
Visualisation: Pan Chen, XiaoQi Chen, DongLing Han
Photography: Jian Zeng, Chun Li
Company: Sichuan Sanlian New Material
Country: China
Category: Products for smokers

SILVER PENTAWARD 2020

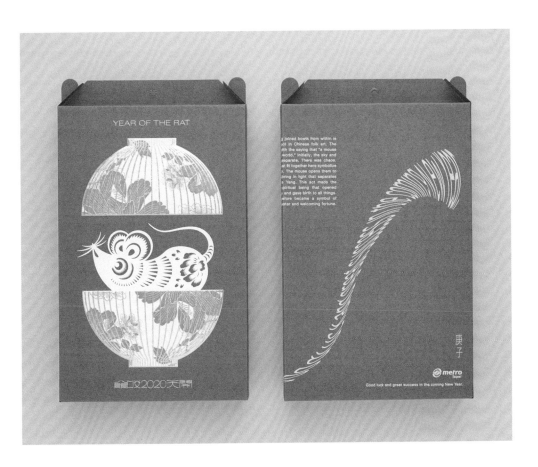

TAIPEI METRO YEAR OF THE RAT COMMEMORATIVE TICKETS

Design: Midnight Design
Creative Direction: I Chan Su
Art Direction: Yi Gu
Photography: Mo Chien
Client: Taipei Rapid Transit Corporation
Company: Midnight Design
Country: Taiwan
Category: Self-promotion

BRONZE PENTAWARD 2020

BURGOPAK

Company and Manufacturing: Burgopak
Concept, Artwork, Design and Photography: Lucy Parker
Copywriting: Alethea Price
Company: Burgopak
Country: UK
Category: Self-promotion

BRONZE PENTAWARD 2019

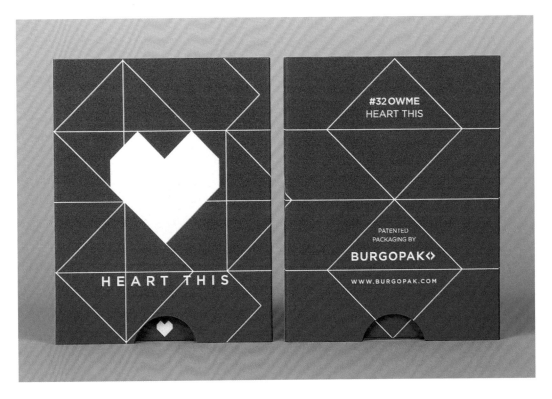

CLAY FIGURE

General Management: Kazuhisa Horikiri
Design: Daisuke Sato
Company: Fujifilm Corporation
Country: Japan
Category: Self-promotion

SILVER PENTAWARD 2019

This company-issued **Rat Apple Cider** was presented as a New Year's gift to the partners of Svoe Mnenie branding agency. The ordinary bottle was made to look like a rat – the symbol of the year according to the Chinese calendar. A cork covered with red sealing wax forms the rat's nose, the whiskers are made of twine and the red eyes and ears are printed on the paper package of the bottle. On the bottle label, an apple-shaped brain holds keywords related to the agency's work and symbolises the taste of the drink itself. It is also worth mentioning that the stem of the fruit takes the shape of a rat, happily leaving the maze of tasks completed in the passing year.

Dieser **Rat Apple Cider** wurde den Partnern der Svoe Mnenie Branding Agentur als Neujahrsgeschenk überreicht. Handelsübliche Flaschen wurden dafür in Ratten verwandelt – laut dem chinesischen Kalender das Tierkreiszeichen des Jahres. Ein Korken, bedeckt mit rotem Siegelwachs, formt die Nase der Ratte, Fäden um den Flaschenhals bilden die Schnurrhaare und rote Augen sowie die Ohren sind auf einen Papierumschlag gedruckt. Es ist noch erwähnenswert, dass das Etikett, ein apfelförmiges Gehirn, die Mottos der Agentur führt und gleichzeitig den Geschmack des Getränks symbolisiert. Der Stiel der Frucht formt eine Ratte, die das Labyrinth aus erledigten Aufgaben des Jahres glücklich hinter sich lässt.

Le cidre **Rat Apple Cider** a été produit comme cadeau de Nouvel An aux partenaires de l'agence de branding Svoe Mnenie. La bouteille a été pensée pour ressembler à un rat, signe de l'année selon le calendrier chinois. Recouvert de cire à cacheter rouge, le bouchon représente le nez de l'animal, alors que ses moustaches sont faites de ficelle et ses yeux rouges et ses oreilles sont imprimés sur l'emballage papier de la bouteille. Sur l'étiquette, un cerveau en forme de pomme contient des mots clés liés au travail de l'agence et symbolise le goût de la boisson ; sans compter la tige du fruit en forme de rat heureux de sortir du labyrinthe de projets accomplis l'année passée.

RAT APPLE CIDER

Creative Direction: Andrey Kugaevskikh
Design: Anastasia Ushnurtseva
Company: Svoe Mnenie
Country: Russian Federation
Category: Self-promotion

SILVER PENTAWARD 2020

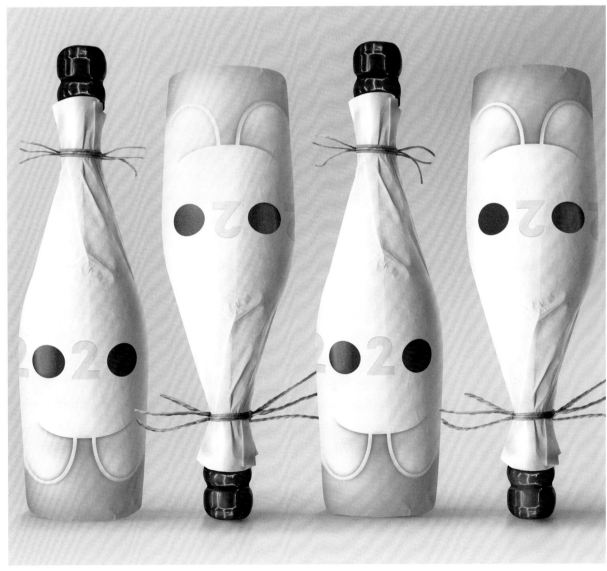

SARISTI

Creative Direction: Antonia Skaraki
Design: Valia Alousi, Evri Makridis, Andreas Deskas
Copywriting: Sotiria Theodorou
Company: A.S. Advertising
Country: Greece
Category: Self-promotion

BRONZE PENTAWARD 2020

NOW EVEN BETTER

Concept, Design and Typography: Bart Nagel
Production Management: Oscar Flier
Box and Wrapper Printing: Drukkerij Aeroprint
Pad Printing of Bottle: Walter Jonkman, MWJ Print
Company: Now Even Better
Country: Netherlands
Category: Self-promotion

BRONZE PENTAWARD 2019

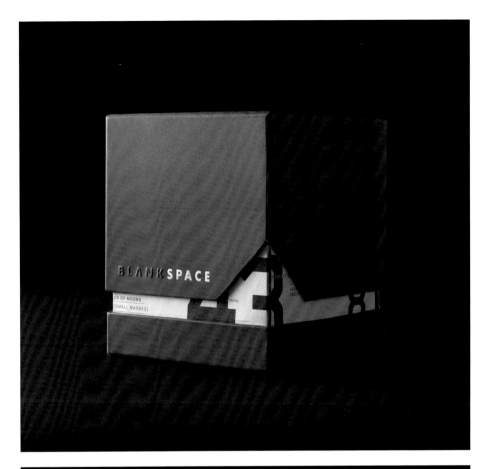

BLANKSPACE

Lead Design: Michael Guite
Design: Sarah Howley, Ben Alpert, Andy Powell
Copywriting: William Burns
Associate Creative Direction: JoEllen Martinson Davis
Senior Production Design: Paula Van Beckum
President and Creative Direction: Shane Breault
Project Management: Carolyn Weatherhead
Company: Ultra Creative
Country: USA
Category: Self-promotion

BRONZE PENTAWARD 2020

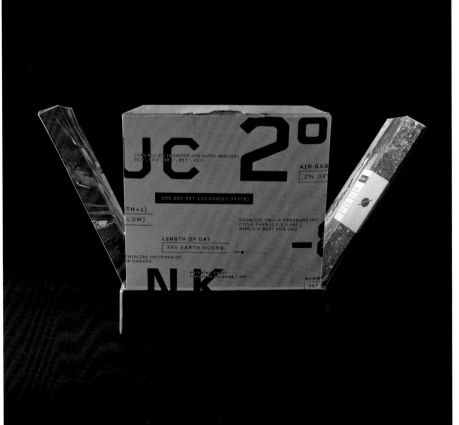

YANGYANGLA

Creative Direction: Xiongbo Deng
Design: Xiaoyu Li
Illustration: Xiaoyu Li, Xing Liu
Client: Yunnan Jianshui Honghui Breeding Industry
Company: ShenZhen Lingyun Creative Packaging Design
Country: China
Category: Baby products

GOLD PENTAWARD 2020

HUGGIES

General Management: Lori Gross
Executive Creative Direction: Valerie Aurilio
Client Direction: Katie Mancini, Phyllis Murphy
Design: Candace Carson, Hannah Mot
Client Management: Marissa Stoiber
Company: WPP
Country: USA
Category: Baby products

GOLD PENTAWARD 2019

A HAPPY KOALA

Brand Management: Alicia Arteaga
Photography: Carles Rodrigo
Company: Creatique
Country: Spain
Category: Baby products

BRONZE PENTAWARD 2020

Conscious hugs for curious kids

A Happy Koala quiere ser un miembro más
de la familia. Arropamos a los peques con un
cuellito suave, de algodón 100% orgánico,
que se confecciona exclusivamente en España.

ahappykoala_kids | ahappykoala.com

SIENNA & FRIENDS

Creative Direction: Patrick De Grande
Design: Sara Gunnarsson, Marloes Zwaenepoel
Company: Quatre Mains
Country: Belgium
Category: Baby products

SILVER PENTAWARD 2020

HOWIES

Art Direction and Graphic Design: Lennaert Stam,
Jasper van Grunsven, Aniek Frölke
Company: maan identity. design. content.
Country: Netherlands
Category: Baby products

BRONZE PENTAWARD 2020

LITTLE FREDDIE BABY FOOD

Creative Direction: Paul Williams
Design Direction: Kevin Daly
Company: Springetts
Country: UK
Category: Baby products

BRONZE PENTAWARD 2019

PICUALIA

Design: Isabel Cabello
Company: Cabello x Mure
Country: Spain
Category: Baby products

SILVER PENTAWARD 2020

NIMBLE

Group Account Direction: Sarah Wildmann
3D Design Direction: Mark Armstrong,
Simon Newbegin
2D Design Direction: Luke Roberts
Company: Marks R5
Country: UK
Category: Baby products

SILVER PENTAWARD 2019

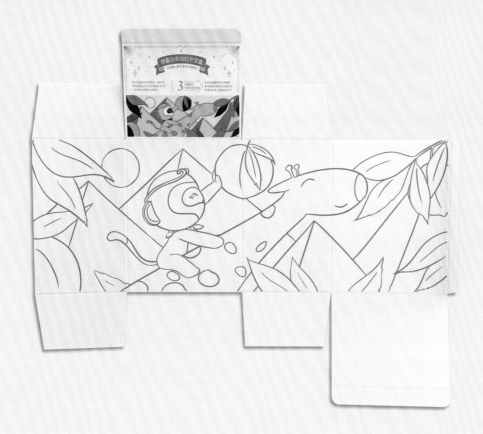

LONGMU ZHUANGGU KELI

Design: SenseBird Design Team
Company: Wuhan SenseBird Design
Country: China
Category: Baby products

SILVER PENTAWARD 2019

SOFTLOVE SUPERTHIN

Creative Direction: Joey Lo
Design: Joey Lo, Lily Li
Illustration: Lily Li
Art Direction: Yvonne Chung
Company: The Box Brand Design
Country: Hong Kong
Category: Baby products

BRONZE PENTAWARD 2019

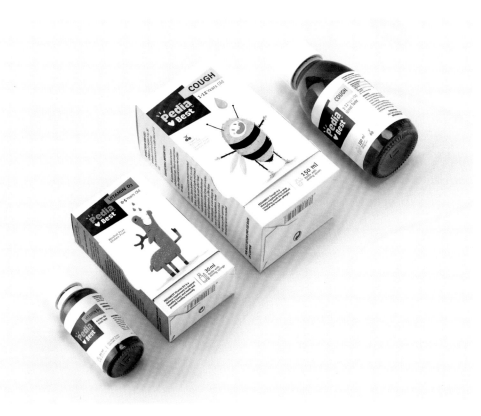

PEDIA BEST

Art Direction: Seyyed Mostafa Seyyed Ebrahimi
Creative Direction: Yekta Jebelli
Illustration: Yekta Jebelli
Design: Yekta Jebelli, Seyyed Mostafa Seyyed Ebrahimi
Client: Pedorifamp, Pedia Best Brand
Company: DEEEZ – Design & Creativity
Country: Iran
Category: Baby products

BRONZE PENTAWARD 2020

WILDLY CRAFTED BOTTLES

Design: Seriesnemo industrial and graphic team
Company: Seriesnemo
Country: Spain
Category: Sustainable design

GOLD PENTAWARD 2020

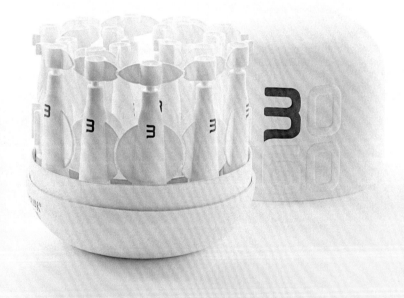

BIOHYALUX

Creative Direction: Zhang Xiao Wie
Design: Xu Jing, Qin Zeng Wei, Li Jing Yan
Photography: Gao Feng
Client: Biohyalux
Company: Beijing Weina Culture and Art
Country: China
Category: Sustainable design

GOLD PENTAWARD 2019

The glass in **Wildly Crafted Bottles** comes from an industrial oven with the highest percentage of PCR (post-consumer recycled) glass in the market. All types of recycled glass are accepted, meaning that slight variations occur, but this is seen to reflect the authenticity and exclusivity of the products. NºT REGULAR Spirits embraces imperfections, thereby reducing waste. The inevitable defects that appear during production are integrated and not considered errors but values of differentiation, creating a unique product.

Das Glas der **Wildly Crafted Bottles** stammt aus einem Industrieofen mit dem auf dem Markt höchsten Prozentanteil von PCR-Glas (Post-Consumer-Recycled, also nach der Nutzung durch den Konsumenten recyceltes Glas). Alle Arten von Glas werden genutzt, was bedeutet, dass kleine Farbunterschiede entstehen können, wodurch aber die Authentizität und Exklusivität widergespiegelt wird. NºT REGULAR Spirits nimmt Unvollkommenheit an und reduziert so Abfall. Kleine Fehler, die während der Produktion entstehen, werden integriert und kreieren ein einzigartiges Produkt.

Les bouteilles **Wildly Crafted Bottles** sont fabriquées dans un four industriel avec du verre contenant le pourcentage PCR (recyclé post-consommation) le plus élevé du marché. Tous les types de verre recyclé sont acceptés, ce qui entraîne de légères variations et rend les produits authentiques et exclusifs. NºT REGULAR Spirits se saisit de ces imperfections en vue de réduire le gaspillage. Ces défauts inévitables apparaissant en cours de production sont conservés et ne sont pas considérés comme des erreurs, mais comme une marque de différenciation au résultat unique.

BIOPAK

Marketing Direction: Fredrik Sverkersten
Design: Karolin Larsson
Project Management: Tatiana Korobova
Company: Duni Group
Country: Sweden
Category: Sustainable design
SILVER PENTAWARD 2020

KEVIN.MURPHY

Founder and Creative Direction: Kevin Murphy
Managing Direction: Christian Jensen
(Pack Tech A/S)
Company: Kevin.Murphy
Country: USA
Category: Sustainable design
BRONZE PENTAWARD 2020

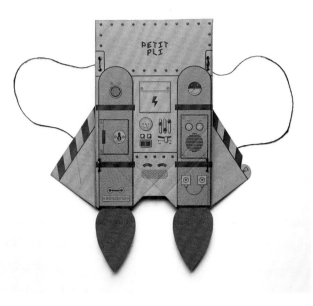

PETIT PLI

Creative Direction: Alan Dye, Nick Finney
Design and Illustration: Sam Pittman
Manufacturing: Box & Seal
Client: Ryan Marion Yasin
Company: NB Studio
Country: UK
Category: Sustainable design

BRONZE PENTAWARD 2019

HUMAN

Design: Linea team
Company: Linea
Country: France
Category: Sustainable design
BRONZE PENTAWARD 2020

CIF BEAUTIFUL BOTTLE

Creative Direction: Mike Webster
Design: Tim Ryan, Toni Papaloizou, Jon Shaw
CAD Design: Sach Chauhan
Company: IHQ Brand Agency
Country: UK
Category: Sustainable design
BRONZE PENTAWARD 2020

ZËRNA

Creative Direction: Farrukh Sharipov
Client Service Direction: Alina mirzaeva
Account Management: Anna Pak
Art Direction: Timur Aitov
Copywriting: Aleksandra Khalimon
Design: Tamilla Mirzaeva, Kristina Popova
Company: Synthesis creative lab
Country: Uzbekistan
Category: Sustainable design

SILVER PENTAWARD 2020

To replace plastic packaging, **Zёrna** came up with the first vegetable-based packaging made from pumpkins. Lagenaria plant, or bottle gourd, is ideal as packaging for dried fruits thanks to its environmental friendliness, moisture and light resistance, reusability, unique pattern, size and shape. In the Middle Ages, lagenaria was used as a vessel for storing water and spices in Central Asia, as the dry vegetable's shape and rigidity made it perfect for transporting these goods. This packaging decomposes in just a year and then serves as an organic fertiliser for new plants.

Als Ersatz für Kunststoffverpackungen hat **Zёrna** die erste moderne Verpackung aus Kürbissen entwickelt. Die Lagenaria-Pflanze, auch Flaschenkürbis genannt, ist umweltfreundlich, feuchtigkeits- und lichtresistent, wiederverwendbar und hat einzigartige Muster und Formen: Sie eignet sich ideal als Verpackung für Trockenfrüchte. Aufgrund ihrer Form und Härte im getrockneten Zustand wurde die Lagenaria schon im Mittelalter verwendet, um Wasser und Gewürze in Zentralasien zu transportieren. Diese Verpackung kompostiert in nur einem Jahr und dient dann als organischer Dünger für neue Pflanzen.

Comme alternative aux emballages en plastique, **Zёrna** a inventé le premier packaging végétal fabriqué à base de citrouilles. La calebasse, ou gourde, est idéale comme emballage pour les fruits secs en raison de sa viabilité écologique, de sa résistance à l'humidité et à la lumière, de sa capacité de réutilisation, ainsi que de son aspect, sa forme et sa taille uniques. Au Moyen Âge, la calebasse était employée en Asie centrale comme récipient pour stocker l'eau et les épices car une fois séchée, elle offrait une forme et une rigidité idéales pour leur transport. Ce packaging ne prend qu'un an pour se décomposer et sert ensuite d'engrais organique pour de nouvelles plantes.

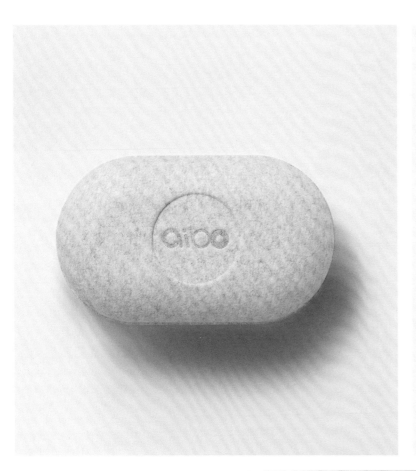

AIBO

Design: Kenichi Hirose,
Daigo Maesaka, Tetsuro Tsuji
Company: Sony Corporation
Country: Japan
Category: Sustainable design

SILVER PENTAWARD 2019

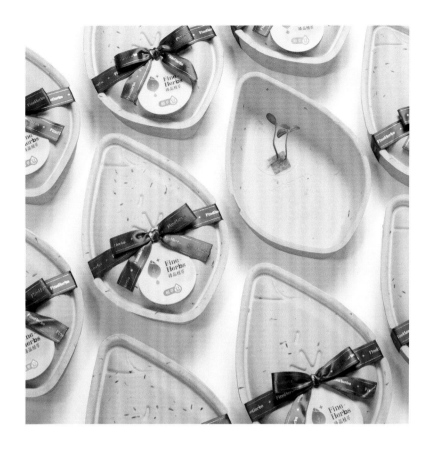

NEW HOPE SEED

President: Yung-Li Chen
Creative Direction: Jigle Tsai
General Management: Kai-Ting Chang
Design Management: Pin Tsai
Stock Management: Tzu-Hsin Wang
Art Management: Ya-Lan Yang
Pchome Chief: Shu-Hui Wu
Post Mall Chief: Pei-Chi Chen
Company: Fineherbsoap
Country: Taiwan
Category: Sustainable design

BRONZE PENTAWARD 2019

METHOD

Direction of Industrial Design: Sean McGreevy
Senior Brand Design: Tammy Dyer
Senior Digital Design: Cat Oshiro
Company: Method Products PBC
Country: UK
Category: Sustainable design

SILVER PENTAWARD 2019

AMPLE

Creative Direction: Jacob Norstedt
Design: Tobias Rehnvall
Design Direction: Jonas Berg
Account Management: Ida Stagles
Company: Silver
Country: Sweden
Category: Distributors'/retailers' own brands/
private labels

GOLD PENTAWARD 2020

ALBERT HEIJN

Design: Tahir Idouri, Jobert vd Bovenkamp
Account Management: Sascha Goutier
Illustration: Fred van Deelen
Company: Millford
Country: Netherlands
Category: Distributors'/retailers' own brands/
private labels
GOLD PENTAWARD 2019

LEADER PRICE

Creative Direction: Melanie Seneze
Design: Léa Bayram
Account Management: Céline Ferreira, Marie Carral
Business Management: Arnaud Kervella
Client: Hélène Bousquet , Marceline Gendry
Company: Surf
Country: France
Category: Distributors'/retailers' own brands/
private labels

SILVER PENTAWARD 2020

EL CORTE INGLÉS

Creative Direction: Paco Adín
Account Direction: Lourdes Morillas
Account Management: Susana Seijas
Corporate Private Brand Management: José A. Rojano
Company: Supperstudio
Country: Spain
Category: Distributors'/retailers' own brands/
private labels

SILVER PENTAWARD 2020

MOTOMASTER

VP Account Direction: Sara Merrifield
VP Creative Direction: Mark Roberts
Design: Paul Scarfo
Company: Davis
Country: Canada
Category: Distributors'/retailers' own brands/
private labels
BRONZE PENTAWARD 2020

STARBUCKS

Creative Direction: Qin Shaohui
Art Direction: Sun Li, Ge Yaqi
Client: Starbucks
Company: Shanghai Heguan Management Consulting
Country: China
Category: Distributors'/retailers' own brands/
private labels
SILVER PENTAWARD 2019

SUSHI VESLA

Art Direction: Ermek Cherkesov
Creative Direction: Oleg Barinboim
Agency Production: Sevda Jalal
Case Direction: Dmitry Kostuchenko
Account Management: Anna Dzhandoeva
Executive Creative Direction: Dmitry Tutkov
Company: TUTKOVBUDKOV
Country: Russian Federation
Category: Distributors'/retailers' own brands/
private labels

SILVER PENTAWARD 2019

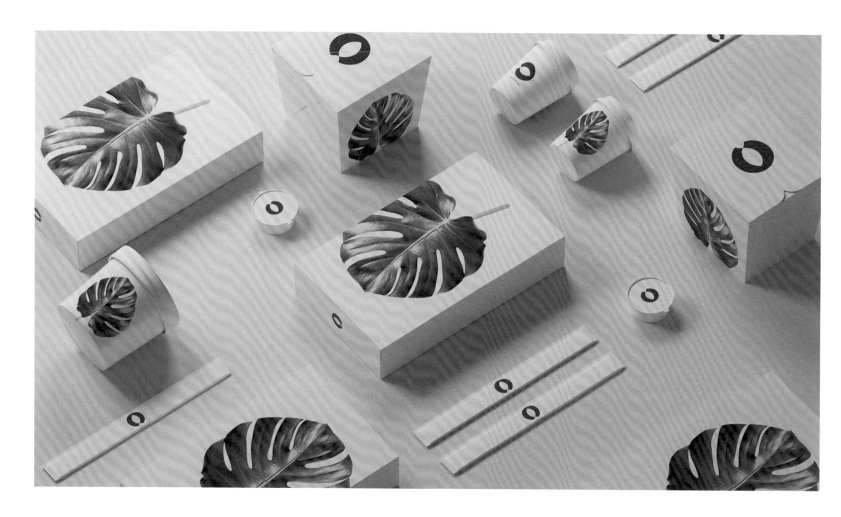

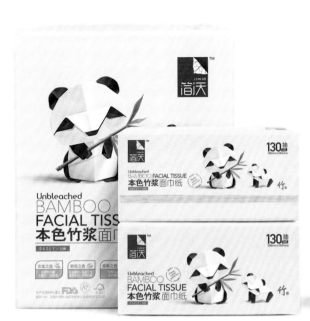

JIAN WO

Creative Direction: Jeff Wu
Graphic Design: Qiong Wu, Juan Ying Zheng
Client: Womai, COFCO
Company: Beijing Perfect Point Design
Country: China
Category: Distributors'/retailers' own brands/
private labels

BRONZE PENTAWARD 2019

DUNHUANG IMPRESSIONISM

Creative and Art Direction: Tom Shi
Project Management: Camelia Leung
Design: Camelia Leung, Tin Liu, Yuxin Liu
Concept Shooting Creative: Camelia Leung,
Zhenghao Fan
Concept Shooting Executive: Tangtu Photography
Concept Photo Assistance: Jiandong Shen
Online Promotion: Num Lo, Ivy Li, Xitong Hu
Copywriting: Camelia Leung
Print Production: Prestige Prints
Art Paper: Lanbiyuan Holding Group
Company: Tomshi & Associates
Country: China
Category: Distributors'/retailers' own brands/
private labels

BRONZE PENTAWARD 2020

BRIGHT MEN

Creative Direction: Yoshio Kato
Art Direction: Yoshio Kato, Eijiro Kuniyoshi
Design and Illustration: Takaaki Hashimoto
Company: Kotobuki Seihan Printing
Country: Japan
Category: Packaging concept (professional)

GOLD PENTAWARD 2019

Bean Playing Tennis is a packaging concept that not only stands out but helps motivate kids to get outside and have fun. Inspired by the green bean, this tennis ball pack takes the shape of a massive bean pod and holds four green bean tennis balls. With a semi-matt finish the hard plastic pod clamps the balls in place but is soft enough to allow the balls to be pulled out of it. A hook extends from the top of the bean pod in an organic shape, allowing it to be hung in shop displays or on the mesh fence at a tennis court.

Bean Playing Tennis ist ein Verpackungskonzept, das nicht nur heraussticht, sondern auch dazu beiträgt, Kinder zu motivieren, nach draußen zu gehen und Spaß zu haben. Inspiriert von grünen Bohnen, hat dieses Paket mit Tennisbällen die Form einer Bohnenhülse, die vier grüne Bohnen-Tennisbälle enthält. Mit einer halbmatten Oberfläche klemmt die harte Kunststoffschale die Bälle fest ein, ist aber weich genug, dass man die Bälle gut herausziehen kann. An der Oberseite der Bohnenhülse ist ein Haken angebracht, an dem man sie sowohl im Schaufenster als auch am Maschendrahtzaun auf dem Tennisplatz aufhängen kann.

Bean Playing Tennis est un concept d'emballage qui ne passe pas inaperçu et motive les enfants à sortir et s'amuser. Imitant un haricot vert, cet étui pour balles de tennis ressemble à une énorme cosse et peut contenir quatre balles-graines. De finition semi-mate, cette cosse en plastique dur retient les balles mais est suffisamment souple pour pouvoir les retirer. La partie supérieure se termine par un crochet de forme organique permettant de pendre la cosse dans une vitrine ou au filet du court de tennis.

BEAN PLAYING TENNIS

Owner and Creative Direction:
Kyanne Bückmann, Kevin Davis
Company: Bowler & Kimchi
Country: Netherlands
Category: Packaging concept (professional)

GOLD PENTAWARD 2020

MINI KEYBOARD PACKAGE

Production: Design Unit, Product Development,
Headquarters, Casio Computer
Direction: Nagayama Yosuke
Design: Kato Shuji, Murata Fumina, Otsubo Yuka,
Company: Design Unit, Product Development,
Headquarters, Casio Computer
Country: Japan
Category: Packaging concept (professional)

SILVER PENTAWARD 2020

GREEN FINGER FOOD

Senior Design: Sandra Wiggers
Company: SGK Anthem – Amsterdam
Country: Netherlands
Category: Packaging concept (professional)

BRONZE PENTAWARD 2019

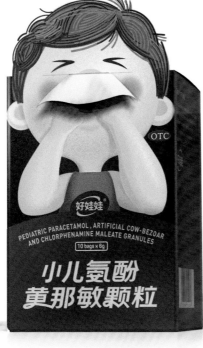

GOODBABY®

Supervision: Cao Xue (Guangzhou Academy of Fine Arts),
Duan Hongli (China Resources Sanjiu)
Art Direction: Chen Jiayi (JiaYi (Guangzhou) Design)
Creative Direction: Xu Mengzhen (China Resources Sanjiu)
Graphic Design: He Ge (JiaYi (Guangzhou) Design)
Communication: Lin Huangtao
(Guangzhou Academy of Fine Arts)
Company: China Resources Sanjiu Medical & Pharmaceutical
Country: China
Category: Packaging concept (professional)

BRONZE PENTAWARD 2020

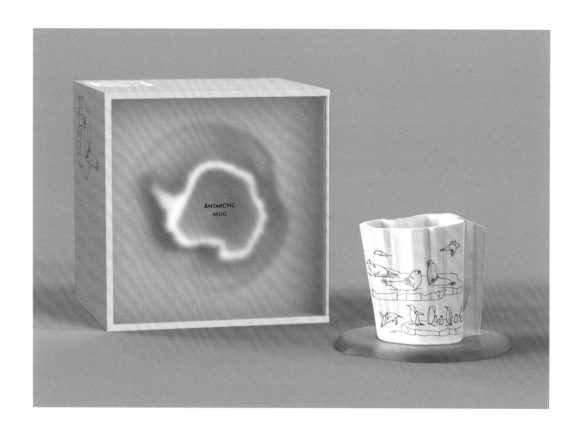

ANTARCTIC MUG

Art Direction: Kim Viktoriya
Copywriting: Yekaterina Padyukova
Design: Raziya Akhmetzhanova
Curation: Igor Medvedskiy
Company: Progression CA
Country: Kazakhstan
Category: Packaging concept (professional)

BRONZE PENTAWARD 2020

WHAT'S THE TIME?
SWATCH WATCHES

Creative Direction: Vyacheslav Nabokov
Senior Art Direction: Pavel Alekseev
Art Direction: Igor Erasov
Company: Kollegi Creative Agency
Country: Russian Federation
Category: Packaging concept (professional)

BRONZE PENTAWARD 2020

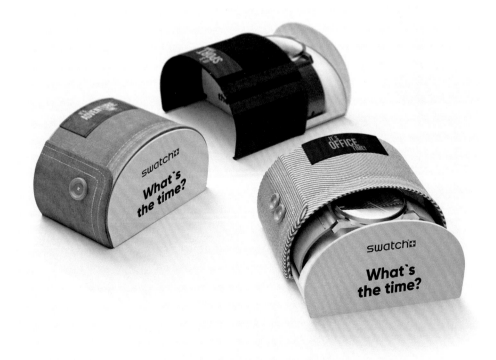

LIKEADOG

Group Head: Andrey Kuklugov
Copywriting: Sasha Chebotareva, Polina Petrova
Art Direction: Anton Saveljev
Design: Olga Fadeeva, Marina Haritonova
Illustration: Marina Haritonova
Company: Art Groove
Country: Russian Federation
Category: Packaging concept (professional)

SILVER PENTAWARD 2019

THE BROOMS

Creative Direction: Yoshio Kato
Art Direction: Yoshio Kato, Eijiro Kuniyoshi
Design and Illustration: Yasunori Wakabayashi
Company: Kotobuki Seihan Printing
Country: Japan
Category: Packaging concept (professional)

SILVER PENTAWARD 2020

CATTITUDE

Design Direction: Sara Jones
Company: SGK Anthem – Benelux
Country: Netherlands
Category: Packaging concept (professional)

BRONZE PENTAWARD 2019

WOODYE

Creative Direction and Design: Alexey Astakhov
Company: Uprise Branding Agency
Country: Russian Federation
Category: Packaging concept (professional)

BRONZE PENTAWARD 2019

SPICE CONCEPT SPACE

Design: Alena Orlova
Art Direction: Timur Saberov
3D Modelling and Visualisation: Alex Avduevsky
Company: Unblvbl Branding Agency
Country: Russian Federation
Category: Packaging concept (professional)

SILVER PENTAWARD 2019

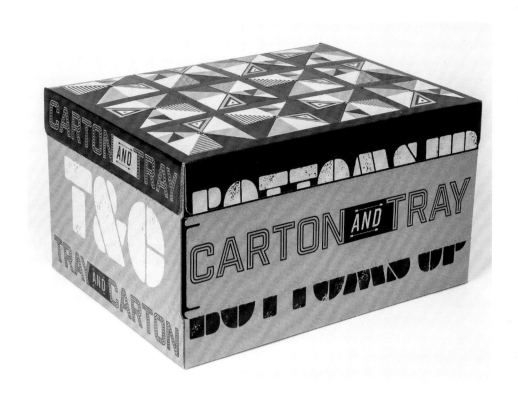

CARTON BOX THAT CHANGES TO A TRAY

Creative Direction and Design: Atsushi Uchida
Design: Yousuke Morita
Company: Toyo Seikan Group Holdings
Country: Japan
Category: Packaging concept (professional)

SILVER PENTAWARD 2019

WASH&PLAY

Design: Anna Kondratova, Natalia Radnaeva
Curation: Oksana Paley
School: HSE Art & Design School
Country: Russian Federation
Category: Packaging concept (student)

NXT-GEN PENTAWARD 2019

Wash&Play is a shampoo for dogs that turns the ordinary process of washing your pet into an exciting game. The concept is based on the similarity dogs can have to children, as both are cute and love toys. The packaging for Wash&Play attracts attention thanks to its expressive shape and bright colour palette, which also allows the user to identify the shampoo type by the attached dog toy and the pattern on the product.

Wash&Play ist ein Hundeshampoo, das den alltäglichen Prozess des Haustierwaschens in ein aufregendes Spiel verwandelt. Das Konzept basiert auf der Idee, dass Hunde, genau wie Kinder, Spielzeug lieben. Die Verpackung von Wash&Play erregt dank seiner ausdrucksstarken Form und der leuchtenden Farben Aufmerksamkeit und der Käufer erkennt die unterschiedlichen Shampoos anhand der Spielzeugs und der Muster auf dem Produkt.

Wash&Play est un shampooing pour chiens qui convertit le nettoyage de votre animal en un moment ludique. Le concept part de la similarité entre les chiens et les enfants, qui comme eux sont attendrissants et aiment les jouets. Le packaging de Wash&Play attire l'attention par sa forme et par sa palette de couleurs vives. L'utilisateur peut identifier le type de shampooing grâce au jouet qu'il intègre et aux dessins sur le produit.

BAYER
INTELLIGENT OTC PACKAGING SYSTEM

Design: Angela Baek
Photography: Jason Ware
Professor: Gerardo Herrera
School: ArtCenter College of Design
Country: USA
Category: Packaging concept (student)

GOLD PENTAWARD 2019

The **LIL'LAMB** brand reflects the idea of a newborn's innocence. It offers granulated and concentrated 0+ detergent based on Marseille soap's 17th-century formula composed of three natural ingredients: olive oil, spring water and wood ash. This soft and gentle soap can be used as a universal cleanser for hand and machine laundry, toys, fruit and surfaces, and as a stain remover or softener – one product instead of six. Cardboard boxes for refills, durable ceramic accessories and reusable dispensers help save plastic, money and the planet.

Die Marke **LIL'LAMB** spiegelt die Unschuld eines Neugeborenen wider. Sie bietet granulierte und konzentrierte 0+-Waschmittel auf Basis der aus dem 17. Jahrhundert stammenden Formel der Marseiller Seife an, die aus drei Inhaltsstoffen besteht: Olivenöl, Quellwasser und Holzasche. Diese sanfte und schonende Seife kann als universeller Reiniger für Hand- und Maschinenwäsche, Spielzeuge, Obst und Oberflächen sowie als Fleckenentferner oder Weichspüler verwendet werden – ein Produkt, statt sechs verschiedener. Pappkartons zum Nachfüllen, langlebiges Keramikzubehör und wiederverwendbare Spender helfen, Plastik und Geld zu sparen und den Planeten zu retten.

La marque **LIL'LAMB** transmet toute la candeur du nouveau-né. Sa gamme 0+ de lessives concentrées en poudre est élaborée à partir de la formule datant du XVIIᵉ siècle du savon de Marseille, qui compte trois ingrédients : huile d'olive, eau de source et cendre de bois. Ce savon doux et délicat peut être employé comme nettoyant universel pour le lavage du linge à la main ou en machine, le nettoyage de jouets, de fruits ou de surfaces, mais aussi comme détachant et adoucissant, soit six produits en un. Les boîtes en carton pour les recharges, les accessoires durables en céramique et les distributeurs réutilisables supposent une économie de plastique et d'argent, ainsi qu'une bonne action pour la planète.

LIL'LAMB

Tutoring: Leonid Slavin, Evgeni Razumov, Denis Shlesberg
Illustration: inspired by artworks of Stacie Bloomfield
3D Visualisation: Pavel Gubin
Product, Packaging Concept and Art Direction: Kate Zakharova
School: British Higher School of Art and Design
Country: Russian Federation
Category: Packaging concept (student)

GOLD PENTAWARD 2020

BOO!
BABY-FRIENDLY BRAND OF
SANITIZING CLEANING PRODUCTS

Design: Evgeniya Abramova
Curation and Tutoring: Leonid Slavin
Tutoring: Evgeniy Razumov
3D Visualisation: Pavel Gubin, Dmitriy Saveliev
Music: Vasily Filipkin
School: British Higher School of Art and Design
Country: Russian Federation
Category: Packaging concept (student)

SILVER PENTAWARD 2020

MAMOLOKO

Design: Alexander Cherkasov
3D Visualisation: Maxim Kadashov
Country: Russian Federation
Category: Packaging concept (student)

SILVER PENTAWARD 2020

KING OYSTER

Creative Direction: Liu Chia-Yu
Graphic Design: Cai Hung-Yu
Technical Direction: Lee Ruei-Yu
Image Editing: Jhang Yun
School: Chaoyang University of Technology
Country: Taiwan
Category: Packaging concept (student)
BRONZE PENTAWARD 2019

TILA

Creative Direction and Design: Hugo de Matos,
Paola Parodi, Yolanda Santamaria
School: Elisava, Barcelona School of
Design and Engineering
Country: Spain
Category: Packaging concept (student)
SILVER PENTAWARD 2019

TASTY STORIES

Tutoring: Leonid Slavin
Art Direction, Design and Illustration: Inna Efimova
Rendering: Pavel Gubin
School: British Higher School of Art and Design
Country: Russian Federation
Category: Packaging concept (student)

BRONZE PENTAWARD 2020

JETPACK

Design: Paul Knipper
Professors: Jessica Deseo, Andrew Gibbs
School: ArtCenter College of Design
Country: USA
Category: Packaging concept (student)

BRONZE PENTAWARD 2019

FINE HERB

Design: Yinan Hu
School: Domus Academy
Country: Italy
Category: Packaging concept (student)

SILVER PENTAWARD 2019

JOY
FRUIT JUICES

Design: Anastasiya Yudina
Tutoring: Leonid Slavin
School: British Higher School of Art and Design
Country: Russian Federation
Category: Packaging concept (student)

BRONZE PENTAWARD 2020

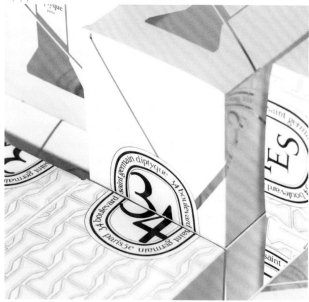

CHALLENGER SPIRIT

Work hard, dream big. For 19 years, global art direction agency **Servaire & Co** has specialised in creative journeys for **leading and disruptive premium and luxury** industries.

Luxury is about emotions. Moments in time which leave an everlasting mark on whoever is willing to experience them to the fullest. For nearly two decades, Servaire & Co has been crafting these experiences through a **sharp and fresh design-making approach, with a challenger spirit**.

As a global creative agency specialising in strategy, branding, design, visual merchandising and content for luxury and premium brands worldwide, we are committed to building brand narratives that provide **impactful and meaningful creative springboards**. We believe that creativity is first and foremost a human adventure. Every day, we mix our talents and various backgrounds to face creative challenges with passion and rigour. As design is strongly rooted in our agency's DNA, we combine our passion for creation with the most up-to-date technological and industrial knowledge to identify and respond to emerging consumer insights.

A multi-award-winning agency, with more than 26 Pentawards, including 2018's Best Designer of the Year for Sébastien Servaire. The paragraph mark § best describes our ongoing vision: writing positive and modern stories for **renewed and sustainable brand experiences**. It is at the very heart of our identity.

DER GEIST DES HERAUSFORDERERS

Arbeite hart, träume groß. Seit 19 Jahren hat sich die weltweit tätige Art Direction Agentur **Servaire & Co** auf kreative Reisen für die **führenden und disruptiven Premium- und Luxusindustrien** spezialisiert.

Bei Luxus geht es um Emotionen. Momente, die einen bleibenden Eindruck bei denen hinterlassen, die dazu bereit sind, sie voll auszukosten. Seit fast zwei Jahrzehnten gestalten Servaire & Co diese Erlebnisse durch einen **scharfsinnigen und frischen Ansatz, Designs mit Herausforderergeist zu entwerfen**.

Als globale Kreativagentur, die sich auf Strategie, Branding, Design, visuelles Merchandising und Inhalte für Luxus- und Premiummarken weltweit spezialisiert hat, sind wir bestrebt, Marken-Narrative aufzubauen, die ein **wirkungs- und bedeutungsvolles kreatives Sprungbrett** bieten. Wir glauben, dass Kreativität in erster Linie ein menschliches Abenteuer ist. Jeden Tag mischen wir unsere Talente und verschiedenen Hintergründe, um kreative Herausforderungen mit Leidenschaft und Hartnäckigkeit anzugehen. Weil Design tief in der DNA unserer Agentur verankert ist, kombinieren wir unsere Leidenschaft mit dem aktuellsten technologischen und industriellen Wissen, um neue Bedürfnisse der Konsumenten zu erkennen und darauf einzugehen.

Eine mehrfach ausgezeichnete Agentur, mit mehr als 26 Pentawards, unter anderem dem Pentaward für den Designer des Jahres 2018 für Sébastien Servaire. Das Paragrafenzeichen § beschreibt unsere fortlaufende Vision am besten: positive und moderne Geschichten für **erneuerte und nachhaltige Markenerfahrungen** zu schreiben. Das ist das Herzstück unserer Identität.

ESPRIT DE CHALLENGE

Travailler dur et rêver en grand. Depuis 19 ans, l'agence internationale de direction artistique **Servaire & Co** est spécialisée dans l'élaboration d'aventures créatives pour les **marques leaders qui bousculent les règles dans les industries premium et du luxe**.

Le luxe est une question d'émotions, d'instants qui laissent une empreinte indélébile chez quiconque est disposé à en faire l'expérience au maximum. Depuis près de deux décennies, Servaire & Co met au point ces expériences avec **une approche novatrice et mordante du design et un esprit de challenge**.

En tant qu'agence internationale spécialisée en stratégie, branding, design, merchandising visuel et contenu pour les marques haut de gamme et de luxe du monde entier, notre engagement est d'élaborer des accroches narratives servant **de rampes créatives pour des lancements retentissants et pertinents**. Pour nous, la créativité est avant tout une aventure humaine. Chaque jour, nous combinons talents et expériences pour relever avec passion et rigueur les défis créatifs qui se présentent. Le design étant profondément ancré dans l'ADN de notre agence, nous allions notre passion pour la création aux dernières connaissances technologiques et industrielles en date pour comprendre les consommateurs émergents et répondre à leurs attentes.

Notre agence a été primée à de nombreuses occasions et a remporté plus de 26 Pentawards, dont celui en 2018 du Best Designer of the Year décerné à Sébastien Servaire. La marque de paragraphe § décrit le mieux notre vision : écrire des histoires contemporaines et positives pour offrir des **expériences de marques renouvelées et durables**. C'est toute l'essence de notre identité.

PENTAWARDS JURY

PACO ADÍN – CREATIVE DIRECTOR
Supperstudio – *Spain*
+ Creative Director and a Partner of Supperstudio, a packaging agency founded in 2003. + Degree in advertising, marketing and design. + Lectures package design classes, teaches workshops and talks at conferences. + Recipient of more than 100 awards and accolades. + Supperstudio was named Agency of the Year at the Pentawards 2016. + Clients include El Corte Inglés, Starbucks, Coca Cola, Danone, Leche Pascual, Young & Beautifood and the Guggenheim Museum Bilbao. + Addicted to packaging, convinced that humour moves mountains and committed to a democratic approach to design.

CAROLINA ALZATE – CEO
OPENLAB – *Colombia*
+ In the packaging and branding industry for over 12 years. + Aims to create and renovate new and existing businesses through strategies, research processes, services and products. + Skills include design thinking, creative techniques, 3D prototyping, deep user-centred research, business strategies, branding perception, benchmarking and identifying trends through "coolhunting" techniques. + 11 recognitions nationally and internationally including four Pentawards: Paris 2012, Tokyo 2014, London 2015 and Barcelona 2017. + Current clients include Grupo Nutresa, Sanofi Aventis, Grupo Gloria, Postobon, SAB MILLER.

JONAS ANDERSSON – MANAGING DIRECTOR
Brand Union – *Sweden*
+ More than 20 years in the branding industry. + Focused on the challenge of how design can change the communicative and creative landscape to create superior brand value. + Work for IKEA has appeared on the cover of the New York Times Magazine. + Team turned Malibu Rum into one of Pernod Ricard global star brands. + Won a Cannes lion with Absolut. + Focus on attracting talent to form a next generation design agency that leverages design as a brand-building tool in the new creative media landscape.

MATTHIEU AQUINO – VICE PRESIDENT GLOBAL BEVERAGE AND BRAND EXPERIENCE
PepsiCo – *USA*
+ Recognised expert in the fields of design and innovation, especially in corporate transformation. + Leads a team that crafts curated storytelling across touchpoints through holistic design-thinking systems and multidisciplinary design tools. + Responsible for developing design strategy, systems and experiences across the entire beverage portfolio globally, and leading new growth initiatives. + Has contributed over the past 14 years to the creation and implementation of two design organisations in two multi-layered international corporations. + Ensures that design thinking is at the core of the business, impacting the internal culture and significantly growing these respective businesses.

STEPAN AZARYAN – FOUNDER AND CREATIVE DIRECTOR
Backbone Branding – *Armenia*
+ Graduated from Yerevan Academy of Fine Arts in 2004. + Founded Backbone Branding in 2009, who have since won over 50 international awards. + Pentawards Agency of the Year 2019 and 2020, first in the region to receive this title and first to win in two consecutive years. + Jury member in professional competitions in China and Europe; speaker to audiences of thousands. + Sees collaboration with his clients as a partnership based on strong communication. + Believes creativity and great quality design have a transformative impact, leading to his mission of revolutionising the branding and overall design scene, starting in Armenia.

MARK BUDDEN – CHAIRMAN (ASIA PAC REGION)
Design Bridge – *Singapore*
+ Joined Design Bridge in 1992 as a designer, later became MD of the Singapore office, which he opened in 2003. + Studied silversmithing and jewellery. + Passionate about developing the future of the design industry in Singapore by providing learning opportunities and long-term career progression. + Design Bridge has become the largest and one of the most respected design agencies in the region, working across multiple touchpoints for famous brands.

MASA CUI – FOUNDER AND CHIEF EXECUTIVE
Marie Dalgar – *China*
+ Founder of Marie Dalgar, Beukay's first consumer brand, starting with her iconic mascara. + Despite not having a background in cosmetics, her dedication to brand development, unique sense of vision and passion for beauty have made Marie Dalgar what it is today. + Committed to building it into "the top-notch artistic make-up brand" in China. + Sincere and strong-minded, with a free and casual attitude towards life; judges fashion with enormous enthusiasm, creativity and artistic perspective.

XIONGBO DENG – FOUNDER AND CREATIVE DIRECTOR
ShenZhen Lingyun Creative Packaging Design – *China*
+ Started in packaging design and branding in 2010. + Founder and Creative Director of Shenzhen Lingyun Creative Packaging (LEADWAY) since 2013. + Believes that brands and designers should create a more enjoyable experience and design service in China. + His work has won many Pentawards and he was named Pentawards Designer of the Year in 2020. + Has helped many brands, including Coca Cola, Snow Beer, Maotai Group, and Wuliangye Group, develop best-selling products in China.

ASHWINI DESHPANDE – CO-FOUNDER DIRECTOR
Elephant Design – *India*
+ Graduated in 1989 from the National Institute of Design, Ahmedabad. + Co-founder of Elephant*, India's largest independent integrated design consultancy with offices also in Singapore. + Creates award-winning work for global brands in diverse segments. + Key member of the Design Alliance Asia consortium. + Editor of Colours of Asia book, which received Design for Asia Special Culture Award from the Hong Kong government. + Co-founder of the Collective, an initiative to create safe workplaces for women. + On Campaign India's A-List. + Mentors start-ups through the "Nurture" initiative of TiE and from the advisory board of Indian Institute of Management CIIE programme.

RAMSES DINGENOUTS – SENIOR PACKAGING AND IDENTITY DESIGN MANAGER GLOBAL COMMERCE
Heineken – *Netherlands*
+ Senior Packaging and Identity Design Manager at Heineken, which he joined in 2014. + Previously worked for various brand design agencies as a creative director. + Responsible for the creative design of award-winning innovative packaging concepts for premium FMCG brands, including Heineken. + Worked on the premium packaging for Heineken and premium sponsor platforms like UCL, RWC, James Bond and Formula 1.

ARRON EGAN – CREATIVE DIRECTOR
ButterflyCannon – *UK*
+ Multidisciplinary Creative Director, with a career spanning over 19 years. + Works in a diverse range of design disciplines: from luxury packaging and branding to creative brand communication, point of sale, print and product innovation. + Belief that all great design starts from a single, instantly understandable big idea, rooted in engaging and authentic brand storytelling. + Has worked on a wide range of global brands and brought numerous start-up brands to life, including Tom Parker Creamery and Unity Beauty Essentials.

PATRICK DE GRANDE – FOUNDER AND CREATIVE FARMER
Quatre Mains – *Belgium*
+ Master's degree in functional design. + Previously worked as a design architect of art books. + Founder and Creative Farmer at Quatre Mains. + Associate and Brand Builder at 4Tops. +Founder and Creator of Opportunities for Packman Packaging. + Winner of many awards, including Gold, Silver and Bronze Pentawards. + Member of advisory board and guest lecturer in branding and packaging design at Luca School of Art. + Active member of the European Packaging Design Association.

CLEM HALPIN – PRESIDENT OF THE JURY AND CREATIVE DIRECTOR
Bulletproof – *UK*
+ Creative Director at Bulletproof, an independent global brand design agency. + Has worked at many well-respected agencies, including nine years as Creative Director at Turner Duckworth. + Many top brand identity and packaging design awards, including D&AD, Clio and Pentawards. + Has worked on some of the world's most iconic brands, including Burger King, Toblerone, Glenlivet, Tick Tock Teas and Kettle Chips. + A regular on the design awards judging circuit.

STEVE HONOUR – DESIGN AND VISUAL IDENTITY LEADER, INNOVATION, EUROPE AND AFRICA
Diageo – *UK*
+ Works in design and visual identity within Diageo Europe and Africa. + Led the creation of new brands, brand identities and packaging of some of the biggest global spirit and beer brands that exist today, such as Guinness, Hop House 13, Smirnoff, Captain Morgan, Roe & Co, Haig Club and many more. + With consumers more brand and design conscious than ever, believes great design has to deliver value and trust, and that brands will win or lose on their ability to connect with consumers through design.

RYUTA ISHIKAWA – ART DIRECTOR AND DESIGNER
Frame Inc. – *Japan*
+ Esteemed Japanese packaging design expert. + Designer and Art Director always thinking about new ways to create communications that generate new value. + Specialises in product and brand development, advertisement production and visual identity development. + Works on projects across multiple disciplines in both domestic and international markets. + Tokyo-based design agency honoured four times, including twice by Pentawards with consecutive Platinum distinctions in 2017 and 2018. + Also works with world-renowned beverage brands such as Kirin Beer and Lotte Sawa.

MARK VAN ITERSON – DIRECTOR GLOBAL HEINEKEN DESIGN, ACTIVATION AND SUSTAINABILITY
Heineken International – *Netherlands*
+ Industrial design engineer by education. + After 13 years in design and brand consultancy, joined Heineken in 2005. + Responsible for design and concept development worldwide. + Work includes brand identity, packaging and merchandise, all designs around the global "open your world" campaigns and sponsorship designs. + Also more experimental activations like the crowd-sourced Concept-Club and Lounge at the Milan and London Design Weeks, and Heineken design competitions in other parts of the world.

TITHA KRAEMER – PARTNER AND DIRECTOR
Bendito Design – *Brazil*
+ Prior to starting Bendito, worked as creative director for important agencies in Brazil, such as MA FrankMeyer, Trio, Competence and Norton/Publicis Groupe. + Has developed a colourful, bright and bold style for Bendito's clients. + Elected Designer of the Year, Promotional Marketing Businesswoman of the Year and Design Businesswoman of the Year by the Rio Grande do Sul Columnists Award. + Shares her creative and strategic knowledge as speaker, teacher or juror at Congreso Diseño Industrial Company, Industrial Design College – Brazil Lutheran University, Polytechnic School of Unisinos, ABRE Award, Bornancini Award and ABEDESIGN Award.

KEVIN MARSHALL – CREATIVE DIRECTOR OF DESIGN
Microsoft – *USA*
+ Over 25 years of packaging design experience. + Microsoft's Creative Director of Global Packaging and Content, leading a world-class team of designers. + Responsible for Microsoft's packaging vision and creative strategy for products including Surface, XBOX, HoloLens, PC Hardware etc. + Leads talented teams that leverage the power of inspired design while launching memorable experiences that delight and build brand equity. + Believes that today's consumers expect intuitive, connected product journeys and that well-crafted packaging is vital to creating meaningful and lasting consumer relationships.

DANIELE MONTI – DIRECTOR, BRAND AND PACKAGING DESIGN | CONSUMABLES PRIVATE BRANDS
Amazon – *USA*
+ Born and raised in Florence, Italy; moved to USA nearly 25 years ago. + Design work has transformed and raised to new levels such brands as Starbucks, Tazo and over a dozen private brands owned by Amazon. + Career splits evenly between agencies and the corporate world. + Has a passion for understanding the customer mindset, online and in traditional retail, anticipating needs and inventing new experiences.

IPPEI MURATA – CREATIVE DIRECTOR
Shiseido – *Japan*
+ A Creative/Art Director for Shiseido, with a focus on beauty product design, including product, space and communication design. + Became Creative Director for Shiseido Europe in Paris in 2009, helping to localise ad and communication plans for the European market. + Currently working at Shiseido China in Shanghai, which he joined in 2015, creating a package design team for the Chinese market. + Believes a greater emphasis on the relationship between the designed product and its surroundings helps to foster affinity through good design.

SAM O'DONAHUE – FOUNDER AND CREATIVE DIRECTOR
Established – *USA*
+ Graduated in industrial design from Central Saint Martins, London. + Runs his own design studio, combining great design with having lots of fun. + Specialises in packaging, identity design and art direction for premium brands in beauty and fashion. + Has spent the last 20 years in the world of luxury design with a client list that includes Marc Jacobs, Rihanna, Calvin Klein, H&M, DKNY, LVMH, Svedka, Evian, Estée Lauder, Black Fleece, Sephora and MCM. + Lectures at Columbia Business School; previously on the jury of Dieline awards and D&AD awards.+ Winner of 30 international design awards, including Gold Clio, Graphite D&AD and the prestigious 2015 Diamond Pentaward.

LU CHEN – MI ECOSYSTEM – DESIGN DIRECTOR
Xiaomi – *China*
+ Graduated from ArtCenter College of Design with a bachelor's degree in graphic design. + Over 14 years' experience in packaging, product and graphic design. + Joined Xiaomi in 2011, headed cross-department team that completed the Mi and Redmi mobile phone packaging series, Ecosystem packaging series, Mi, Mijia and Mitu brand designs, and Mi Home flagship store, CES and MWC Xiaomi exhibition area, and Mi branding products. + Led the team to create packaging suitable for the Mi e-commerce platform, one that serves the product and also the needs of platform development.

YOJI MINAKUCHI – SENIOR GENERAL MANAGER
Suntory – *Japan*
+ Graduated from Kushu Institute of Design. + Joined Suntory as a graphic designer in 1989. + Creates outstanding packaging design and astonishing concepts using various metaphors. + Awards include Package Design Award 2003; ADC in Tokyo 2005; Pentawards 2007–08 and 2010–18. + Work includes the Suntory corporate logotype, Iyemon Green Tea, Green Dakara and Gokuri.

DAVIDE MOSCONI – CREATIVE PARTNER
Auge Design – *Italy*
+ Partner and Creative Director (since 2016) of Auge Design, a creative studio with a focus on branding and packaging design, based in Florence, Italy. + National and international awards such as Cannes Lions, ADCI, Dieline and Clio. + Special edition project for Mutti won the Best of Show – Diamond Award in the 2018 Pentawards. + More than 15 years' experience in communication and design, working with global clients such as Vodafone, Disney, Diesel, Nescafé, Wall's, Martini as well as curating projects for various exhibitions within international museums.

ANGELINA PISCHIKOVA – GRAPHIC DESIGNER
Pearlfisher – *Belarus*
+ Award-winning graphic designer from Minsk, Belarus, with international experience in branding and packaging design. + Joined Pearlfisher London design team in June 2018. + Participated in international festivals, has won outstanding distinctions, including a Platinum Pentaward, Silver Cannes Lion, Graphite Pencil D&AD Awards, Bronze Epica Awards, Gold Dieline Awards, Gran Prix and Gold White Square International Advertising Festival.

JON RATHBONE – PACKAGING DESIGN LEAD
Facebook – *USA*
+ Background in industrial design; has brought products and brands to life through thoughtfully crafted packaging experiences over the past 14 years. + Multifaceted approach to design, exploring the interplay of 2D and 3D touchpoints and the journeys that allow seamless transitions between physical and digital space. + Packaging strategies that deliver equally across brand, business, and consumer needs. + On both agency and in-house teams, developed for some of the world's leading CPG and tech companies, including Proctor & Gamble, Mars & Co., Microsoft and Oculus VR.

DAVE ROBERTS – CREATIVE PARTNER
Superunion – *UK*
+ Multi-award-winning Creative Partner at global brand agency Superunion since 2011. + Responsible for strategic and creative leadership across a number of programmes. + Work with Nespresso across dozens of projects aimed at repositioning as a new luxury brand – from strategy, identity and packaging to in-store experience and communication campaigns. + Developed some of the world's most iconic brands, including Nespresso, Samsung, HSBC, M&S, Investec, Molton Brown and Kew Gardens.

JOSÉ ANTONIO ROJANO LOPEZ – HEAD OF PACKAGING AND DESIGN SERVICES COMMUNICATIONS

El Corte Inglés – *Spain*

+ BFA in industrial design, MA in product design, Istituto Europeo di Design. + Master's in marketing management and sales, IE Business School, 2012; graduated top three and won Beta Gamma Sigma award. + Joined El Corte Inglés in 2007 as Designer on the Packaging Design team. + Head of Packaging and Design Services since 2011; developing over 30,000 new packaging designs with a team of 10 . + Has worked for Imaginarium and Sony Spain. + Specialist in brand development and FMCG-SMCG packaging, focused on creative direction, communication and marketing strategy, design and co-creation processes, innovation and own brand portfolio management. + 20 international design awards in the last four years.

TATIANA RYFER-EMBERGER – HEAD OF BRANDING & VISUAL IDENTITY

Carrefour – *France*

+ International design career, from Rio de Janeiro and New York to Paris in 2006. + Head of Branding & Visual Identity at Carrefour for over eight years, contributing to building design culture inside the company. + By managing the brand's visual aspects, creates consistency through all customer touchpoints. + Prior three-year experience at the Decathlon Group as Branding & Packaging Manager, creating and developing some of the group's own brands and collaborating with its 160-member design team. + 360° design approach and a passion for building authentic brands that talk, share and understand their audience.

SEBASTIEN SERVAIRE – CEO AND CREATIVE DIRECTOR

Servaire & Co – *France*

+ Trained as a designer with an early interest in brands, as they associate the creative concept with the business aspect. + Head of an agency of 30 people, started 14 years ago as R'Pure. + Renamed Servaire & Co in 2015, after merge with Blue Factory retail design agency. + A family business that cultivates the collective spirit, marking a new chapter with strong foundations, commitment, solid values and a sharp global expertise. + Long-term collaborations with major players in the luxury sector, including Veuve Clicquot Moët & Chandon, Guerlain, Rémy Martin and Lancôme.

DENISE SIEBERT – VICE PRESIDENT DESIGN

Global Kellogg Company – *USA*

+ Joined the Kellogg team in August 2017, after 18 years at Procter & Gamble. + BSc in industrial design at the University of Cincinnati College of Design, Architecture, Art and Planning. + Has applied design expertise to global brands such as Always, Crest, Pampers and Oral B, and the P&G corporate brand including the Olympics Sponsorship. + End-to-end design mastery includes upstream innovation, brand positioning and concepts, iconic asset creation, product and packaging development, and in-store/e-commerce experiences. + Builds creative organisations, identifies and attracts top talent, develops creative and efficient design processes and nurtures a positive and inspiring culture.

BRUNO SINGULANI – GLOBAL HEAD OF BRAND IDENTITY AND DESIGN

Nestlé – *Switzerland*

+ Brazilian designer, currently the Creative Leader for all Global Food Brands at Nestlé. + Graduated as a product designer, works in roles with strong focus on branding and strategic design management. + Works with major brands that range from beauty care to food and beverages. + Believes in the essential value of anthropology and human-centric innovation to develop stronger design cultures and build long-lasting brands. + In four years at Nestlé challenged iconic global brands to reinvent themselves, while also pushing Nestlé to empower and enable start-up-like initiatives, achieving positive business results through design-led innovations.

HELLE SØEGAARD RASMUSSEN – SENIOR CREATIVE MANAGER

Lego – *Denmark*

+ Senior Creative Manager at The LEGO® Agency. + Leads the Design Innovation Team, focused on the creation of visual identities that stand out and serve as a foundation for multi-channel, multi-platform global communication. + Creative energy comes from spotting untapped potential and nurturing new talent. + Has worked in the toy industry for the past 25 years, with a leading role on many of the LEGO® Group's global launches. + Fierce advocate for the power of play and boosting creativity in kids, a personal philosophy that carries over into her work.

JANE STRUK – ART DIRECTOR

Depot Branding Agency – *Russian Federation*

+ Art Director for multinational clients at the Depot Branding Agency in Moscow. + Specialises in branding and packaging design, working successfully with major international and Russian brands, Nestlé, Unilever, Pepsico, Bayer, Danone, Heineken etc. + Team has won prestigious awards at international design and advertising festivals. + Inspired by minimalist art, Scandinavian aesthetics and functionalism, interpreting them her own way via the medium of graphic design. + Love and passion in every project ensures a breakthrough.

FRANÇOIS TAKOUNSEUN – DESIGN MANAGER AND CO-FOUNDER

Partisan du Sens – *France*

+ Graduated from the Ecole Supérieure de Design Industriel, Paris. + Founder of Partisan du Sens, together with Gérald Galdini in 2003, a global design agency in Paris. + More than 20 years' experience in the luxury sector. + Winner of the Platinum Pentaward 2015, several Gold, Silver and Bronze Pentawards, Red Dot Design Award, Grand Prix Stratégies du Luxe, among others. + Believes design is not simply about creation, it is a philosophy. + Instilling desire, transforming the material and subtly stimulating innovation through the fostering of intense brand loyalty is the essence of fine work.

RICHARD WALZER – HEAD OF DESIGN, EMEA

Mars Wrigley – *UK*

+ At Mars Wrigley for over five years, Head of Design, EMEA. + Previously at various design agencies building design strategies and unlocking the innovation potential for clients spanning various sectors, including Dell, Diageo, GSK, Nestlé Purina, P&G and Vodafone. + As design leader at Mars, charged with designing and innovating on some of the world's most loved treats, including M&M's, Snickers, Galaxy, Skittles and Orbit Extra. + Strives to unlock growth by building meaningful and coherent brand experiences, from establishing opportunities to delivering design solutions to shelf.

INDEX

IMPRINT

EACH AND EVERY TASCHEN BOOK PLANTS A SEED!
TASCHEN is a carbon neutral publisher. Each year, we offset our annual carbon emissions with carbon credits at the Instituto Terra, a reforestation program in Minas Gerais, Brazil, founded by Lélia and Sebastião Salgado. To find out more about this ecological partnership, please check: *www.taschen.com/zerocarbon*.
Inspiration: unlimited. Carbon footprint: zero.

To stay informed about TASCHEN and our upcoming titles, please subscribe to our free magazine at *www.taschen.com/ magazine*, follow us on Instagram and Facebook, or e-mail your questions to *contact@taschen.com*.

© 2020 TASCHEN GmbH
Hohenzollernring 53, D-50672 Köln
www.taschen.com

Pentawards
Adam Ryan, Head of Pentawards
Jennifer Clements, Marketing Manager
Ying-Ying Chen, Marketing Executive
Emmelie Evans, Project Executive

Design
Andy Disl and Birgit Eichwede
Layout
Jon Cefai, Collaborate, London

English Editing
Thea Miklowski, Cologne
German Translation
Lea Buseck for Delivering iBooks & Design, Barcelona
German Editing
Katharina Kümmerle, Munich
French Translation
Valérie Lavoyer for Delivering iBooks & Design, Barcelona
French Editing
Serge V. G. Dambrine for Delivering iBooks & Design, Barcelona

Printed in Slovakia
ISBN 978-3-8365-8502-6